THE NORSEMEN

the
norsemen

ERIC OXENSTIERNA

Translated and edited by

CATHERINE HUTTER

New York Graphic Society Publishers, Ltd.

GREENWICH, CONNECTICUT

Library of Congress Catalog Card Number 65–16464

Printed and bound in the United States of America by Halliday Lithograph Corporation and The Book Press. Designed by Peter Oldenburg and Sophie Adler.

CONTENTS

LIST OF ILLUSTRATIONS

1

The Vikings — Heroes
or Raiders?

WHY ARE the Vikings so often portrayed as roving scarecrows with straggly fur strapped haphazardly around their bodies? Actually they were the greatest fur traders of their day. They wore beaver and sable, breeches, tunics and jackets, with smartly cut cloaks swinging from their shoulders. Must they always be depicted wearing those ridiculous horned helmets? The Vikings were skilled in the art of warfare; their conic helmets were immune against the stoutest sword. The horned helmet, the masquerading as berserkers or wolves, was a part of their tribal ritual which supposedly gave the wearer the strength of the mimicked animal. Must every wooden trough with the superdimensional head of an animal on its prow be classified as a Viking ship? The most impressive oceanic travelers of world history should not be shown sailing the seas in tubs. The Vikings have a right to the same historic accuracy in illustration, theater and opera as the figures of other epochs.

Today you can make capital from a show of violence. Uninhibited cruelty is *en vogue*. Motion pictures, books, articles, revel in the crimes of the Vikings. We no longer know whether their rapaciousness is being lauded or condemned. In their day, however, the monastic chroniclers who had settled down on the vulnerable Occidental coast naturally had nothing good to say about the attacking heathen. "The dead lay everywhere," reads one report. "Priests and laymen, women, children and infants. The Franks were filled with despair. The Christian lands seemed doomed to annihilation." Or: "The town of Noyes on the Seine was attacked by night. The heathen took the bishop and nobility prisoner, laid waste to the town, led the prisoners off and killed them on the way." Or: "The inhabitants of Trier conferred with the wise men of the city and buried the treasures of the church in the earth. The caskets of the saints were lowered deep into the ground so that the relics might not be mocked and jeered at by the barbarian."

Over a period of five hundred years, only accounts like these could be read. But then sailing vessels came from Iceland, bringing parchment volumes that had been handed down from generation to generation and read on that island. They told of heroic deeds of the pagan ancestor; of pride, honor and valorous military expeditions in foreign lands. Gustavus Adolphus II (1594–1632) could see in the old Goths or Götars—as they were called in those days—the dauntless forerunners of his Swedish soldiers of the Thirty Years War. It fortified his national pride, and he created an office until then unheard of in Europe—"historian of the realm." He ordered all rune stones and monuments of prehistoric days to be collected, and encouraged epic-form poetry to glorify Goth and Viking. But after the catastrophe at Poltava in Russia, which led eventually to the end of Swedish power in 1718, heroic deeds lost their fascination. Again the chroniclers had nothing but contempt for the Norsemen.

This change of heart and mind was followed, in the late eighteenth and early nineteenth century, by the stimulating nationalism—in Germany—of Arndt and Fichte, and a wave of nationalistic romanticism swept across Sweden, too. But here you could find no inspiring hatred of Napoleon. Scandinavian romanticism had no political goal for the future; it groped its way back into its own historic past. The Vikings were brought out of oblivion and raised to the status of heroes and mighty swordsmen. In the year 1811, the *Götiska Förbundet,* or Gothic League was formed. Its members adopted old Nordic names, drank out of horns, and practiced so-called manly virtues in a ridiculously boyish fashion. Per Henrick Ling (1776–1839) never spoke; he bellowed "like a Viking," and developed a program of calisthenics to toughen the body. All Europe honored his system of gymnastics at the Stockholm Lingiade in 1939, but tactfully refrained from mentioning his old Nordic poetry.

Erik Gustave Geijer (1783–1847), member of the Gothic League and great classicist of Swedish poetry, studied Old Nordic so that he might read the Icelandic sagas in the original. He had a fine ear for poetry; he could appreciate the old language, and created a new Swedish, free of French, German and Latin sentence structure; clearly phrased in short, energetic sentences that centered around the verb. He favored an unadorned style with no abstractions, which eventually became the standard language pattern. He wrote his most beautiful poem about the freeholding peasants, the yeomen, whose faith was rooted firmly in their national soil; and he sang the glories of the Vikings who roved far afield, driven by the wild yearning of the Northerner. But even he, the poet, failed to fathom the mystique of the Vikings.

A great army of jubilating warrior maidens, in the shape of Valkyries, rode across the stage as the Vikings experienced a totally unexpected musical glorification in Wagnerian opera. All hail to a new, radiant hero—and heroine! But again the vision was shattered, this time, in 1945, by a *Götterdämmerung* of unprecedented proportions, to be followed once more by a monotonous chorus of chroniclers who saw the Vikings as barbarians, bandits or pirates.

How are we really to evaluate them? Must their fame always remain a controversial issue?

They were first and foremost human beings whose behavior evolved from their historic situation. Heroism and the lust to kill are secondary manifestations that appear in conflict; they are never the prime historic or psychological causes of an event. The Vikings founded colonies in foreign lands—not pleasant for the native population. But what we want to know is *why* did they wander off looking for land? What was their social order like? To be just, we must find this out without measuring them against the standard of Roman law or Christian morality, of which they knew nothing or very little.

The Vikings were brilliant traders and returned home rich with treasure. On this point all written sources are silent, but twentieth-century archeological research—working slowly, with a methodical precision equal to that of the technical sciences—has brought to light an enormous amount of findings from graves, settlements and hoards. In the last twenty years discoveries have been made that have not yet been incorporated into general knowledge; top-quality artifacts are piling up in museums. This book will tell of them.

Before we work our way through to a new conception of the Viking, let us pick out a few genre pictures from their legendary history, as handed down to us in Snorri Sturluson's *Heimskringla* (Orb of the World).

A Viking ruler had his three half brothers brought before him, sat them on his knees and made fearsome faces for their benefit; he frowned and looked at them angrily. The two oldest ones were frightened, but the youngest stared straight back at him fiercely. When the king tousled the boy's hair, the little hands grabbed the king's beard and ruffled it. The two oldest boys wanted land and a cow; the youngest wanted to lead warriors when he grew up.

"You are raising a future king here, Mother," the king said with satisfaction. And in time the boy became the powerful successor of his half brother.

These were the standards by which the Vikings evaluated their children. Toughness and self-reliance were considered the most laudable attributes, and were encouraged in play, sport and speech.

A twelve-year-old boy called Egil was raised in this spirit. Once his father meted out to him a severe punishment, which was undeserved. Egil refused to reconcile himself to it and behaved according to the example set him. When his father "sat down at table with his entire household, Egil had not taken his place." He took his revenge on his father's highly valued overseer in the brutal way customary in days when the only way to avenge an insult was by an act of violence. The boy crept up on the overseer and killed him. The account of what followed is terse: "Father and son never spoke about it, neither angrily nor calmly. And thus the winter passed."

The people of the North lived side by side, yet isolated by their own reticence. Rash deeds constantly involved life or death; sudden rebellion was followed abruptly by peace and calm. Uncommunicatively they worked out in their own minds what had taken place. Should a father reprimand his son for the latter's proud confidence in himself? On the contrary, he admired the boy and could sense in him the spirit of one of the most famous Vikings.

> His mother said a warship was his due,
> With virile oarsmen, as a Viking, to bring home the spoils.
> Standing at the prow, he should be steering his ship dauntlessly,
> A hero when in harbor he smote other men.

This is Egil Skallagrimsson, who has become Iceland's national hero—warrior, seafarer, brilliant poet and freedom fighter. He was born in A.D. 904. In the *Egil's Saga* (attributed to Snorri Sturluson) we learn about the everyday life of the Vikings and catch a glimpse of the restless North when it was all-powerful, in the era that was to have such an important influence on the continent of Europe at the hour of the Occident's birth. It was a time when every man cultivated his land and tended his home, yet none of them stayed there. All of them were in the grip of a new ideal. In a brief summing up, the old Northern saga gives us a picture of those days:

"In the summer they went on Viking voyages, conquered land and divided the spoils among themselves. In the winter they stayed at home with their fathers. In those days it was easy to gain riches and honor."

Egil, too, went to sea with his brothers. "In the spring they readied a long ship, took on a crew; in the summer they voyaged to the Baltic Sea and plundered, took booty, and gave battle. Then they sailed to Kurland and made landfall there. They signed a truce and trade pact. But when the time had passed, they started to plunder again and attacked in various areas."

Egil, taken prisoner by a Kurland peasant, managed to escape, taking all the peasant's treasure of silver with him. As he fled, it occurred to him suddenly that he had stolen the silver like a thief, behavior unworthy of a Viking. He put down the box full of silver, about-faced, went back to the peasant's house and set fire to it. He called the man out and killed him and the other inmates as they issued forth. Then he took up the box of silver again—now the justly earned reward of a fight—and sailed away with an easy conscience. . . .

In the winter, the men faced the care of their own hearths or were the honored guests of a friend. This involved an exchange of presents. One person, receiving a silk gown from the Orient, reciprocated with a strong, brilliantly colored sail that was praised by expert seamen and recognized with fear and awe whenever it appeared on the horizon in years to come.

The wear and tear on ships, gear, and weapons was tremendous. The winter months at home were therefore employed in the repair of the sensitive "sea stallions." New masts had to be cut from the highest trees in far-off forests. Steering gear, rudders, small parts had to be carved; sails had to be woven, rope spliced and rewound. Weapons had to be forged; animals had to be hunted for their fur; wounds had to heal. Many a man managed to crawl home in miserable condition after suffering all sorts of hardships; others were saved only by swimming or clinging to the wreckage of their ship until they were picked up. There was a lack of soldiers and laborers. Sword and storm shortened an average life span that was already brief. Only too often, in saga and rune stone, we read of a father's grief for his sons, or a similar lament for a fallen brother. As the grave mound, under which Egil's brother was buried, was being raised, Egil wrote:

> Dark suffering closed the eyes
> Of Grimm's fierce son.
> Dreadful sorrow. Ne'er
> Can I lament enow. . . .

But the sea dealt Egil his worst blow in the death of his favorite son, Bödvar. A storm struck the young man's ship, dragging him and his entire crew into the deep. To commemorate the tragedy, Egil composed a lay which today, a thousand years later, speaks to us more convincingly than any other poetry of its time.

The narrator starts with the bereaved father's burial of his son, during which his grief caused him to swell so that shirt and trousers tore with the pressure of his blood! "This was the way Egil was dressed: his hose were strapped close about the leg, and he was wearing a red, fustian kirtle, tight-fitting in its upper part and laced at the sides. But men report that he so swelled, that the kirtle split off him, and the hose too." He also ate no more, but shut himself up in his room. His daughter, Thorgerd, was sent for hurriedly, and he allowed her to enter, so that she might die or starve to death with him.

"For a while they were silent, then he said, 'What is it, my daughter? Are you chewing something?'

" 'I am chewing seaweed,' she replied, 'or I would live too long. I think it is making me feel worse.'

" 'Is it harmful?'

" 'Very. Do you want some?'

"After a while, they gave her water to drink because she was thirsty. 'Do you want to drink also, Father?' she asked.

"He took the drink. It was in an aurochs' horn. He drank in great gulps. Then his daughter admitted, 'They have deceived us. This is nourishing milk. And that is the end of our intention to die. Now, Father, I would prolong our life by having you write a lay in honor of Bödvar.' "

After these two preliminary items in prose, the one melodramatic, the other subtle, the tragedy in its sparse poetry, is doubly effective:

> Too heavy my heart   to send aloft
> A song scale's   airy meter.
>
> A man can't laugh   who filled with grief,
> Bears his son's body   to the grave.
>
> For at home   my house is dying,
> Like a branch   in groaning storm.
>
> Grim is the gap   the furious sea
> Tore in the tribal   row so firm.

The old man's thoughts wander back and forth. He speaks in metaphors; he reflects upon his progeny, and the kindness of his son:

> His father's words   did please him most,
> E'en when all people   spoke against it.
>
> They tell me   to replace this son
> Is possible only   if I sire others,
> One born to fill   his brother's place.
>
> Always he helped   the old man in his house;
> Always his strength   was a support at home.
>
> The feebleness   of this old man
> Is clearly there   for eye to see.
>
> Human companionship   I gladly shun,
> E'en if I see all men   in kindly spirit.

There is no mention of a mother, yet she too was grieving for her son. It was the cruel fate of all Viking women: to wait at home for their fathers, their husbands, their sons. Who would come back to them in the autumn? When the gray mists began to roll over the land, the same painful questions were being asked in thousands of homes: Are the men wintering away from home or shall we never see them again? Will a lonely seafarer bring us the answer? Stalwart, silent, dry-eyed, the fishermen's wives of the twentieth century on the west coast of Sweden—proud by necessity, controlled unto death— still receive the news that their men are lost forever. For nine hundred years, the sea has been master, enemy, disciplinarian, for the women living on the coast. The sea made them strong and reserved so that they might have the fortitude to wait for months, years; to care for farmstead and harvest alone; to manage their slaves and cope with the envy of their neighbors. Life was kinder to the men. A law permitted a man to have a wife in Iceland and one in Norway. There was no binding law for seamen in other harbors; situations were dealt with from case to case.

We chose the *Egil's Saga,* one of the finest poems of Old Norse literature, to demonstrate these everyday events, but its subject matter is subordinate to a more grandiose theme—the pride of heroes, the importance of the tribe. To illustrate this, let us turn to another tale from the saga.

Egil Skallagrims' brother, Thorolf, had just collected taxes in northern Norway for the Norwegian king. This was a coveted office because there was no way of controlling the tax collector; he could keep as much of what he collected as his conscience permitted, and the king had to be satisfied with a share of costly furs. No wonder Thorolf invited his king and master to a sumptuous feast.

No house was large enough to contain it, so the king, with three hundred men, was quartered in a huge, festively decorated barn, where Thorolf received him with five hundred men. This could not end well, for the king was Harald Fairhair (*circa* 860–*circa* 940)—ambitious, distrustful, anxious to do away with every possible opponent to his newly won and by no means secure dominance of Norway. There were rumors that Thorolf was planning to attack the king, that he had enriched himself beyond all fairness with the taxes collected, and the king was filled with envy. Negligible incidents, involuntary slights, led to ineradicable hatred. A few years later, the two men faced each other in battle. "Thorolf was wounded by sword and spear; the king himself struck the fatal blow."

For us the conflict between the two men would herewith be ended. Not so in times when the clan represented the only political and legally valid unity. Thorolf's tribe was weakened by his death. Vengeance was compulsory to restore a balance of power. Thus began one of the long tribal feuds which are the leitmotif of all the Old Norse family sagas. In the case of Skallagrim, however, the feud was of special importance because his adversary was such a mighty Norwegian, with the ambition to unify the nation.

After many acts of vengeance on both sides, Skallagrim chose to leave Norway a free and independent man, and settle in Iceland. Egil Skallagrimsson was born in Iceland, in the image of his father's hatred of the Norwegian royal house. His opponent was no longer Harald Fairhair, but his son, King Eric Bloodaxe. Long before they met both men had automatically taken upon themselves all rights and obligations—and animosities—of their tribes. Ridiculous little episodes had been interpreted as insults; a tense self-consciousness had grown oversensitive.

Egil's ship was driven on land by a heavy storm. Soaked to the skin, he and his men came to a manor which was being cared for by Bard, a steward of King Eric. Bard was of lowly origin but very efficient, and the king valued his services highly. He regretted that he could serve his unexpected guests nothing better than milk, sour milk and cottage cheese. The more they partook of the food, the more their host brought of it; there seemed to be an endless supply of the stuff. With wet boots, sour stomachs, and in a foul mood, the men lay down to sleep on their straw pallets.

Suddenly King Eric appeared with his spouse, Gunnhild, and Bard hastened to serve them his best beer. "The repast was very fine and there was plenty to drink."

Infuriated, his face getting redder and redder, Egil sat facing the royal pair. He was insulted, yet he could not abuse Bard's hospitality while he was under the man's roof. Not until they were outside could they have it out with each other. In the course of the fight—to the great annoyance of the king—Bard was killed.

The Vikings traveled into the most far-flung regions, driven by the miserable harvests of their cold homeland; borne along by a youthful restlessness and an uncontrollable yearning for what was far away; by the urge to seek strange lands, to discover and settle them. Life beckoned and enticed. Every summer offered its own horn of plentiful experience. Who had seen Gibraltar or the Bosphorus? Who knew the feel of a good sharp blade when it struck home? Was there anyone present who could walk outside the railing when the oarsmen were rowing full speed? No chance for adventure was permitted to pass by. The Vikings were always vibrant, always creative, always ingenious, shaping each situation in life brilliantly. And there—in the boundlessness of their activities, the exuberance of their lust for action—lies the fascination of their exploits.

Every year uncountable dragon ships sank to the bottom of the sea. With their wealth of wood carving and grinning dragon-post heads, they remain in a good state of preservation because—with water flowing over it, not exposed to the air, and without too great changes of temperature—wood possesses excellent durability. Thousands of these ships lie at the bottom of the Baltic and North seas; hundreds in German and French rivers; in the Atlantic Ocean and the Mediterranean. Some may be found in still more distant waters. Only a small minority of the Viking ships were burned or rotted; most of them are preserved to the present day in slime and silt.

There they lie, fascinating, tempting, but too deep down for even the most modern diving apparatus; inaccessible evidence of the birth of the Occident, an era when the Vikings were mobile, were everywhere. The goal of a voyage might have been England, Ireland, or the Orient. In the Far North an inheritance had to be claimed, a meeting of the *thing* assembly seemed of vital importance; an injustice had to be avenged in blood. Swedish colonies were developed in Finland and the Baltic provinces. Viking ships dominated the Slavonic coast east of the Elbe. The Baltic was a landlocked Swedish sea nine hundred years before Gustavus Adolphus II. And the first question we ask ourselves is one that will occupy our minds often in this book: How was it possible for these Norsemen to find their way to such far-flung waters? How could such far-off land conquests take place? How could the isolated, distant, primitive North suddenly be capable of fostering such exploits?

1. *Map of the European peoples in Viking days.*

2

Barter and Trade

Beginnings (150 B.C.–A.D. *650)*

The Romans loved the spectacular. To be able to offer them something new, Emperor Nero sent forth one of his so-called Amber Knights, Justinianus, via Carnuntum—on the Danube, between Vienna and Pressburg—northward, into territory that was later to be East Prussia. Justinianus returned with such a tremendous amount of booty that the hedonistic emperor declared a special Amber Day for the gladiator games on which the arena may well have been decorated with the semiprecious stone. Such natural treasure was easily found and brought back in incredible quantities from the Ancient Germans.

Tacitus writes: "For a long time the amber lay there with everything else cast up by the sea, until our affluence made it famous. They [the Teutons] had no use for it themselves. They collected the raw material, brought it to market uncut, and were surprised when it fetched such profit." Thus, hesitantly and naïvely, Germanic trading began. In the days of the Vikings it was to dominate the world market.

The Baltic Sea did not have the benign warmth and azure blue of the Mediterranean. Its stormy waves mirrored the eternal gray of cloudy skies; they broke on rocky reefs or sand banks, neither very inviting to the peasant farmer. On the whole, the Scandinavian peninsula did not offer settlers a welcome. The giant trees of its forests grew on morainal land; the high mountains were inaccessible; cool, barren summers and humid autumns made farming a hazard. That was why cattle breeding predominated; milk soup was more common fare than bread. Loaves made of rye or wheat were a rarity, sometimes an unknown delicacy.

The people lived isolated in small communities. It was a long journey to the Celts and Romans in southern Europe. The Baltic had to be navigated in rowboats because sailing ships were still unknown in northern waters, and to row long distances, strong arms and endurance were needed. And the sea had to be calm, or the waves would have destroyed the keelless boats. That was why the few men who voyaged far had to depend on detours that led along the coast. On boat expeditions such as these, the modest barter trading of simple iron ware took place with the South.

Under the Roman Emperors, however, all this changed. Traders from the South reached the North with goblets, buckets, platters, sieves, bronze ladles, with glass and silver. And such luxuries were what the Norsemen coveted above everything else. Happily they offered their wares in exchange: fine furs and amber.

The furs had to be brought from far away; and it came about that the southern and northern trade routes met on the centrally located Danish archipelago. Here the bartering thrived. The rich findings of Roman tableware in innumerable Danish graves is proof of the prosperity of those days.

Oarsmen were a familiar sight. They traveled along the coast; pushed on to the northernmost bays of the Baltic; felt their way along the Norwegian oceanic littoral as far as the Lofoten Islands, to Harstad. Spits of land, reefs and bays impressed themselves on the eyes of these skilled seafarers. The retina was their most reliable map. Across the continent, the Vistula, the Oder, the Elbe and the Rhine transported merchandise quickly, conveniently, and in comparative safety, southward and northward. On the latest chart registering all the Roman finds from Old Germania, we can see exactly how they grow more numerous along some of these waterways, and become rarer inland. For more than five hundred years, the rivers of Central Europe were the main arteries for trade and barter.

The first tribes we hear of are the Cimbri and the Teutons. In 120 B.C. they abandoned the peninsula of Jutland and wandered up the Oder River. In surprise attacks they defeated the heavily armed Roman legions only to be finally destroyed themselves in northern Italy. Next came the Burgundians, from the island of Burgundarholm (today Bornholm) and the surrounding coast; and the Vandals from Vandilsyssel (today Vendsussel in North Jutland). The two tribes settled first in north Germania before moving on southward—more slowly now—giving their names finally to the provinces of Burgundy and (V)Andalusia. And the Goths left their original homeland, which, all signs indicate, must have been in West Sweden, beyond Göteborg. During the first two centuries of our Christian calendar, they settled in the Vistula delta, then moved on to southern Russia. The Lombards forsook the region around the mouth of the Elbe and settled finally in Lombardian North Italy. One wave of peoples after the other moved from north to south. The saga scholars are still quarreling over the written sources. Some doubt their value, others swear by them. Let us leave the argument to them. We prehistorians have to evaluate our archeological findings independently, and must include the Saxons, and the Anglians who did not wander off to England until the fifth century A.D. The powerful expansion of the Vikings to southeast and southwest was the last migration of ancient Nordic days. It should be seen as part of the whole great migration of peoples which took place over a period of a thousand years, in this case a human stream that originated around the Baltic—in those days the Eastern—Sea. With one difference: unlike the uniform tribes who had migrated before them, the Viking moves were made up of people from all Scandinavia. What took place before the year A.D. 800, however, should not be termed Viking migrations, as the expression "Viking" was not formulated until about that time.

In this prehistoric period we may also include the host of Swedish soldiers who became Roman mercenaries and were paid in gold coin or bars. They returned to their northern homeland, buried their purses, their gold necklaces, all their treasure, in the earth—and died. No one knew the tree or stone where the treasure lay or is lying today, to come to light utterly unexpectedly when a road is built or a foundation dug. It was the Gold Age of Europe (*circa* A.D. 200–600) as immortalized in the legend of the Nibelungs. Actually the gold may have come from Roman gold discoveries in Africa, but most of it has been preserved for posterity in—of all places—Scandinavian soil! Today it fills the museums of northern capitals with its glittering glory, especially the Gold Room in Stockholm. For the Scandinavian settlements had long ceased to be purely farmer's land. We find reflected in grave excavations a society of warriors, chieftains and kings; the slaves, those without property, laborers and children disappear from our findings. We are dealing suddenly with early Germanic states, with an art-appreciative people, men and women who could be ostentatious, who took a lively interest in life on the continent, and who also fought each other bitterly. But around A.D. 650 the entire influx of Roman gold and import pieces traded along the German rivers breaks off. An event then took place in Europe that was to change the face of that continent for centuries.

The Birth of the Occident (A.D. 650–800)

At this point the Slavs penetrated the West. With them came tribes from the eastern steppes, the Avars, for instance, moving forward from Asiatic areas into the Danube basin.

The Slavs' home was in central Russia around the Dnieper, a relatively small settlement area, surrounded by Finns and Turks. Now they began to move, zone by zone, into unpopulated central Europe. First they crossed the Vistula, and all trading ceased on the River Oder, which had once been so lively. When they reached the river that was to form their westernmost boundary—the Elbe—this river, too, was abandoned as a north-south trade route for the Occident.

The Slavs lived in villages and tribal communities, split up politically and underdeveloped as merchants, with the result that traffic on the big continental rivers came to an end. In these dark centuries, the center of Europe's cultural life shifted so far west that the once-vital barter between Scandinavia and the South could take place only on the Rhine and along the Atlantic coast. The "West" had been just as menacingly reduced and narrowed down as it is today.

East of the Elbe, Slav and Scandinavian ruled; in Spain, the Arabs. The latter, defeated at Poitiers in A.D. 732, nevertheless made trading with the Orient difficult. Only the Jews were still able to carry on to some extent. Believers and nonbelievers sought their wares. Business associates in every city and harbor assisted them. Their ships dared to cross the Mediterranean, which was swarming with Mussulmen pirates. Jews turned up with merchandise of the West in Seville, Athens, Damascus and Baghdad, and went back to the buyers of the Occident with the spices, silk and luxuries of the Orient. No wonder they were permitted to cross all boundaries, unharmed, and were welcome wherever they went. No wonder the Frankish kings—Pippin, Charlemagne and his son, Louis the Pious—gave them trading privileges and asked in return that they appear personally in Aix at least every two years.

There is a story that throws light on such events. It concerns Archbishop Richulf, in Mainz (A.D. 787–813), who craved earthly goods above everything else. Charlemagne ordered a Jewish merchant "who traveled regularly to Palestine" to trick the archbishop in some fashion or other. The merchant took a common mouse, treated it with aromatic herbs, decorated it in bright colors, and offered it for sale to Richulf, declaring that this extremely valuable and hitherto unknown animal had been imported from India. A wild bargaining ensued. The merchant indignantly refused to accept three pounds of silver and declared that with ten he would still be out of pocket. The archbishop raised his offer and finally acquired the mouse for a bushel of silver. The Jew settled up with the king who had wanted to punish the avaricious Richulf in such a realistic way. At the next conclave, the silver was carried into the palace and the deeply shocked churchman was laughed to scorn.

What is important to us in the story is the fact that the Jewish merchant "traveled regularly to Palestine." Since our sources of direct information on these days is so scant, this is a vital detail. We also see that these widely traveled merchants were in the habit of offering their rare treasures for sale to princes, bishops and kings. They were no mere peddlers; they were skilled voyagers, who knew how to navigate the southern trade routes. And they could count on being paid well for their time-consuming efforts and the considerable dangers they faced on their long journeys.

The Jewish trader was not so familiar with the northern territories, by which I mean the world of the Vikings, which interests us most. Here all trade was in the hands of the Frisians, a race of coastal people living on the mouth of the Rhine, who, in the eighth and ninth centuries experienced a golden age of their own and enjoyed a leading position in Europe. It was impossible to by-pass them. They were masters at combining littoral, sea and river voyages, and wove a far-flung mercantile network that could compete on an equal footing with that of the Jewish and Oriental traders. A strange combination—Jews and Frisians—yet together they controlled the European markets at the hour of the Occident's birth.

The Frisians organized their business trips from bases well known to us. Dorestad, east of Utrecht, was their most important trading center; from it they controlled the old (Krumme) Rhine, the Vecht and the Lek—three of the four arms of the Rhine in those days. Documents tell us that Pippin built a fortress here in 689, and that the settlement around it became the tariff and mint center of the Frankish Empire. Today the Old Rhine is covered with sand, and a small town called Wyk-te-Duurstede lies on the Lek. But the Dutch, in the course of their excavations under the leadership of Professor J. H. Holwerda, mainly in the 1920's, were able to reconstruct the pulsating life of this extraordinarily important trading town. (*See ill. 2.*)

Today a street in Dorestad runs northward from the state church, far out

2. *The Frisian mercantile city of Dorestad.*

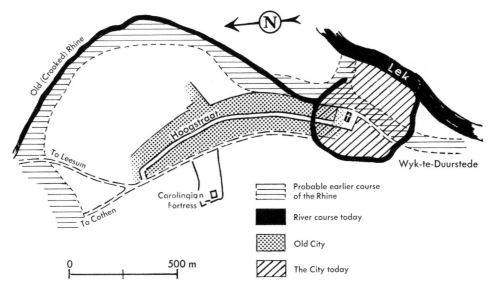

into the fields. It is called Hoogstraat, and innumerable parcels of land jut out from it. Oddly enough, they are all the same length, which results in the formation of two boundary lines—one east, the other west—running parallel to the Hoogstraat. Here excavations uncovered the former ramparts. The outlines of ancient Frisian Dorestad may, therefore, be quite clearly seen today on the land-registry-office map. The settlement was a long and fairly narrow commercial town, about thirty-three acres in all.

Ramparts, wall and trench offered good protection, not so much against enemy attack as against the flooding of the Old Rhine. Excavators found the houses of those days mainly on the west side of the Hoogstraat; on the east, down to the banks of the river, lay only a few scattered larger buildings. This seemed strange. Houses usually tend to stand on both sides of a village main street. Here, however, we are not concerned with a village but with the first harbor and mercantile city of the early Middle Ages. The native Frisians lived west of the Hoogstraat; the east side was reserved for the traveling merchants. There is documentary evidence that officers of the king were permitted to charge harbor dues. The actual anchorage area was probably on the Rhine, outside the city walls.

On one side, the roofs of houses; on the other, shipping anchorage. What intensive life there must have been on the narrow strip of land in between, during the hectic market and trading weeks. We know all about it because at that time there was no such thing as an orderly removal of refuse. Bones, leftovers, offal, pottery shards, every manner of waste was left to lie where it fell in a so-called kitchen midden, forming a "black earth" or humus of considerable depth. Unfortunately, ignorant people coming upon it and evaluating it, declared it to be manure. In 1843 alone, 2,750 bushels of bones were dug up in this area, with which activity Dorestad's most valuable archive was uprooted and destroyed, the cultural earth of a brilliant trading epoch scattered to the winds. How we would have liked to study the individual weavers, combmakers, smiths, shoemakers and potters, in their homes; the noblemen; the Frisian voyagers with the treasures brought back from their travels! However fragmentary the remains, they would have been invaluable documentation of their day.

The Frisians could boast a whole row of important commercial trade centers. From written sources we know of the Baltic sea port, Quentovic, mint town and asylum for pilgrims; through excavations we are familiar with Domburg on the island of Walcheren. Today the place where it once stood is mainly covered by water and could be studied only when the tide was very low, for the last time in 1867. Traces of traders, artisans and a wharf have been found in Emden and Hesse. Dorestad, though, remains of primary importance.

In the *Vita* of English Benedictine missionary, Wynfrith Boniface (*circa* 680–755), a short but graphic note on Dorestad harbor activity records his last mission to the continent in 716. (He was never to see England again.) "Boniface traveled by boat from London to Dorestad . . . with the captain's permission he boarded the ship—a strange passenger for the bustling crew— paid his fare, and with a good wind reached Dorestad." This doesn't sound different from the accounts of any harbor in those early days. It indicates peaceful passenger and freight service in precisely defined forms.

For a continuation of the trip up the Rhine to Cologne, Mainz and Speyer, the missionary, Alcuin, left a vivid account, written in the year 781, in verse. It is of special interest to us because the river lane it describes—the only river trade route still in existence from the north southward at that time—was of such vital importance to the Viking traders. In his letter, Alcuin gives all the necessary advice for the dangerous and laborious Rhine trip, beginning with the English Channel. Quaintly, he addresses himself, not to the recipient of the letter, but to the missive itself:

> Hurry, fleet as the wind, little missive, across the wide sea,
> In the wild foam striving to reach the mighty mouth of the Rhine
>   with its treasure of fish,
> The river that's tossed by the rushing wave as it meets the sea.
> See to it that the stream's power wash not thy quarterdeck forward.
> Then let thy prow glide upstream from a long hawser,
> And if on the river trip my Alberich should come to meet you,
> "Oh, powerful cattle-rich Prince!" say to him quickly, "Greetings!"

Apparently cattle husbandry was already thriving in Friesland in those days, and the following lines concerning the treatment of guests in the pagan cities of the Rhine delta are informative:

> Hadda, in Utrecht, will scarce treat you
> To more than one night of honey, vegetables and yellow butter;
> For neither oil nor wine are decanted
> In the land of the Frisians.
> Let thy sail therefore swell, and hasten to circumvent Dorestad.
> Rotbert the Black may scarce be expected to give thee a welcome,
> Since he, the miserly merchant, will not be enraptured of thy song.
> Turn thy keel rather t'ward the shores of Ionas, the seer.
> There you will find rest offered to him who is weary of travel,
> As well as vegetables, fish and bread in richly amount.

Alcuin's account then takes us to the most famous stretch of the great river:

> Cologne, I know, will also ope wide the gates of its houses to thee.
> Here greet respectfully Father Rikvulfus.
> Say to him: "Beloved, praise of thee lieth fore'er in my heart."
> On gliding keel hie thee hence then, through the wild waves
> 'Till thou hast reached the mouth of the friendly Mosel.
> Travel the river, rowing. . . .

The letter brings greetings to friends on the Rhine:

> Shouldst thou mayhap come to Mainz, crown of all cities;
> Vouchsafe to Lullus, the teacher, undying greetings,
> Since he doth count as a churchly example, a jewel of wisdom,
> And greet the pride of the people of Speyer, good Father
>   Bassinus. . . .

> Then, O missive, go back to thy waiting ship. . . .
> Let neither castles nor houses nor towns nor blossoming landscape
> Keep thee filled with astonishment for e'en an hour;
> Hurry, ne'er tarrying, with the stormy strides of man fleeing;
> Hale, hearty, happy, and filled with the zest of life
> May thou set eyes on our friends in a friendly spirit. . . .

Thus versified a man who was familiar with the sanctuaries of the Church, the footholds of the great travel and trade routes of the early Middle Ages. But archeological findings are going to bring to life for us the commerce that is scarcely mentioned in the written sources of those days—an example of the complementation possible between these two sources of modern scientific research.

The Frisians, as already mentioned, dominated the trade of the Rhine and the northern seacoast. In Mayen, west of Coblenz, is found a type of basalt especially suitable for making millstones. Traces of a thriving stone industry are therefore found in this area, and we recognize its products at once whenever they turn up in our findings. The same can be said of certain double-conic clay pots, and the so-called Badorfer vessels that came from the north Frank district west of the Rhine. They were easily transported on that river. We come upon them regularly in the eighth-century findings of littoral settlements all the way to the Ems and Weser—unmistakably trading objects. East Friesland, however, between the Weser and Eider, was strictly avoided.

The flat marshes and violent North Sea storms made this strip of coast forbidding, but on the island of Föhr, a single vessel was found; also a gold coin from Maastricht, struck before 650.

Coins are practically talking witnesses. We find Frisian coins all along the Rhine to Constance on Lake Constance, westward to England, northward to Jutland. Dorestad coins from before 689 have been found on the island of Sylt; on the Lim Fjord, Pippin's pale Madelinus coin dated after 689. Quite clearly you can trace the enterprising Frisians, feeling their way along the Scandinavian littoral, coming to a standstill before the Jutland peninsula barrier to the Baltic Sea.

The people of these dark ages knew practically nothing about the Scandinavians. Could there possibly be a rewarding market in these unknown territories to the north? Could this cold zone produce anything desirable? Could there be native traders here with whom contact could be established?

Emergence of the Viking World (A.D. *650–830*)

In Old Uppsala and on Lake Mälar, a tribe emerges victoriously from innumerable battles with its neighbors: the Sveas, founders of a future Sweden. We also have some knowledge of Danish kings and petty Norwegian rulers along the coast and in the valleys; they introduced luxuries and a certain degree of splendor in their court life and their warriors were ever ready for action not only in Scandinavia, but beyond the Baltic and North seas. For in the meantime they had made a decisive technical discovery: the art of sailing.

Strange, what a long time it took these seafaring people to hit upon such an obvious idea. The Norsemen may have seen Roman sailing vessels, which certainly didn't incite the northern mariner to imitation because they were designed for the calm waters of the Mediterranean, and the Romans were poor sailors. The oak ship from the moor of Nydam (*circa* A.D. 300; now in Schleswig) had 36 oars; sail and keel are still missing. (*See ill. 3.*) The somewhat earlier portrayals of ships on gravestones on the island of Gotland are similar to it. (*See ill. 4.*) They too lack sails; the men are rowing, the sternpost swings up in the form of a sickle. The sail demanded an entirely new principle of balance, a securing by way of a keel. This totally different sailing-ship construction was not created overnight. A drafting board was unknown to the men who lived so close to the primitive powers of nature. What they designed had to be tested by the sailor in storm and on the open sea. We can only guess how many faultily constructed ships foundered in storms and sank to the bottom of the ocean with their crews.

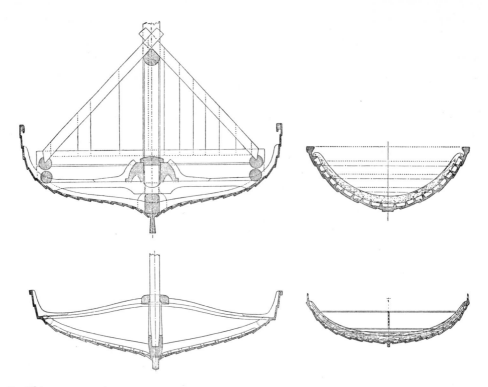

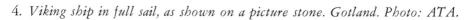

3. *Ship cross sections.*
      RIGHT: *From Nydam and Kvalsund. Circa 600.*
      LEFT: *Fully developed Viking ships from Gokstad and Öseberg. Circa 800.*

4. *Viking ship in full sail, as shown on a picture stone. Gotland. Photo: ATA.*

A fortunate ship finding from the year A.D. 600 shows the struggle with the problem still going on. The ship of Kvalsund has reinforced floor planking and a mast for a sail. (*See ill. 3.*) With a strong keel, a ship was capable of riding the waves easily, of cutting through them, of defying the gales of the open sea. With a keel, a ship could carry sails and with the right wind reach astounding speeds. It could be built twice as broadly, permitting it to carry a far greater cargo of provisions and men. With the discovery of the sail, the Norsemen took a giant step forward.

5. *Viking ship from Gokstad. Ship Museum, Bigdoy, near Oslo. Universitetets Oldsakssamling, Oslo.*

It is not surprising to find the new art of sailing also represented in grave findings. At all times and the world over, grave ritual has reflected the ideals of nobleman and prince. The powerful ones of this world have had themselves interred in driving or riding posture, standing or sitting, dining, or enjoying other pleasures of an earthly life. So why not sailing? The Hird people of the Svea kings turn up suddenly in our findings and from the seventh century on, quite logically, the peasant princes north of Stockholm sail into eternity in the full regalia of their armor. In Vendel, Valsgärde, Tuna and Ulltuna, the ships were drawn up on land and covered with earth after the burial. Long, narrow depressions betray where the men lay, side by side in their ships, while the women were still being cremated, according to ancient custom. The practice of burial in one's ship was not adopted by the Svea kings themselves; for this—to our astonishment—we find an example in an English royal grave near Sutton Hoo, in Suffolk, northeast of London. It is the richest find of its kind ever to have been excavated north of the Alps. Apparently the last semipagan East Anglian king, Aethelhere, who died in 655, is being honored in this ship grave.

A new inspiration spreads quickly, and can catch the people of this earth like a brush fire. Thus it was with the passion for sailing. To be able to branch out in open sea voyages; not to have to creep along the coast any more; to discover strange lands by crossing the sea directly, to dominate the North and Baltic seas—these were the unmistakable realities behind the custom of ship burial.

6. Stones in ship formation, adjacent to the king mounds of Badelunda, west of Stockholm. Photo: ATA.

7. *Scabbard trim with profile of two horses rearing, in Irish interlace design. From Vendel, north of Uppsala, Grave 1. State Historical Museum, Stockholm. Photo: ATA.*

8. *Irish illuminated script, with animal interlace design. Codex Aureus in the Kungliga Library, Stockholm.*

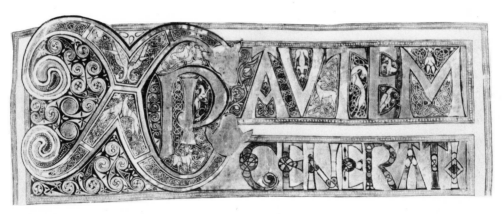

Sword, shield and helmet of Sutton Hoo could have originated in Old Uppsala, so similar are they to Swedish findings. How close was the relationship existing between the Anglo-Saxon kings and Sweden, across the sea? Were there political friendships, or were the princely houses related? We have no definite answers yet to these questions, but we know that the art of Old Uppsala was strongly influenced by Anglo-Irish style forms, although we find examples of the latter only on the illuminated scripts of monastic chroniclers, of the former on the metal accouterments of the pagan Norse warrior.

In several ship graves dating from the beginning of the eighth century, sturdy triangular horses can be distinguished trotting along the metal fittings of armor. (*See ill. 7.*) But they do not move freely. They are chained to the background by so-called Irish interlace which fills the remaining space. One

9. *Two horses ornamenting a scabbard. From Grave 5 in Valsgärde, north of Uppsala.*

may also see two horses facing each other as if in battle, their jaws fiercely locked. We find illustrations like this in the *codex aureus,* a copy of the gospels presented to the abbey of St. Maximin by a reputed sister of Charlemagne. (*See ill. 8.*) It would almost seem that the heathen smiths had leafed through holy books. But from the shaping of the animals' jaws, hoofs and similar details, we realize that these armor fittings were definitely wrought by native Norse artists. (*See ills. 9, 10.*)

Around the middle of the eighth century, we find animals on narrow metal bands which are closely related to the serpentine animals in the sacred volumes of the monasteries of Lindau (Bavaria) and Lindisfarne (Ireland). These are followed later by grotesque humans, hideous crossbreeds between animal and man, similar to those so popular in the Irish Book of Kells. (*See ill. 11.*)

Unlike the hard granite and gneiss of the Swedish mainland, the Baltic Sea island of Gotland is composed of fine sandstone. Artists discovered its advantages in prehistoric times and from it created innumerable elegantly formed and decorated monuments to honor the dead. (*See ill. 12.*) In the eighth century, they were especially rich in decoration, and by their Irish interlace we can date them fairly precisely. A rectangular fenced-in courtyard depicted on one stone is exceptionally interesting. (*See ill. 13.*) The homestead is being attacked, and its owners are defending it. We see cattle and the gables of houses with their ornamentation. A similar scene may be found on an English

10. *Interlace horses on both sides of a sword pommel. Liland, Norway. Original size.*

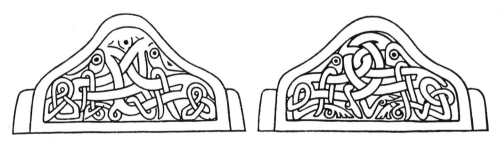

11. *Grotesque human figures on an oval brooch found in Norway. Östnes, Bjarköy, Tromsö. Universitetets Oldsakssamling, Oslo.*

whalebone casket, Frank's Casket. (*See ills. 14, 15.*) The finer material makes possible more delicate carving.

The design on the Gotland memorial stone is so obvious it requires no explanation. At this point the Scandinavians were fascinated by ornamentation, yet so poorly schooled in the art of depicting the human figure that even the simplest motif could count as an innovation. Only very few regions were willing to incorporate the human figure in their art, among them the always pictorially minded Gotlanders. On the English casket we see illustrated the *Edda* lay of Volund (Wayland) the Smith. And we find it repeated on another Gotland memorial stone. Here, as revenge for his captivity, Volund has

12. *Picture stone of Ardre VIII, Gotland. Height about 7 feet. State Historical Museum, Stockholm. Photo: ATA.*

13. *Battle scene from picture stone of Klinte Hunninge I., Gotland.
Photo: ATA.*

14. *English whalebone casket (Frank's casket.) 9 by 7½ inches. British Museum, London, and 15. Battle scene from Frank's casket.*

killed the king's sons, who lie beheaded at his feet. The king's daughter visits him with her handmaidens. He seduces her and flees in the shape of a swan. On the right, his brother Egil is preparing the costume out of four living birds. On the Gotland stone, you can see, between the smith and the beheaded princes, the smithy with its thatched roof. Volund has already assumed the shape of a swan; the king's daughter is on the left, her back to him. Through seafarers, a casket like the English one, or another similarly illustrated object,

16. *Volund Saga on Frank's casket.*

must have fallen into the hands of some ambitious Gotland stonemason. (*See ills. 16, 17.*)

Art was apparently the cultural contribution of the Anglo-Irish, while the activity of the Norsemen was being played out on the sea, even far beyond the North Sea, westward. What could be more natural for them than to reach out eastward as well, across the Baltic? Which is just what they proceeded to do.

In the early 1930's, before modern-day politics put a temporary end to research, excavations brought to light findings of an era poor in written documentation. The first inkling of these discoveries came in 1929 when Swedish and Lett archeologists—the former under the leadership of Professor Birger Nerman—exhumed two barrows approximately three and three-quarter miles east of the city of Libau (Liepaja in Latvia). The mounds gave every indication of being Swedish and were of considerable size. Probably there were once

17. *Volund Saga on Gotlandic picture stone.*

a thousand such hill graves, although now barely half that number are left, and only thirty-three were opened. All of them covered Swedish cremation graves. The funeral pyres had raged ruinously, still we can easily recognize bent, brittle pieces of metal as the remains of swords with Irish interlace design, shield-bosses, the points of spears, belt buckles, fittings and other accessories of clothing and armor. (*See ill. 18.*) Here the Svea founded, on the other side of the Baltic, a settlement which existed from A.D. 600 to 800, in a

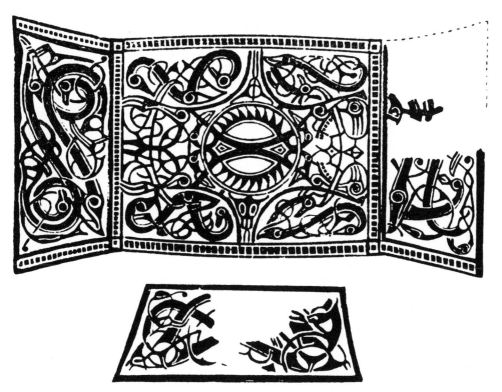

18. *Ornamentation on a sword hilt. Ihre, Gotland. Original size. Drawing: ATA.*

development area that was Kurlandic. The graves of the Kurlanders of this era look quite different from the immigrants' and can therefore easily be distinguished.

Of still greater importance, a third burial ground was found, almost the same size but more difficult to recognize because it was hidden under the ground. All the sod had to be removed, after which a hundred graves could be examined. Here men were buried with and without armor; also women, with their trinkets, brooches, clasps, buckles, bracteates, necklaces, pendants, keys, bracelets, finger rings and beads, like those found on the Baltic Sea island of Gotland. (*See ill. 19.*) Similarly the level-earth burial ground uncovered here is originally Gotlandic and not to be found on the mainland of Sweden. No doubt about it—this is a burial field of Gotlandic settlers who pushed forward across the Baltic, *circa* A.D. 650–800, not as marauders or warriors, but with their wives, to found a colony in a thinly settled immigrant area. They remained in close contact with their Gotlandic motherland. A similar development of jewelry in Gotland over the same 150-year period is indisputable proof of this. That is why we may speak here of true colonization.

In the course of these migrations, the Gotlanders and Sveas were on good terms with each other. We find often that they settled down together. Their burials, however, remained separate.

They settled in the small town of Grobin, where a magnificent earthwork fortress, bounded on three sides by the Alande River, offered a safe haven. Later, the medieval Ordenburg was built of stone, close to it. They penetrated farther into Kurland. On five different sites, to east and north, Swedish or Gotlandic objects of the same period were found, all crying out for a more thoroughly organized excavation, which unfortunately could not take place because of the Second World War.

And what was the relationship of these immigrants to the Kurlanders? After all, the Norsemen were the politically active ones and supreme in military affairs. They probably demanded tribute. In those days, everybody who had the power exacted tribute from an alien people. This helped to make life far from home pleasanter. They were probably also avid traders. The organized trade policies of the Sveas—about which we shall hear more later—point to this. Gradually Kurlandic jewelry found its way into Swedish graves. This is not as obvious as one might think, because in those days jewelry was part of the native costume. When, therefore, Kurlandic chain necklaces, bracelets and spiral neck rings turned up in our findings, it was, indicatively, in later graves, which were dug at a time when the colonists had finally, to some extent, lost touch with their motherland, had begun to feel at home on the sandy Kurland coast, and had married Kurlandic women.

Highly revealing is the fact that the evidence of colonies closely follows the first boat graves and the period of the king barrows in Old Uppsala. Kings —at their sides warriors who felt superior to the native peasant fighter and therefore adhered to their own customs and ritual—seem to go historically right along with the first overseas voyagers, proving that an active colonial policy was evolving beyond the Baltic. We find the material proof of this in the graves of that period, and may confidently conclude this political reality even though we have no documentary evidence of it.

We are in the fortunate position of being able to find out quite a lot about

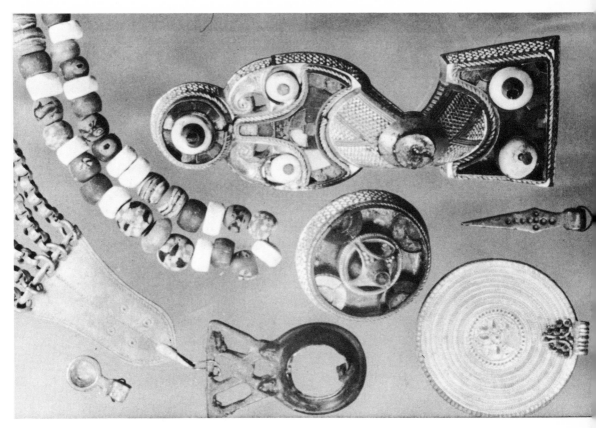

19. *Jewelry from Gotland,* circa A.D. *650–800. Ihre Grave 159. State Historical Museum, Stockholm. Photo: E. Oxenstierna.*

the kings of the Svea in Old Uppsala. In approximately the eighth century, Ivar Vidfamne (the Far-Reaching), his grandson Harald Wartooth, and Harald's nephew, Sigurd Ring, ruled. The Ynglinga Saga, written by Snorri Sturluson as introduction to his *Heimskringla,* tells us about them: "Ivar conquered Kurland, Saxland, and Estland, and all the lands east to Gardarike [the Russian settlements, of which more later]. He also ruled over West Saxland, and won that part of England which was called Northumberland. . . . Harald Wartooth subjugated all the aforementioned lands which King Ivar once possessed. . . ."

Here Kurland is mentioned specifically, and one-fifth of England as well. We therefore have to accept the idea of Swedish activity also beyond the North Sea, especially after having found such strong Anglo-Irish influences in the boat graves of Uppland, and after discovering a boat grave similarly appointed in Sutton Hoo. The seizures in both East and West were probably of a warlike and political nature, with the added impetus of trade interests. But what was the fate of the colony in Kurland?

In 1931, after the successful finds in Grobin, digging was resumed near Apuole, in Lithuania, about twenty-five miles southeast of Grobin, on the Barte River. Here, too, several Gotlandic level graves of A.D. 650–800 were uncovered, directly adjacent to a fortress, about 50 feet above the river, with a 25-foot rampart. During a siege, no one tarried long in such refuge fortresses. They were built primarily to serve as protection for retreating or evacuated women, children, cattle and treasure. They often lay outside the village or town precincts. The remains of settlements and "black earth" are consequently scarce. Just the same, a wall conceals traces of collapsed wooden palisades, often of several fort foundations built one on top of the other. Especially remarkable in this ninth-century stratum are 150 non-Baltic iron spearheads, giving proof of a mass attack.

Archbishop Rimbert, who had been in Sweden, knew all about these events and in 876 wrote: "Far from the Swedes, a people called Kurlanders once were subject to them. But this is long ago. For they rose up and threw off the Swedish yoke."

This information corroborates the Grobin finds, which go only up to the year 800. Rimbert reports that the Danes, on a warlike expedition to Kurland, suffered a bloody defeat. He goes on to recount the events of *circa* 850: "When the Swedish King Olaf [barely one hundred years after Harald Wartooth] and his men heard of it, they decided that they would also try it [to subdue the Kurlanders]. Olaf assembled a mighty force and set out for Kurland. At first, and unexpectedly, they came to a city in a kingdom called Seeburg, in which they found 7,000 men ready for battle. They laid waste to this town, plundered it and burnt it to the ground. Their courage grew through this action. In a state of wild excitement, they left their ships and set out on a quick expedition of five days, and hastened to reach another city, named Apulia. In this city they found 15,000 men ready for battle. When they had reached the town, and the others had retired inside their fortress, Olaf's men launched a powerful attack on the city from the outside while the men inside defended it manfully."

Seeburg, in all probability, is our Grobin; Apulia is unmistakably the Lithuanian-Kurland town today called Apuole. For eight days Olaf's men fought bitterly, until the defenders of Apulia sent delegates and declared: "First we will give you, as alliance tribute, all the booty in gold and weapons that we took from the Danes in the year gone by. We moreover offer half a mark in silver for every man residing in this town, and beside that we are prepared to pay the taxes we once were wont to pay; to furnish hostages; and from now on to obey and follow your leadership as in earlier days." After that, only the cocksure young warriors still wanted to storm Apulia; the Swedish king and his trusty old soldiers were agreeable to the conditions specified, and we archeologists are delighted to find documentary evidence and archeological findings again complementing each other.

We see Sveas and Gotlanders settling on the banks of the Alande and Barte rivers, but not directly on the Baltic seacoast. That would have been too dangerous. Marauders from the sea could attack too easily. Rather, inland, so that sentinels on the coast could give the alarm by fires. Besides, the Libau Haff—one of those long, shallow Baltic lagoons, separated from the open sea by a sand bar—offered the mariner an immense, excellently shielded harbor.

We feel our way down the Baltic littoral, because now we know which settlement areas the Swedes of the seventh and eighth centuries preferred, and the first thing we come to is the Kurische Haff. In those days it did not open up near Memel, but at the southwest end, near Wiskiauten. Once there were 500 barrows here, and archeologists have been excavating since 1870. Gotlandic trinkets and jewelry typical for women shortly before the year 800, also innumerable contributions of the Svea point to a colony with the same organized installations as the one in Kurland. Encouraged by these findings, German and Swedish archeologists examined a few more barrows in 1932. Many more should be dug. Where is the Gotlandic level burial ground? Could this settlement predate the one in Grobin? One difference between the two is obvious—Wiskiauten was not abandoned shortly after 800, but remained in Swedish hands throughout the entire Viking era.

We continue to sail down the coast to the Frische Haff. Scattered Viking findings are often discovered in a wide area as far south as Elbing (today Polish Elblag). We also hear of Old-Prussian settlements and burial fields. On New Year's Eve, 1936, when (then German) Elbing was about to usher in its seven-hundred-year jubilee, it was proclaimed that the town would have to move the hour of its birth back at least five hundred years! The typical Gotlandic level grave field had been found west of the railway station. It contained round box-brooches, open-work metal plates, arm bands, keys, and so on—a rich find which has not yet been publicized sufficiently because of the intervening war. Typical Swedish forms of jewelry and Old-Prussian graves were also found. (*See ill. 20.*)

A settlement at Elbing on the Drausensee (Lake Drausen) is mentioned in King Alfred's translation of the Spanish historian, Orosius. Into it he inserted the story of two voyages of discovery (*circa* 880) as described to him by the Norwegians, Ottar and Wulfstan. Here we can read:

"Wulfstan reported that he sailed from Haesum (near Schleswig) and in seven days and nights arrived in Truso, his ship having run under full sail all

20. *Gotlandic jewelry from Elbing on the Frische Haff. Original size.*

the way. During our entire voyage to the mouth of the Vistula, Wendenland lay on our starboard side. The Vistula is a great river, dividing Witland and Wendland; and Witland belongs to the Aisten [Old-Prussians]. But the Vistula comes from Wendenland and flows into the Aisten Sea [the Frische Haff], and the Aisten Sea is about fifteen miles wide. Then the river Elbing flows from the east into the Aisten Sea from the water (Lake Drausen) on which Truso lies. . . . Aistenland is very big. There are many castles, and there is a king for every castle. The king and the wealthiest men drink mare's milk; the slaves and the needy drink mead. There is much warfare in the region."

Wulfstan's geographic information is most exact. His town Truso on the Elbing is today's Elblag. It seems to have been the most prominent goal of the eastern Baltic even if Wulfstan tells us nothing of merchants there. We find no evidence, however, of a Svea colony before 800 in the *haff* at the mouth of the Oder, perhaps because this is Scanian-Danish water, and the Swedish pioneers favored the more northern reaches of the Baltic.

Fur dealers from Drontheim (Trondheim, Norway) had formed a settlement in Finland, near Vaasa, on the opposite side of the Gulf of Bothnia, in the days of the Great Migration of peoples. It is of interest to us that in the decisive seventh century, they were replaced by the Svea. A great number of finds—swords, helmets, jeweled plates with the typical Irish interlace patterns, and a more recent adoption of middle-Swedish style forms in Finnish artifacts —give clear indication of Swedish radiation in every direction across the Baltic. Some must have settled down, but we find no evidence of typical colonies. Here the Swedish minority chose to develop through a quite different form of exchange with the people who were its hosts.

We can safely call the Baltic of the eighth century a Swedish inland sea, just as it was in the seventeenth century. What chance did the Frisians have of developing their trade northward? There could be no thought of a Frisian *Hanse* or merchant guild. In the North they now faced traders as skilled as they. They must have been in regular touch with them for quite some time because we find Rhenish glass and other Southern wares in Svea boat graves. How this intercommerce took place was a mystery until recently, because all we knew about were the Rhine and Dorestad routes. Of the great trade centers of the North we were quite unaware.

In 1953, by chance, there were finds on an island called Helgö in Lake Mälar, west of Stockholm, not far from Drottningholm Castle. Since then, and with increasing enthusiasm, excavations have been going on in Helgö with Docent William Holmqvist the inspired leader of the project. In today's pine woods, certain terrace formations have turned out to be the artificial transformation of a slope. Once houses stood here, living quarters, workshops, warehouses, side by side. Those who are digging have to keep track of innumerable post-holes and a thin charred strata in order to be able to follow the plan of the settlement. But all this is well worth the most meticulous care because here dwelt the traders who kept the Svea kings and chieftains supplied with the luxuries of the South. Here they discarded all the glass broken in transport. That is why the earth contains so many glass fragments as well as the refuse of metal and more perishable materials. Magnificent goblets and jewelry such as we find undamaged in boat graves and exhibit lovingly in our museums, are found in shards and fragments in the ground of this former market town. But they are just as vital to our research. They form indispensable complementary parts and make their considerable contribution to our knowledge of the cultural history of that period.

Helgö was already settled in the fifth century. In the eighth century it reached the height of its activity. Archeological research will go on there for many years to come, and the graves on surrounding hills tempt us to find the masters of Helgö themselves. The small island dominates the water routes from the Baltic into Central Sweden, as Stockholm Old City has done since the thirteenth century. Helgö is strategically the oldest mercantile-political predecessor of the Swedish capital. Its masters could afford the dazzling luxuries of the South only because they controlled the Swedish-Finnish fur market in the North. They were the middlemen, in the same favorable position as the people on the Danish islands, five hundred years before, in Roman days.

About forty-three miles to the north ruled the King of Old Uppsala, whose "colonial" activities reached out beyond the Baltic Sea. No private merchant house therefore settled this strategic city of Helgö, we may be sure of that. Helgö existed by royal command, and the royal policy was practical, carefully organized and far-reaching. No savage barbarian was playing a tough or capricious game here. The findings of archeology point to a sensible, versatile operation.

The rapid development of Norse power is obvious, and the demands of the upper classes for luxuries so apparent, that trade from the Rhineland across Finland to Scandinavia could not possibly have been satisfied by one empowered trading center alone. The point at which the extensive northern and southern trade routes met head on was the Schleswig-Holstein isthmus. It stood in the way of all through traffic for shipping. If it could be mastered, it would be possible to organize foreign trade in a way inconceivable until then, and a much greater quantity of goods could be expedited across greater distances. And this is precisely what happened in the dramatic years around A.D. 800.

3

~~~

First Raids – First Settlements
(A.D. 793–830)

IN THE RUINS of Hamburg after the Second World War, it was difficult to satisfy even the most primitive needs of daily living. All cultural activity seemed senseless and far removed from the harshness of reality. But there were a few scientists in Hamburg who realized that here was a unique opportunity to study the core of the old city. It had always been possible to work out on the city map the decisive points where excavations should take place: they lay between marshes and sandy uplands along the city limits, and under the former cathedral; but now there were ruined areas where this desk work could be practically applied, especially since the Johanneum on Cathedral Square had been reduced to ashes during the holocaust of 1943.

The layout of the big new traffic artery, called the East-West Axis, which was being run straight across Cathedral Square, turned out to be of major advantage to the investigations. The energetic head of the project, Dr. Reinhard Schindler, stood on twelve-foot deep, black, slimy, cultural earth that was rich with datable refuse. He found an enclosed rectangular wall exactly where he had expected to find it, encircling the Cathedral Square area. It was the site of the old Hammaburg, and in the center—without doubt—were traces of Ansgar's Baptismal Church. Underneath the site, he found trenchlike depressions with pottery shards, and the waste of Saxon settlers of the seventh and eighth centuries, and something totally unexpected—*Slavonic* ceramic fragments with undulating patterns. Written sources had to be studied all over again until these finds could be clarified.

Charlemagne had dealt with the Saxons in an extraordinarily stern and cruel fashion, converting them to Christianity by force, or annihilating them. In order to assure himself complete victory, he had allied himself with the Slavs beyond the Elbe and had threatened the Saxons with a two-front war. Finally, in the year 798, he faced the North Elbe Vigmodians on Swentinefeld, near Bornhöved in East Holstein, defeated them, and carried off ten thousand men, women and children. In 804, he received his ally, Prince Trasco, chief of the Slavonic Obotrites, in Hollingstedt, showered him with lavish gifts, and handed over to him all the territory beyond the Elbe. Apparently this was when the Slavs moved into the strategically advantageous city of Hamburg, an event corroborated by the undulating patterned clay vessels found on the site of old Hammaburg. Again documents and archeological findings complement each other, and we have moved a step closer to the threshold of the Baltic scene at the beginning of the actual Viking era.

The Schleswig-Holstein isthmus between North and Baltic seas was a tritribal triangle: on either side of the Elbe, Saxons and Slavs; to the north, on the Jutland peninsula the Danes. The energetic Danish king, Godfred, kept a cautious eye on what was happening in Holstein, prepared for battle, and in 808 issued forth against the Slavonic Obotrites who had become more powerful than suited him. The expedition was only partially successful, and he had to be satisfied with destroying the Slavonic town of Reric, in which he had until then "levied taxes with great advantage to the Danes." We find such terse but important information on the subject in the annals of the Frankish kingdom. Why did Godfred choose to destroy such a prosperous center?

Reric has unfortunately not yet been found. A few explorers have looked for it in the neighborhood of Wismar, others near Lübeck. According to what we know today, the latter seems more likely. It must have been a trading center on the Baltic that served the transit trade from the North Sea. Godfred, afraid of the growing power of Charlemagne and the Slavs, feared also to lose the tariffs of Reric. He therefore did the only sensible thing from his point of view. Near Sliesthorp (today Schleswig), on the river Schlei bordering his Danish realm, he founded a new mercantile city of his own. In documents we find it mentioned most frequently as Haithabu; today it is called Hedeby. Godfred secured it by running a rampart (the Dannevirke) straight across the Schleswig isthmus and with this move created a land barrier between the world of the Vikings and the Occident. (*See ill. 28.*)

Thus Godfred found a solution for an expanding mercantile activity that was still only feeling its way along the peninsula of Jutland. The regions farther south were being too hotly disputed to be suitable for peaceful trading, and to sail around Jutland was not only time consuming, but highly dangerous. According to statistics, the number of shipwrecks as recently as one hundred years ago was still frighteningly large. A replica of a Viking ship foundered in 1951 northeast of Helgoland, taking seventeen young people down with it. The North-East (Kiel) Canal, only a few miles south of the former ninth-century crossing, is the modern solution for an age-old traffic problem which Godfred solved in the year 808 in a relatively ingenious way. In those days the Treene River, flowing into the North Sea, was suitable for ship traffic inland as far as Hollingstedt; even the narrow Rheider Au could carry a ship a stretch farther. On the Baltic coast, the Schlei penetrated deep into the land. These waterways were separated by only a little more than eight miles of land across which ships could be dragged, their cargoes carried.

Haithabu on the Schlei therefore attracted the entire still-disorganized trade in that area. Frisian traders from Dorestad felt at home there and paid taxes to whoever was ruler, at first to the Danish kings. Here they could meet in an orderly and safe commercial atmosphere with Norwegian and Swedish traders who shared their interests.

All this was promising, but it was by no means all that was taking place on the threshold of the Viking era. We begin to hear of strange surprise attacks, at first isolated events in far-off regions, but they resulted in a storm of protests and horror in the entire Christian world. Devout Irish monks had built a monastery on the Holy Isle of Lindisfarne, between England and Scotland. Here they wrote the holiest and most beautiful of all books, the Lindisfarne Gospels, and venerated the relics of Saints Cuthbert and Aidan. Who would dare to do these good brothers any harm? But on the eighth of June, 793, a number of dragon ships appeared on the horizon, and the men in them did not behave like normal traders or mariners. They stormed on land, tore the monk's clothing off their backs, ran their swords mercilessly through the good men's bodies, drowned them, knocked over the stone cross of Bishop Ethelwold,

21. *The ruins of the monastery of Lindisfarne.*

22. Memorial stone of Lindisfarne.

seized all the monastic treasure, set fire to the buildings, slaughtered the cattle, dragged the carcasses on board their ships, and were gone as suddenly as they had appeared.

The bloodthirsty deed aroused horror in the entire world. Fearfully and hesitantly, those monks who had managed to flee crept back to the smoking ruins. Laboriously they rebuilt their monastery, which had been robbed of all its treasure. They even tried to raise the stone cross of Ethelwold. They felt that the dreadful day had to be commemorated by a stone memorial. (*See ill. 22.*) We are strangely moved by the reliefs that reach out to us in their direct, pictorial language. On one side, two men kneel before the benign, heavenly powers: cross, sun, moon and God's hand; the other side of the picture stone depicts the frightful heathen horde—seven men, sword and ax raised. They move in closed formation, terrifying symbols of evil paganism.

But what really happened?

Men who have been on the open sea for weeks have to go on land from time to time to rest and find provender. Very often the alien native population doesn't welcome them. Fresh meat and water have to be gained by force. *Strandhugg* was the Nordic word for this type of operation, and it is still practiced today by tourists of the sea, in harmless forms and against payment. On that summer day in Lindisfarne, the Norsemen acted according to the old seafarer's law. It is indicative that they slaughtered the cattle and took the carcasses with them. With that bit of information, the written sources give us the true purpose of the landing. To murder the monks, who did not defend themselves like men, and to take booty was just too tempting and therefore irresistible.

How these Norsemen must have boasted of their prowess when they returned to their homes in Scandinavia, presumably on Norway's west coast, and handed the valuable booty around to be admired. Everyone must have been astounded. So it was as easy as that to acquire such treasure. It lay on the British coast across the sea, completely unguarded! And all of them could sail. . . .

The following summer, Cloisters Jarrow and Monkwearmouth on the British North Sea coast were attacked. The latter foray failed, but a year later Rechru, Skye and Iona—islands of Saints Patrick and Columban in the Irish Sea—were devastated and plundered. From 799 on, even the Frisian-Frankish coast was threatened, and Charlemagne had hastily to organize a coastal watch.

The tactics that developed from the *strandhugg* were far superior to the military strategy being practiced by the Christian states of Central Europe. In the spring, sailing vessels appeared on the horizon; in a few hours, the huge square sails had grown to menacing proportions. The coastal watch could not get to their positions fast enough once the grinning dragon posts and the powerfully armed men on board had been sighted by a terrified civilian population. The surprise attack was quickly over.

All organized defense proved unavailing against the mobility of the Vikings, and their loose system of government made any diplomatic protest or counter-measures impossible, for every peasant and warrior of the North was his own master. The only tie recognized was that of clan and family. Even their kings had no more power than they were able to assume with the aid of their subordinates. They could not practice any sort of state jurisdiction since the modern idea of "the state" was still nonexistent. The crew of a ship could wage its own war if it seemed advantageous, and a fleet of as much as a dozen ships was already a threatening power. These men carried on what might be termed petty warfare, similar to the encounters in which individual knights fought each other in the Middle Ages.

Monastic chroniclers quite naturally saw these events in a different light. For two hundred and fifty years, they bewailed the Viking scourge and called the Norse warriors pirates, murderers, robbers, heathens, devils, blasphemers, plunderers, barbarians and bloodthirsty villains. When we read about the wars of the Middle Ages, we don't side with one knight or the other, but when we consider the Viking raids, we invariably side with the Christians because they were the weaker and because we allow the monastic annals to influence us. Today we wage large-scale wars and are inclined to evaluate the small sea-foraying Viking groups as really nothing better than pirates. But as a result of these early raids for booty, there gradually evolved truly grandiose field expeditions, land conquests and a dominion over land and sea lanes.

Out of the great technical discovery of those days—the fast sailing vessel that could cross the open sea—grew two major activities: Viking raids and Viking mercantile voyages. The two achievements are curiously interwoven, for those were the days when every trading site was designated by the word

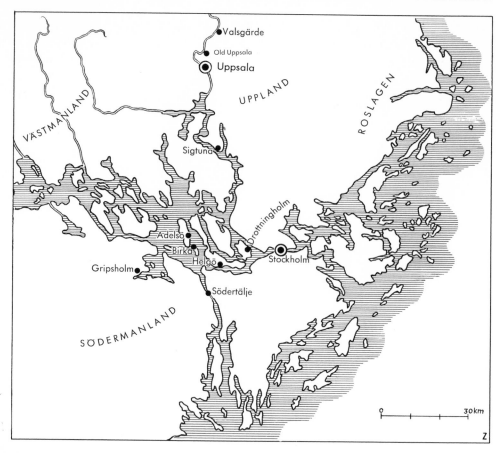

23. *The political heart of Sweden: the Lake Mälar region.*

vik, which comes from *vika* (Swedish), meaning to yield or withdraw; therefore a place to which to yield or to withdraw. According to this, to go "a-
Viking"—in a word formation similar to our modern "shopping" or "camping"
—could mean visiting or trading in a *vik*-place. In western Europe we find 870
vik-localities; for instance, Wyk-te-Duurstede, Braunschweig, Schleswig, Lun-
denvic (London), Bardowic (near Lüneburg). But many hundred *vik*-locali-
ties in Scandinavia are purely natural names, since a *vik* is also a place where
land yields to water, a bay or a fjord where ships may anchor, and the Vikings
could therefore settle and live. The west Swedish landscape of Bohuslän, north
of Göteborg, once was named Viken; its inhabitants were Vikings in the most
literal sense of the word. The name was derived from and became popular in
an era of *vik*-localities and *vik*-waters. At times it was misunderstood and
abused, yet in the end it became a highly expressive designation for the Norseman in his dual role as warrior and trader.

The Viking expeditions from 793 on, and their trading in far distant countries from 808—the two greatest achievements of these brilliant seamen—take organized shape in the hour of the Occident's birth. The coronation of Charlemagne in 800 can very well serve as the commemorative date. Rarely has it been possible so clearly to establish an epoch as beginning with three major events within a span of fifteen years. They were to change the entire political and economic structure of Europe, yet they crystallized quite logically out of a century-long development. We have read about the activity of the Svea in the Baltic Sea and have seen them settle along the continental rivers and haffs, protecting themselves from attack and ready to take possession of this land beyond the sea. What happened in the year 793 was nothing more than that the quick sea raids were now conducted also against Christian lands and recorded in monastic annals.

For twelve years, we have known about Helgö, focal point for the Baltic Sea trade of antiquity; in the 1920's, Frisian Dorestad was reconstructed for us; written sources tell us about Haithabu. What could be more probable than that trading centers like them should be founded in Scandinavia itself? Very soon—we dare not try to date them more exactly than at the beginning of the ninth century—Skiringssal on the Oslo Fjord, and Birka—today Björkö on Lake Mälar—were burgeoning cities. With Haithabu, they appear quite chronologically (*circa* 800) as the first mercantile cities to be founded in the north.

Whoever wishes to visit Birka must go by boat, now as then. East of Stockholm lie about thirty miles of skerries, rocky islands; west of Stockholm you can sail for eighteen or nineteen miles between the islands on Lake Mälar. (*See ill. 23.*) From the royal seat of Old Uppsala in the north, the River Fyris points directly to the island, which is Björkö—Birch Island. The neighboring islands are called Ekerö—Oak Island; Adelsö—Alder Island; Kersö—Bush Island. The

24. *The barrows of Birka on Lake Mälar.*

25. *Birka.*
  ABOVE: *Air view with the fortress in the foreground, and the city to the left, in the fields.*
  BELOW: *The fortress.*
  RIGHT: *Remains of the city wall. Photos: ATA.*

name Björkö is justified, for here two thousand burial mounds—part of what was once the city population—lie in light birch glades. A silence, broken only by the soughing of the wind in the trees, reigns on this well-preserved historic site. You may clamber over grave mounds nearly 2 feet high and nearly 20 feet wide, circumvent those that are more than three feet high, and measure the length and breadth of this unique cemetery. These mounds were excavated in the 1870's by Hjalmar Stolpe, fortunately very conscientiously in this early period of archeological research. Professor Holgar Arbman has published his findings. In them, the wealth of grave furnishings and wares collected from far and wide is astounding.

In the extreme western part of the island is a hillock where a fort once stood. Nothing but stone and a little earth now mark the modest installation. Below, between fort and graveyard, lies the former city, surrounded by a wall, which was not added until the tenth century. (*See ill. 25.*) The town area is easily recognizable because of the black humus. In barely two hundred years, it grew more than 8 feet in depth from the refuse that was never removed but on which the residents lived unconcernedly. Small trial shafts have been dug here and there, but for the most part this first-rate research archive has remained untouched, waiting for the most expert methods modern science can provide. All we know is that the strata is rich in fragments of merchandise and workmanship, that blockhouses once stood here, and houses with walls woven of rush and calked with clay.

26. *Haithabu.*

ABOVE TOP: *Dannevirke. The earthworks of the Viking era included a wooden palisade. A brick wall from* A.D. *1160 is visible above the dry river bed.*

ABOVE BOTTOM: *The wall of the Viking city.*

RIGHT: *The 1936 excavations in the city's center, showing the river bed. Photo: Herbert Jankuhn and the Land Schleswig Holstein Museum.*

The city was only about 32 acres in size. The bay served as the harbor in which the dragon ships with their costly wares were beached. Other harbors were: Saltvik, Korshamn and Kugghamn. The later was probably once called Kogghamn, reminding us of the Frisians, whose Kogges—forerunners of the Hanseatic freighters—here had their own harbor. It is quiet on this birch-green island now, almost a thousand years after it fulfilled its historic mission. With the documentary evidence on hand, one's fantasy can conjure up a picture. And that is the specific value of these three Nordic sites—that they were not destroyed by the building of later centuries, as is the case with every one of the prehistoric towns of the European continent.

Haithabu—Hedeby, as already mentioned—lies on the River Schlei. (*See ills. 26, 27.*) A semicircular wall surrounds the black earth. It is much more imposing than Birka, and of a later period. The visitor can't see the level graves at all. Here, too, a fort lies just outside. We found four rune stones, three of them now in the Schleswig Museum. The long wall (Dannevirke) westward across the Schleswig isthmus begins outside the city. In 1931, Professor Herbert Jankuhn, with other German archeologists, started excavating in this virginal region. In 1960, after the long interruption of World War II, work was resumed on the large-scale project. We know that the black humus can answer decisive questions for us, not only those concerning age, site and dimensions of this oldest trade settlement of Godfred's time. Haithabu, too, at first was small and not fortified. Not until the tenth century did the town cover an area of more than sixty-five acres.

The Swedish contribution to the findings of Haithabu is striking: two rune stones, many women's graves with oval brooches, and above all a wooden chamber grave. The burial did not take place in the ship itself, but below it, in a carefully carpentered and buried wooden chamber with an invaluable inventory. (*See ills. 29, 30, 31, 32, 33.*) Underneath the jewelry we came upon a matrix (not illustrated here) with which a gold plaque found in east Sweden was stamped.

27. *Haithabu. Aerial view, showing semicircular wall. The fortress lies to the north, in the wooded area. Photo: Land Schleswig Holstein Museum.*

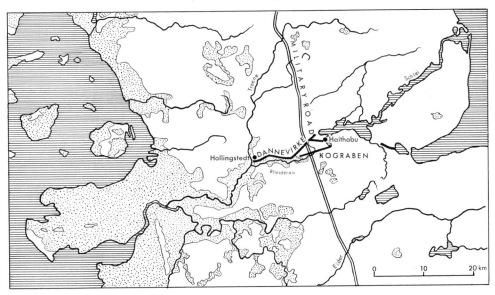

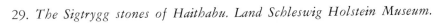

28. *The land barrier between the Baltic and North seas, showing main defense points and age-old military route northward. Dotted areas indicate
marshes.*

29. *The Sigtrygg stones of Haithabu. Land Schleswig Holstein Museum.*

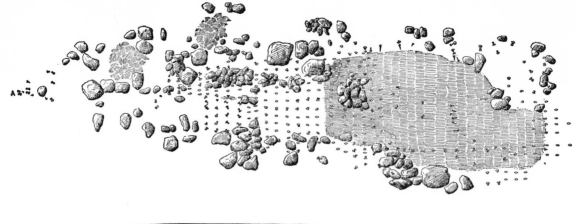

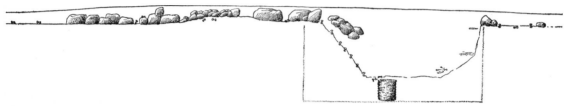

30. *The richest grave in Haithabu. The rivets from the rotted ships lie in long rows. At the extreme right are three horse skeletons. Under the middle of the ship, shown in profile, is the wooden chamber. A plan with accessories found in the chamber is also shown.*

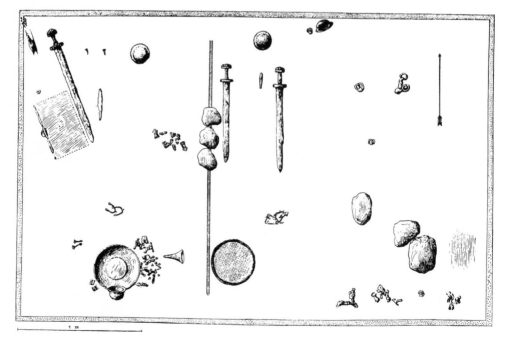

31. *Oval brooches. National Museum, Copenhagen.*

32. *Jewelry from Haithabu. Land Schleswig Holstein Museum. Photo: E. Oxenstierna.*

The objects are a little larger than actual size. The pin on the right, the gold coin beside it, the buckle and the small pendants (LEFT) probably came from a destroyed ninth-century grave, the accessories of which had been collected in Byzantium and Ireland. The Byzantine gold coin (TOP, THIRD FROM LEFT) was minted for the Emperors Theophilos and Michael Constantine (circa A.D. 829–842) and reworked into a pendant with loop. This coin is rare, because Russian-Byzantine objects were usually found in Birka; the trade of Haithabu flowed in a different direction. The plaited band ornamentation on the bronze buckle is foreign to the Baltic Sea lands; it probably came from Ireland. Traces of the original gold plate still show on the buckle.

33. *Gold disc, Thor hammer and small animal head from an East Swedish silver and gold hoard. State Historical Museum, Stockholm. Photo: E. Oxenstierna.*

We don't know nearly so much about Skiringssal. The place is rarely mentioned in documents. Its establishment on the western entry of the Oslo Fjord was arrived at very gradually, and only in the 1950's was it possible to start organized excavations. They were carried out by Charlotte Blindheim, after Norwegian scholars had discovered the rich level graves and defined the outlines of the former city area. Natural mountains protect it, but the thin layer of humus has been farmed constantly, just the same, we can wrest valuable knowledge from it. Norway's political disunion may have contributed to the fact that Skiringssal did not attain the same importance as Birka and Haithabu.

It is quite obvious that Scandinavian kings played a strong part in the life of these cities. The energetic Godfred took the initiative, brought all trade together at one point, laid down a formidable land barrier in the Dannevirke, and secured for himself the best profits of commerce—the tariffs. We can't vouch for the names of the kings of the Swedish royal house in Old Uppsala in the years around 800, but we can recognize their policies. An entirely new and bold outlook, unheard-of perspicacity and initiative were required to establish the first mercantile cities in a purely peasant-warrior land. If they were to fulfill their purpose, they had first and foremost to guarantee commercial peace, so that Frisians and traders traveling with costly wares might feel safe. For the first time, two categories of people, merchants and artisans—who did not nourish themselves solely and directly by their own labors, but who had to trade their produce for food—settled down together.

Trading had always been sacrosanct in Scandinavia. On certain days friend and foe converged on holy places; no blood might flow; each man brought his offering to the gods. These feast days were at the same time active market days during which all forms of barter thrived. In the thinly settled northern lands these annual market days played an important role even after the Christianization of the land. We have only to think of the market on the north Swedish river, Torne, which Olaus Magnus visited in 1519 and described, or of the *Dis-thing* near Old Uppsala. On sleds and across the ice, even the Lapps brought their horn and leather work for sale, and only in recent times have these market days become festive fairs rather than important trading events.

With Haithabu, Birka and Skiringssal, a new conception became reality: commercial peace the year round, with no ritualistic ties, granted especially to foreign traders with alien beliefs, who had no way of protecting their wares. Only an energetic king could guarantee peace, and the normal equivalent was for the merchant to pay him appropriate tribute. On an island east of Birka lies Helgö; the island to the west is Adelsö. (*See ill. 34.*) Here the king of Old Uppsala built a royal residence in order to be able to look after his interests in Birka, where we know that he frequently visited. To protect his rights he appointed a royal governor who officiated side by side with the city adminis-

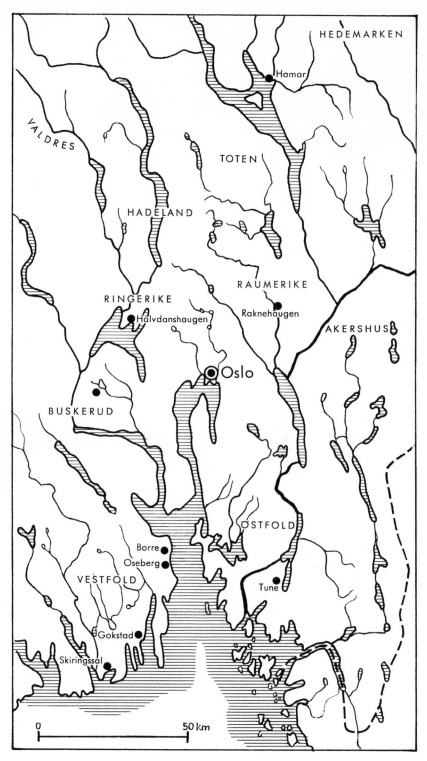

34. *The political heart of Norway: Oslo Fjord region.*

tration. Similarly we find a *comes vici* in Haithabu; in London a *vic gerefa;* in Hamburg a *comes praefecturam tenens,* and so on, titles which we translate as viceregents.

Birka-Björkö's law for commercial peace has not been handed down to us, but in the Middle Ages, innumerable Nordic towns had a "Björkö law." The name unmistakably betrays its origin. The form is archaic, suitable for word-of-mouth use at a time when judge and assessor had to learn paragraphs of law by heart.

And this mercantile peace had the desired effect. Traders came and went unhindered. Rimbert tells of a Christian woman named Friedeborg and her daughter Katla, whose name sounds Frisian. They lived in Birka, and the mother had bought some wine which she kept in a bottle. When her last hour approached, she told her daughter—who was also a believer and pious—to pour some wine into her mouth, since she could not receive last rites. In this way her passing would be recommended to the mercy of God.

So you could buy wine in Birka. . . .

The woman told her daughter to divide all her worldly possessions among the poor. " 'Since there are so few poor people here (!) sell everything that you have not given away after my death, take the money and journey to Dorestad at the first opportunity. There you will find many churches, priests and holy men; there you will find many needy people. When you reach Dorestad, find some believers who can instruct you how the money should be divided, and give everything away as a merciful offering for the salvation of my soul.'

"After her mother's death, Katla eagerly carried out the instructions that had been given her. She speedily got under way, arrived in Dorestad, there sought and found several pious women who visited the holy places with her and advised her what she should give away in each case."

Friedeborg had apparently been quite well off; her husband must have made his fortune as a Frisian-Christian trader. The details of this little story show living conditions in Birka in a favorable light. It was closely allied to Dorestad. Traders from far and wide told of it.

And Emperor Louis the Pious listened. Up there in the North there were enlightened people; there was religious freedom; life was protected. It should be possible to bring Christianity to Haithabu and Birka. To convert the Vikings —*that* was the genial solution for putting an end to the annoying coastal raids. As Christians the Norsemen would willingly give up their bloody forays and never plunder monasteries again.

Actually, missionaries had already pressed forward to Scandinavia and reported that the Danish king was "harder than a stone and wilder than any beast." No misunderstanding that terse description. Just the same, Willibrord, the Northumbrian, (known as "the Apostle of the Frisians,") returned from the North with thirty young Danish men who were to be educated as Christians. We have this fact from written sources and may expect these early missions to leave their traces in archeological findings.

In Denmark, seven rectangular plaques of gilded bronze have been found. (*See ill. 35.*) Some of them are about 6¾ inches long and very ornate. On the back they have a pin and must therefore have been worn as brooches. But that was not their original purpose. For each plaque has eight rivet holes and must therefore once have been fastened to a base, probably wood. For two decades, scholars studied these plaques, compared them, discussed them. Their ornamentation is not Scandinavian. The division into rectangular or diamond-shaped areas, the ring-chain pattern in the border and the animated, sometimes

35. *Ornamental plate from a reliquary casket, with screw holes. Gilded bronze. Found in Lyngby, Jutland. National Museum, Copenhagen.*

confused animal motifs are Anglo-Irish. They may have been applied to small, house-shaped reliquaries, once the object of household veneration. We find similar small reliquaries in the British Museum. They were especially suitable for missions to people whose social order was based on family and clan. They can be classified with other, related metal fittings, among them a triangular one that may have served a reliquary or as a book corner. They are of the period when Willibrord lived, *circa* A.D. 700. His mission can't have been very successful. The Norsemen decided to use the relic fittings as brooches. . . .

Not until nearly one hundred years later do we find further brief reports of missionary activity in Denmark. Of the year 777 we read: "Many more people were baptised in one place, named Orhaim, on the other side of the River Obacrum." And in 789, Alcuin sounds discouraged when he wonders "if there is any hope of converting the Danes."

Just the same, it was possible to exact certain conditions from the trader in distant lands for the privilege of buying and selling his wares in the Carolingian Empire. For instance, only Christians were supposed to trade in Christian lands. But the merchant's conscience adapted itself easily to his gainful profession. A baptismal shirt of fine Frisian cloth might be a present that would influence a merchant to conversion. Suddenly there was such a demand for these shirts that the Frisian home industry couldn't keep up with the royal orders. The unexpected boom and conversion furore forced the Frisians to turn to sackcloth as a substitute material. But the merchants noticed it at once, and one man about to be baptized cried out angrily, "Twenty times I let myself be washed [baptized] by you, but nobody ever offered me such miserable stuff!"

No. The thing definitely had to be settled by higher politics. A favorable opportunity offered itself when Godfred's sons banished a petty king, Harald Klak, from Denmark. He begged Roman Emperor Louis the Pious for sanctuary, always a good card in the diplomatic game. This was followed by various conferences with Godfred's reigning sons, until the Emperor gave them a demonstration of how brilliantly Northern rulers were rewarded if they came to terms with him. A stupendous show was put on when Harald, with his wife, son, and entourage, were baptized in Ingelheim, in the Palatinate, in 826, in the presence of the Emperor and his nobles. The climax came when Harald was given Rüstringen on the mouth of the Weser as fief. This was a good piece of land, the rich cattle pasture and active Frisian trade of which assured him a life of luxury. The Emperor felt he hadn't given away too much, for he hoped he had found a vassal whom the Vikings would leave alone. The Norsemen would not attack a Nordic king. That's what he thought. And King Harald was just the man to accompany the Emperor's missionaries to Denmark and lend them the necessary authority.

A fearless man of God was also found; Ansgar was his name. Equipped with religious articles and royal gifts, the two men set out on their journey north, accompanied by a monk called Autbert. They sailed the route we already know so well, down the Rhine. In Cologne they boarded their own ship with two cabins—Harald Klak was delighted with it—and set sail for Denmark via Dorestad. They may have stopped at Haithabu. Archbishop Rimbert, however, does not report that they succeeded in their mission.

But the Emperor did not drop his favorite project. It was his intention to destroy Viking audacity from within. The missionaries were to form a "fifth column." A conquest in faith would at the same time be a stupendous political success.

An opportunity arose when ambassadors of the Svea king appeared at the conclave in Worms in 829. In those days trade and war were usually the main themes of any diplomatic negotiations. In this case a trade agreement for the new mercantile center of Birka may have been under consideration, and the Svea king might have taken this opportunity to assure the safety of any missionary expeditions to Birka. The delegates are even supposed to have declared that quite a few of their people wanted to be baptized, and that the Svea king himself was ready to welcome the Christian priests.

The Benedictine monk, Ansgar, thus became the first official missionary to the North. Allegedly born in Lower Saxony in 801, he was brought up in the monastery of Corbie, east of Amiens, and was educated in the new Westphalian Cloister Corvey. He received his instructions for the mission from the Emperor personally, and set out on his second journey, this time with a monk called Vitmar. We know some details of this mission from Archbishop Rimbert's report, which also describes the perils of the journey:

"Halfway there, they were beset by pirates, and although the merchants who were traveling with them defended themselves manfully and were at first victorious, they were defeated in the second attack and subjugated by the pirates who plundered their ships and robbed them of all their possessions. They had to leave behind the royal gifts which they had intended bringing to the land of the Svea, and were able to save only the few worthless things they could carry on them as they jumped from their ships. Among other items, they lost almost forty volumes that were intended for religious service and which fell into the hands of the pirates."

The picture is vivid. The monks had evidently attached themselves to some merchants. They may have been traveling with the first group resulting from the bilateral trade treaty of Worms, in spite of which they were attacked by Viking ships somewhere along the south Swedish coast.

We are further told about their arrival in Birka: "With great difficulty they continued their journey on foot, traveling whenever possible by boat across the waters that crossed their route, and arrived finally at a harbor town in the land of the Svea, called Birka. Here they were welcomed by the king, whose name was Björn. The delegates told the king the purpose of their journey. When he knew it and had discussed it with his faithful followers, he gave them permission to stay—with the former's approval—and to preach the gospel of God. He also gave permission to anyone who so desired to participate freely in this instruction."

All this is so simply told that every word rings true. The friendly reception was probably aimed first and foremost at the contractually expected foreign traders. Did the Swedish delegates who had attended the conclave in Worms have to remind their king of a promise given rather casually? Be that as it may—King Björn had no reason to reject his visitors. Ansgar and Vitmar knew the Emperor personally, and in Birka there were many gods and many religions. Why shouldn't Christ have his advocate, too? Even the royal prefect, Hergeir, "advisor to the king and loved by him," was pleased with the new teaching of Christianity and submitted to baptism. On his ancestral estate he built a church for the community. This was the most noteworthy success of the year-and-a-half-long mission.

Rimbert says, "On his ancestral estate," but Birka was a newly founded city, and none of the graves excavated can be dated earlier than the ninth century. Did this *Vik*-count Hergeir perhaps reside on the neighboring island of Helgö? The theory is tempting, especially since a remarkably beautiful Irish crozier was found on Helgö. (*See ill. 36.*) One sacramental accessory naturally doesn't give us a conversion church, but a "Coptic" ladle, a silver platter and the fragments of a wine jug—all of Ansgar's time—do form a quite conspicuous accumulation of church implements in one spot. Clay jugs with handles are especially curious

36. *Irish bishop's crozier, found on the island of Helgö. Approximately 4½ inches long. State Historical Museum, Stockholm. Photo: ATA.*

37. *Wine jars with tin-plate ornamentation, from Birka. Height approximately 9½ inches. State Historical Museum, Stockholm. Photo: ATA.*

finds, because they are ornamented with tin plate, and in most cases a large cross can be found in the geometric pattern. (*See ill. 37.*) Worldly utensils don't look like this and, indicatively, they are missing in all Frisian settlement finds. These pieces may have been manufactured for liturgical purposes in Cloister Lorsch, in the Worms region. They were found in Dorestad and Haithabu, and in pagan Birka graves, which isn't very surprising, since the brittle vessels were more enduring than the early conversions. We are reminded of Friedeborg who kept wine in a bottle and used it for the holy sacraments. Since there is still much to excavate on Helgö Island, we may hope for some fortuitous finds in the near future, and a clearing up of the question as to whether or not the *Vik*-count lived ,there and built the first church in Sweden on Helgö.

After his return to the Emperor, Ansgar sent his co-workers to Birka while he proceeded to Haithabu. In Denmark, in the meantime, one of Godfred's sons, Horic, had made himself sole ruler of Denmark, and in his turn permitted a church to be built in his kingdom. "There were already many Christians there who had been baptized in either Dorestad or Hammaburg, some of whom could be counted among the most eminent citizens of the town."

Ansgar became the first archbishop of the North in Hammaburg, the new trading city on the Elbe. Thanks to the unique and fortunate excavations in Hamburg's ruins after World War II, the Hamburgers were able to familiarize themselves with archaic Hammaburg. They found out that the Slavs had been forced to withdraw and that the northern frontier of the Carolingian Empire had been secured with innumerable fortresses. The excavations clearly and unequivocally uncovered a somewhat rounded, quadrangular wall, about 328 feet in diameter on the inside, in some places nearly 23 feet high, which cleverly made use of the unevenness of the terrain. (*See ill. 38.*) It was supported and reinforced by strong wooden palisades. To create it, 26,160 cubic yards of earth had to be moved, and 7,000 trees felled—a considerable achievement. Proudly Ansgar was able to build his baptismal church in the center of the Hammaburg.

This seems to be a highly satisfactory picture, yet the Emperor's success did not fulfill its promise. For after seeing how immensely fruitful their small raids were, the Norse warriors had quite different things on their minds than Christian behavior. We know that the first decades of the ninth century show only minor coastal forays, one might call them "private enterprise" attacks. Their invariable success must have been discussed at home and mulled over. Equipped more thoroughly and with forces unheard of until now, would it not be possible to achieve far greater conquests?

38. *Reconstruction of the Hammaburg.*

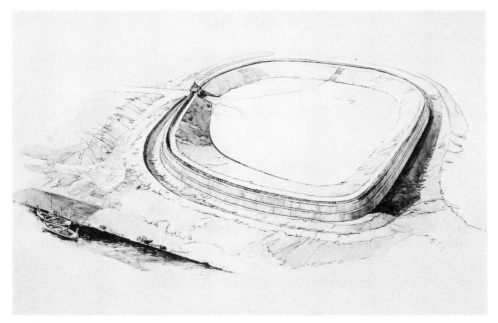

4

~~~~~

The Roving Vikings
(A.D. 830–850)

CATASTROPHE had already overwhelmed Ireland in the year 820. The Annals of Ulster report: "The sea spewed a flood of strangers over Erin, and there was no harbor, no landing place, no fortification, no fortress, no bulwark without fleets of Vikings and pirates." The poor petty Irish kings, who weren't even capable of keeping peace among themselves, could not agree on how to repulse the peril from across the sea. On top of all this, the Norsemen suddenly gained unified leadership in the person of a daring chieftain called Turges, who, in 839, had himself declared King of Ireland and sacrificed to Thor in Dublin, Armagh and Clonmacnois. "A land with no priest, no credo, no Gaelic, only foreign tongues."

Until 834, the continent of Europe was spared, but then came the storm which was to thunder across the world for the next seventy-two years. Louis' son Lothair, who had shared the throne with him, rebelled against his father and replaced him. But he had made one decisive mistake: he had hired Danish mercenaries. In the end he had to hand over to them Rüstringen, which had once more become Frankish territory—land changed hands frequently in those days. Soon after that he had to relinquish Walcheren. This was followed in 841 by the bloody fratricide of Fontenoy and the Treaty of Verdun in 843 which gave the kingdom of the Western Franks—corresponding practically to what is France today—to Charles the Bald; the eastern part of the empire, as far as the Elbe, to Louis the German; and to Lothair the narrow strip in between, from Friesland southward into Italy.

"For the younger brothers it was a miserable victory. Their quarrels gave the enemy outside their borders renewed strength. The watch on the coast was abandoned. The numbers of Normans grew beyond all bounds."

Here we have an example of the eternal Occidental game of the balance of power that enabled the dread Vikings to conquer and keep the initiative for so long.

The events themselves were dire. The organized Viking raids on the continent of Europe came as a profound shock. Every year the Norsemen set themselves more grandiose goals. On May 12, 841, Danish Vikings sailed up the River Seine; Asgeir was the name of their leader. Rouen was burned to the ground. They reached St. Denis, but decided for the moment to avoid battle with the approaching Frankish army. In 842, the Frisian harbor city of Quentovic was destroyed. In 843, Norwegian Vikings sailed up the Loire in 67 ships, and the people of Nantes experienced the Feast of John the Baptist in a way they had not expected. The Norsemen spent the winter on the island of Noirmontier, on the mouth of the Loire, and "settled down as if they intended to remain forever." They even sent for their wives and children. The surrounding countryside was expected to nourish them. "Oh God, protect us from the Norsemen and their wrath!"

The tri-division of the Holy Roman Empire proved advantageous to the Vikings. In the year 845, organized attacks against all three parts took place simultaneously. The royal brothers had brought their own misfortune upon themselves at Fontenoy and Verdun. Ragnar Lodbrok, legendary Viking hero, sailed up the Loire with 120 ships and conquered Paris. He defeated half the army of Charles the Bald on one side of the river while the other half stood indecisively on the opposite bank, watching in horror as Ragnar strung up 111 of their men as a sacrifice to Wodan. Charles the Bald paid his unwelcome Paris guests 7,000 pounds of silver to get rid of them.

It was a dangerous way of placating the Norsemen. Gradually it was to cost the Christian lands fortune after fortune. But that was the way the Counts wanted it, because a victory in open battle would have strengthened the power of the Emperor, and that was as undesirable as the presence of the Vikings. Moreover, the silver could be collected from peasantry and subjects, in the course of which a goodly part remained in the nobles' pockets.

A Viking fleet set out for Dorestad which, from 834 on, was ransacked almost yearly; another set sail for Hamburg. Rather characteristically, *Vikcount* Bernhard was away, and the garrison was weak. Again we quote Rimbert:

"Ansgar realized that he could offer no resistance with his men. He took measures to remove the holy relics to safety and was barely able to escape, and had to do so without his cloak, whilst his priests scattered in every direction. The civilian population also fled wherever it could. Most escaped, some were taken prisoner and most of these were killed. By now the enemy had taken possession of the town and ransacked everything in it and in the surrounding countryside. They came in the evening, stayed the night and the rest of the following day. After they had set fire to everything, they withdrew. The church which had been erected with such magnificence under the leadership of the bishop [Ansgar] was reduced to ashes, together with the wonderfully equipped monastery. The Bible which His Majesty the Emperor had given to our Holy Father went up in flames with numerous other volumes. And everything he had owned in the way of church vessels and other valuables was destroyed, either by plunder or by fire, so that he escaped almost naked."

The chroniclers count 600 ships. Since we must give every ship a crew of 40 men, we arrive at the fantastic figure of 24,000 men. We need therefore have no qualms about crossing out the last zero of this obviously legendary ship count, as did the excavators of Hammaburg. The only weapons of the battle which we found were Viking swords, dredged out of the Elbe.

The charred strata of the short-lived Hammaburg, however, led to more precise conclusions. Innumerable little wings of insects were discovered, telling us that bugs and Vikings swarmed on the same night in June. A posthole of Ansgar's church could be identified. More could hardly have been expected. And yet—the merchant's settlement outside the fort site did not go under in this surprise attack. To see how it ran uninterruptedly along the *Reichenstrassenfleet,* where the oldest harbor was situated, is one of the most interesting results of the excavation. A hitherto unauthenticated commercial prosperity in Hamburg in the ninth and tenth centuries may be deduced from the finds. Jugs with handles and ornamented in tin plate, Badorf vessels, Mayen millstones, and Norwegian soapstone are some of the typical wares, as they are in other harbor cities of the Baltic and North seas.

The loss of a magnificent riding spur on a piece of land on the wide Reichenstrasse must have vexed the owner. What was he to do with the one spur left him? He must have looked for the one lost everywhere except where the excavators found it nine hundred years later—in a heap of manure. Unfortunately we now miss the spur the rider kept. . . .

Messengers came from Louis the German to Denmark to negotiate for peace, but they arrived at a highly unpropitious moment—just as Ragnar Lodbrok came home with the 7,000 pounds of silver given him by the brother of their Emperor. He also showed the shocked ambassadors the lock of the gate to the city of Paris which he had in his pocket.

That year three Viking fleets were able to threaten the entire Empire, while Ireland was swamped with Normans, and a fourth fleet of a hundred ships sailed past Spain to North Africa. After the German delegates, Arabian legates turned up in Denmark. The new great powers of the North were quite obviously beginning to develop an active foreign policy.

Ansgar, now a bishop without a see, sorrowfully retired to Bremen, and the future conversion of the North now emanated from that city. Since there had been no mission to Birka for some time, Ansgar decided to travel there once more, in the year 849. But this time his plea for permission to revisit Birka was inopportune. It was made just as the Norsemen were in a state of pagan ecstasy. Ansgar's petition had to go through the usual administrative channels. The king gave his consent, but he did not have sole say in the matter, since "it is customary for every public event to depend on the unanimous will of the people rather than on the power of the king."

Ansgar's petition was passed on to the city administration and from there to the *thing* in another district—presumably Attundaland, which included Birka. Only then was the religious freedom granted according to the same administrative policies that prevail today.

The words of an old man, written while this popular vote was taking place, reveal quite clearly how warlike unrest on the seas had increased. "Now and then a few people from this area have been in Dorestad and of their own free will adopted this form of faith in God, because they thought it might be useful to them. But now there exists much knavery on the way there and the journey has become dangerous because of attacking pirates."

Quite naturally more Norwegians and Danes took part in the western voyages; Sweden does not figure in our written sources. But it was the Swedes who, by boldly—one might almost say nonchalantly—penetrating "upriver" into Russia, opened up the barriers in the east to a world that was still farther away and utterly different. They must have discovered the lower reaches of the Southern Dvina, the Memel and the Vistula even before the year 800. Now they penetrated farther and farther inland, also through Finnish populated areas, up the Svir and past the big lakes Ladoga and Onega. The source areas of these river lanes proved to be no problem. On the other side of the divides lay the sources of other rivers. Just as they had done on the Schleswig peninsula, the Vikings dragged their ships across land and sailed down the Volga and Dnieper.

It was a wild, desperately risky adventure. These pioneers couldn't possibly have had any idea how much longer the eastern rivers were than those of their homeland. Nothing but empty river banks for days, for weeks on end, strips of land thinly settled by Slavs and Turks who had these first daring explorers completely at their mercy. Somehow the Vikings fought their way through and proceeded onward. Somewhere these rivers had to empty into a sea. Here we have a good example of Viking audacity: no retreat; forever forward. Until, after superhuman exertion, they sighted the wide horizon of the Black Sea.

Thus, as early as 830, they reached Byzantium, and arrived—truly strange strangers—at the court of the Emperor Theophilus. But the men still comprising their decimated ranks were shy of a return trip home through the same

wild country, so they chose to accompany a Greek legate (in 839) to the court
of Roman Emperor Louis in Ingelheim. From there they returned to their
homeland.

Here we have an exact date for a time when the upper reaches of the Russian rivers were already known to the Swedes, and their first men reached
Byzantium. Our sources are the *Annales Bertiniani,* written by the scholarly
and conscientious Bishop Prudentius of Troyes. In them he says:

"When the Emperor questioned the reasons for their journey, he found out
that they were Sveas, but . . . he considered it necessary to keep them there
until he was convinced that the reason for their arrival was actually the one
stated by them."

Theophilus was Emperor of Byzantium at the time, and in Birka grave No.
632, a coin of the Emperor was found. This is a great rarity; we know of only
two other similar finds in the North. (*See ill. 39.*) We also have two small

39. *Oriental and Scandinavian pieces from the hoard of Varby, southwest of
Stockholm.*
The coin (LOWER RIGHT) *is Arabic. The circular plate with cross* (UPPER
LEFT) *and the three filigree pendants are of native Nordic craftsmanship.
The beads and the remaining objects, which probably formed part of a
necklace, originated in the Sassanide-Khazan area of southeast Europe
and the Middle East; one might even venture that Chinese influence
made itself felt here. State Historical Museum, Stockholm. Photo: E. Oxenstierna.*

silver fittings which originated in the territory of the lower Volga. They are ornamented with kidney-shaped leaves. All three pieces, with hooks attached to them, have been inserted in a woman's bead necklace. (*See ill. 40.*) We counted 34 such pieces in 6 Birka graves that were grouped together and of the same period. How would it be if we concluded that they were brought there, all of them, also the coin from Byzantium, by the Vikings returning from Byzantium via Ingelheim, perhaps on an ornate belt? Sometimes we come very close to recognizing historic personalities in the anonymous graves of antiquity, but the final proof still eludes us. Instead we are delighted with the beauty of the other pendants on this chain of beads. The origin of one must have been an Anglian book cover; another has been cut out of an Arabian silver platter, the rest are Nordic, among them a little curled-up snake and a pretty little chair. One may well say that this one piece of female jewelry reflects the entire European activity area of early Viking days. With the necklace we found an Anglo-Irish ladle and a Frankish knife beside numerous Swedish artifacts.

With their return the Norsemen could declare triumphantly that they were the first men to sail around the continent of Europe. They had covered unheard-of distances, from Russia in the east to Spain in the west. Now they could really trade! The dominant enterprise of an epoch was theirs to command. There were opportunities in these foreign lands for every man, woman and child in an overpopulated homeland. Now we understand why the settlements in Kurland were abandoned in 800. The people in them moved on to better positions in more distant lands. Grobin on the Libau Haff no longer fulfilled a purpose in this far-flung network, whereas Wiskiauten on the Kurische Haff did, since this was a settlement that secured the river lane of the Memel leading into Russia. It was therefore preserved. Only now could trading in far-off lands expand in a way hitherto undreamed of. Merchandise from Scandinavia and Russia could pass through the hands of the Norsemen and be exchanged for Frankish wares. Everyone profited from this dealing, and the middleman came off best of all, though his was the greater hazard. He had to travel for months, years, at risk of life, but he had the fatter part of the profit coming to him. A program of trading and dealing was created, a program of great significance, and the Vikings brought the full value of their triumph home.

They dealt in luxury items. The seaworthy but comparatively small dragon ships could not take on grain, foodstuff, or bulky cargoes. They were suitable only for highly valuable but light merchandise and this became a determining factor in the trade interests of the ninth and tenth centuries.

From the south came costly hand-made industrial products. Cloth was in great demand. We noted this in the conversion zeal which was aimed at the procuring of a good shirt. The Annals of Ulster also betray it when they re-

40. *Necklace from Birka.*

  The silver coin (UPPER LEFT) *was minted by Emperor Theophilos in Byzantium* (A.D. 829–842). *To the right of the coin: Two Khazar pendants from the Volga district. They are followed by two silver wires strung with one bead and five beads respectively; a piece of an Arabic silver bowl; two silver wires, strung with one bead each; a silver wire, rolled to form a circular disc—Nordic work; a silver wire with three beads; a book mounting from southern England with animal-band interlace design (same piece enlarged,* LOWER CENTER); *two shield-shaped pendants and a tiny silver chair. The beads are carnelian and crystal.* (UPPER CENTER) *A Frankish strap tag, remodeled into a piece of jewelry. State Historical Museum, Stockholm. Photo: ATA.*

port that the Vikings, in their landing on Lindesfarne, tore the monk's clothing off their backs. So-called Frisian cloth enjoyed an exceptionally fine reputation. The sheep-grazing pastures on the North Sea coast have been famous from Roman days to the present. We hear that Charlemagne sent Caliph Harun-al-Raschid, among other gifts, Frisian cloth, "white, red, green, and blue, which counts in your land as rare and very costly." Louis the Pious gave his officials "colored Frisian coats" on high feast days, and in other sources there are further references to the same material. But when were we finally going to get a look at this so perishable stuff?

In the 2,000 Birka graves we often found women wearing jewelry made of curved, ornate metal that we call oval brooches. Under these 3- or 4-inch-long brooches especially around the pin, scraps of material are often so interspersed with verdigris and well protected by the metal that they have been preserved for posterity. (*See ill. 41.*) It is not possible to reconstruct entire skirts and

41. *Cloth piece from Birka. A piece of pleated, fine woolen material, probably "Frisian cloth," found preserved under an oval brooch in Birka Grave 517.*

42. *Funnel-shaped drinking glass and Viking swords from a ship chamber grave in Haithabu. Land Schleswig Holstein Museum.*

tunics from these fragments, but we are able to ascertain the quality of the material and the weaving technique. Many are coarse, simply woven, and certainly originate from ordinary Swedish sheep. But a great many scraps differ in that their wool is fine and of uniform quality. They are made of worsted, in most cases twisted to the left and woven in a 3- or 4-thread twill on looms with a hanging chain. Many are dyed blue, quite likely with woad coloring. Here we probably have the popular Frisian cloth itself. "Frisian cloth" may have been a quality term in those days, as "English cloth" is today. The grave finds prove that it was in great demand, and this is the sort of information we are after.

Glass drinking vessels were just as popular. (*See ills. 42, 43, 44.*) Glass was being blown in Frankish-Rhinelandic glassworks in the days of antiquity. The shape of the conic glass is appealing. It can't stand upright when full, but must be held and drained at one go; then it can be put down upside down. Most of the glass was found in Birka graves, one good piece in Haithabu. Dorestad, Groningen, Sylt, Föhr and Helgö turned out to be other decisive points of excavation for this type of ware, all of them lying along the popular trade route. The gently rounded glasses encircled by fine glass threads of a different color are especially beautiful. When the rim is a still different color, the thin receptacle has a marvelously shimmering delicacy. Glasses with applied

43. *Man drinking from a funnel-shaped glass.* Wandalbert-Martyrologium, *November Issue, Vatican Museum, Rome.*

44. *Glassware from Birka.*
    (TOP LEFT) *Arabic glass with animal and geometric ornamentation, about 3½ inches high. The other glasses are of Frankish-Rhinelandic origin. The round objects* (LOWER LEFT) *are amber game counters. State Historical Museum, Stockholm. Photo: E. Oxenstierna.*

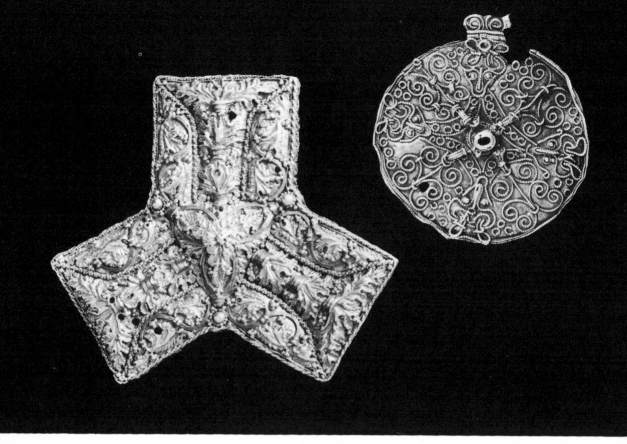

45. Ornate Frank brooch and pendant from the gold hoard of Hon, Norway. Universitetets Oldsakssamling, Oslo.

glass thread, grapelike knobs and colored rim, or those of veined glass, are evidence of a flowering industry that could command a good market.

Other type vessels were also in demand: jugs with handles, ornamented with tin plate, were used perhaps solely for liturgical purposes, but in our trade centers we often find clay vessels with small wheel-like ornamentation, and amphoras with decorative bands in relief. Since the Swedes had only poor raw material at their disposal, it is not surprising that the residents of Birka, who could afford luxuries, preferred West European vessels to the Swedish clay ones. In modern research, every type has to be recognized, catalogued, "read" or understood—time-consuming work which is nowhere near conclusion, especially since new finds often bring valuable supplementation.

The goldsmiths of the continent delivered exceptionally desirable and costly material. The most valuable treasure unearthed in Scandinavia is undoubtedly the great hoard in Hon, Norway, weighing 2,548 grams, nearly all gold, only a little silver—spiral neck rings, arm rings, buckles, pendants, and 19 coins, 5 of them Frankish. Did such a magnificent hoard really get to Sweden via honest trading? Could it not, perhaps, be the result of tribute paid by Charles the Bald, or part of the booty gained during raids on the Seine or Loire? This we shall probably never know. Among the finest artifacts in this find we must definitely classify the large trefoil buckle with its beautiful leaf work. Here the Norsemen, who were devotees of animal ornamentation, probably saw for the first time the floral ornamentation that was being cultivated in the Frank Empire. And suddenly there was a market in the North for trefoil clasps and brooches with floral design, all of it, of course much simpler than the magnificent example from Hon. (*See ills. 45, 46.*) It is interesting to note how the artisans of Haithabu caught on to the new patterns. Molds found in the black earth demonstrate that they picked up the Frank motifs and worked them up themselves. Offshoots of these wares are found often in Norway and Sweden.

Another profitable business was in weapons. Frankish swords were especially sharp and therefore much sought after by the Vikings. They were especially suited for attack—against the Franks! No wonder Charlemagne and those who succeeded him again and again forbade the export of Frankish swords, and made death the punishment for such export. In vain. The profit on smuggled weapons doubled. In our finds, the swords from Ulfberht's famous smithy are easily recognizable because they are signed, but apart from them, proving that weapons are of Frankish origin is tedious work for the researcher. Sometimes a Nordic handle was attached to a Frankish blade, or a Frank handle was given a new blade. In those restless times, no objects wandered from hand to hand to such an extent as weapons.

The Vikings bartered the products of Southern industry for the raw materials of the North. What they had to offer was for the most part perishable produce; we therefore cannot hope to find much proof of such trading in Southern Christian graves, especially since Christian graves were not rich with accessories. But we are on the track of some with Northern pieces. In the last eight years, one important Northern export article has been unearthed in the South, namely iron.

An analysis of the ore and slag finds in Haithabu showed Swedish bog-iron. Evidently the low-grade ore in Schleswig-Holstein, which was easily available on the spot, was spurned, and a finer grade was imported from Sweden. The prosperity of the south Swedish mainland in the days of the Vikings may very well be attributed to this new trade. Forges and iron slag have been unearthed also, in the past years, on Helgö. The export of bog-iron from the territory northwest of Lake Mälar can only have been controlled in Helgö. The local smiths undoubtedly profited through appropriate tariffs, and Sweden in all probability had already gained its reputation as an iron land in Viking days.

The results of a fresh investigation by Dr. Olaf Arrhenius came therefore as a surprise; 350 tests proved that two thirds of the iron forged was so poor

46. *Clover-leaf brooch and rein fittings from a gold-plated silver hoard found
in Sweden. The large strap tag, front and back view shown, is 5¼ inches
long. All objects have floral ornamentation in the Frank style. State Historical Museum, Stockholm. Photo: ATA.*

47. *Norwegian soapstone ware.*
Universitetets Oldsakssamling, Oslo.

in phosphor content that we have to count on its being mined ore; indicatively it turned up in the middle-Swedish iron-ore fields. Apparently iron was already being mined and smelted, and this type was much in demand because of its greater flexibility. In the near future we hope to have more exact knowledge on the subject.

Conditions were probably very similar in Norway. There is an effective discrepancy between the great quantity of iron utensils in Northern graves and the inventory, for instance, taken from an estate of Charlemagne in France: 2 axes, 2 spades, 2 augurs, 1 hatchet, 1 plane. And that is all. In those days a man paid 6 oxen or 12 cows for an iron breastplate; the same amount for a helmet; a sword cost a little more—7 oxen. The smith of course had to live, too; even so, iron was a rare commodity on the continent. The Northern Vikings could be sure of customers willing to pay well for it.

Some territories in southern Norway produced soapstone, a soft stone which could be cut with a knife and shaped into fire-resistant cooking vessels (pot-stone). Deep in the heart of virgin territory, today's hikers still come across mountain walls of the material and may count the abandoned, round, half-completed articles, for they were best cut directly out of the rock. The ground is covered with shavings, waste, cracked vessels. On one wall the stone masons may have cut deep, into another they may have carved veritable grottoes be-tween veins of hard basalt. Often they erected high wooden scaffolding to get at the desired material. (*See ills. 47, 48.*)

48. *Soapstone wall with molds and fragments.*

To transport these vessels was a laborious procedure. The Viking graves in Norway contain hundreds of soapstone pots. They mark the inland retail-trade route. Eight traders buried their store of merchandise in eight different places, never to raise them again. The cooking vessels were an excellent export article for Skiringssal on the Oslo Fjord, the trading center mentioned in the preceding chapter. Here the number of finds increases constantly. They are also found in Denmark, and on the German coast, in Birka, Haithabu; recently also in Hamburg. When the vessels cracked, they were simply worked over again into molds.

Soapstone had its local boundaries and was a humble product, but the costliest and most spectacular merchandise that could be brought down from the far-off forests was fur.

It is difficult to form an adequate picture of the abundance of game of this early period when we see the hundred-mile-wide forests today, still, and stripped of wild life. A few years ago, a Finn proved to us that Kemi Lappmark did not lose his fur wealth in the Far North until the sixteenth century, and then only due to the rivalry of English and Dutch buyers, at a time when the North Russian market, all the way to the Urals, was already exhausted by the Novgorod and Moscow trade. Today beaver and otter have receded to the Bering Straits. Catherine of Russia secured Alaska for her empire, and a single ship brought her 5,500 beautiful skins of sea otter, an animal that has almost disappeared from the forests of the North. The same ship also carried 1,385 ordinary fish-otter skins, 4,181 beaver, and 4,727 fox. In the end the cleared hunting grounds were sold to the United States in 1867 by needy Tsars.

The Vikings, who had begun to feel at home on the great eastern rivers found their most magnificent merchandise in the Russian forests. Today we have to be satisfied with breeding animals for their fur, with mink and fox in cages. We may know more about dressing fur than the dealers of those early days, yet we speak with awe of wild mink, ermine and semi-wild beaver, and no longer know what sable, sea-otter and Siberian squirrel look like. Listen to the romantic version of a writer of the early Middle Ages, and get a small idea of the wealth that has been lost:

"Black sable, red fox, ermine and beaver in quantities; lynx like the leaves of spring, sprinkled with a hundred thousand violets. (!) Soft beaver, black sable too, came to us ass-borne, until we could no longer count the skins. So many ermine pelts bound together, you could not tell how many there were. Shiny squirrel and ruby-colored fox; also wild filly; lynx fur that brightened your sleeping chamber and made light the dark of the night when it had fallen on the countenance of the day. . . ."

Soon northern Scandinavia was opened up for the hunting of fine fur animals. The Swedish finds move farther and farther north into the Bothnian Sea coast area, as well as inland. The coast of Norway had been explored some time before; now mountain hunters penetrated deep into the valleys to the icy Jotunheims. Arrowheads of the early or later Viking period have remained lying on the stony ground to the present day, once fortuitously in a bear trap, by chance together with a socketed ax.

At the ends of the valleys of Valdres and Gudbrandsdalen we even find hunters' graves, containing quite different furnishings from those of other graves. Dozens of arrowheads, a fish fork, rarely swords, but instead, useful strong knives, socket-axes, spears, a buckle perhaps, but no jewelry. Professional specialists may often be recognized by their grave accessories—the smith has his hammer and ambos, the trader a scale with weights. From this we may conclude that hunting implements would be buried with a professional hunter, one who made his living by selling the furs of the animals he killed, and who

49. *Weapons from a hunter's grave, Norway. The knife at bottom is 14 inches long. Eighth century. Universitetets Oldsakssamling, Oslo.*

50. *Shin bone of a pig, worked into a skate, from a Birka grave. State Historical Museum, Stockholm. Photo: ATA.*

must of necessity have worked mainly for the foreign buyer, in other words, a regular Norse trapper. (*See ill. 49.*)

Brisk hunting for the coveted animals went on all winter. Through buyers and middlemen, the soft, warm, feather-light skins came in bales across the small marts of the Far North to Birka and Skiringssal. What can we hope to find left of such perishable material? As much, anyway, as of the Frisian cloth from the South, and in the same place—hidden under the protective bronze shell brooches of a woman's jewelry. There we often find the hairs of squirrel, martin, beaver.

In the black earth of Birka we found something else—a conspicuously large number of ice skates, not made of iron in those days, but of pig's legs. (*See ill. 50.*) The bone was flattened out a little, two holes were made for the laces, and the smooth winter lakes could be crossed.

It is reasonable to believe that the yearly fur market was held after the winter hunting season had ended, when the perilously gray-blue ice was still traversable. Thus the furs could change hands in plenty of time for the sailing of the Viking ships. For these easily transportable, costly luxury items, the fine ladies and gentlemen in the land of the Franks and in Italy were prepared to pay horrendous prices. It is interesting to note that the Latin names for martin and beaver were replaced by the German designations in the Italian, French and Spanish languages. *Zobel* (sable) is a Slavonic word in German dress. The name wanders with the merchandise. But with a valuable cargo like this, the Viking ships suddenly became cautious freighters that avoided armed conflict, and their crews considered themselves lucky if they reached their destinations unharmed.

We still haven't mentioned the most important traffic of all, the most cruel, yet ever in demand—slaves. Living human beings, hands to work for one, bodies to satisfy one's lust. They took up a lot of room on a ship, but had the advantage of fetching a very high price and if necessary, could be counted on to help with their own transport. An extraordinary demand for slaves on the continent was advantageous to the Vikings. This important commodity had suddenly become scarce. For all major projects—the building of castles, forts, feudal mansions—hands were needed. In the days of antiquity, the situation had been no different, but a rapidly developing Christian church turned sharply against slavery. Among the Mohammedans in Spain there was a tremendous demand for slaves, for strong men and beautiful women; the church fathers first demanded therefore that no Christians be sold beyond the borders of the realm. The European slave-trading center in Lyons regulated all sales to the south and also took care of a third category: some left the city as docile eunuchs for far-away harems.

But where was all this living merchandise to come from? The letters of safe conduct of the first Roman Emperors gave the Jews all travel privileges, but forbade categorically that they trade with Christians. Pagans had therefore to be found, and here the Viking could help the Jew. A part of the Scandinavian population had meanwhile sunk to the status of thralldom. *Trälar* is the Swedish word for it: *Treller* in Danish. Overpopulation being what it was in those early Viking days, we may safely say that there was an abundance of human beings. But this was not enough. Cruel slave hunts were therefore initiated, writing a new chapter in our cultural history which carries us well into the nineteenth century. If we are to understand the events of that early era at all, we must not view them from today's moral standards, not even with the tolerantly critical eyes of a freshly organized West. We have to take into consideration the social structure of those days. That all men are created equal is a modern concept. We cannot expect to find it among the Vikings.

Slave hunts began east of the Elbe and in all Russia. Slaves were rounded up most easily among the Slavonic tribes. Recently the story of the founding of Magdeburg was clarified, in the east of the Holy Roman Empire, directly on the Elbe River boundary. We must not visualize a true city, not at first. The Diedenhof Ordinance of the Emperor in 805 permitted slave dealers to come to Magdeburg where nothing but a few inns surrounded a market place which came to life only on regular market days, when traders from the East offered their chained merchandise to buyers from the West. By a strange coincidence, we have an eyewitness to such a slave transport. His account has been woven into a legend and is mentioned casually, which makes it sound all the more plausible. The Benedictine abbot Sturm is looking for a suitable place to found a monastery:

"On his wanderings he one day came to the road along which merchants from Thuringia traveled to Mainz; and just where it crossed the River Fulda, he came upon a large number of Slavs bathing in the river. . . . In their heathenish way, they jeered the man of God, and showed signs of wanting to do him harm, but the will of God held them back. One of them, their interpreter, asked the pilgrim where he was going. The latter replied, 'Into the upper regions of the wilderness.' "

Obviously a slave transport had stopped for a refreshing pause on its way west. The goods had to be well cared for so that they might fetch a good price. Research seems to prove two further market centers for the slave trade: Regensburg on the Danube (Tariff Ordinance of Raffelstädten for slaves of the year 906), and Haithabu, situated so conveniently on the Baltic.

In slave transports such as these, human beings wandered back and forth as they had done in the Great Migration of Peoples; ravished men and women; booty and oarsmen for the Viking fleets traveling homeward; Christians and pagans in an endless stream. The more numerous the Vikings who left home, the greater the need for farm help at home. The slaves were dragged back and forth, sold, bought back. What Ansgar saw on his mission was an oft-repeated scene: "And he began at once to buy boys of Danish and Slavic origin their freedom, so that he might teach them to serve God." Or, "When a few poor prisoners from Christian lands were abducted and carted off to barbarian territory, they fled to the peoples north of the Elbe . . . where they were received mercilessly and thrown into chains. Some were sold back to the heathen, others were kept as slaves, some were offered to Christians." Or, "When Rimbert came to the land of the Danes, he saw, on a spot where he had once built a church for a newly formed Christian community, a great number of Christian prisoners tottering in chains. Among them was a nun. . . . The holy man, moved by fear and love for her, began to offer the heathens in charge of her various objects of value to pay for her freedom. They however would have none of his offerings unless he gave them the horse on which he was riding. This he did not refuse to do, but leaped out of the saddle at once and gave it, with the harness, in payment for the prisoner. As soon as he had bought her, he gave her her freedom and let her go wherever she wished."

Rimbert's informer was a bungler. That would have been the stupidest thing the bishop could have done—let the woman go unprotected in a heathen trading town. But his readers may not have thought so far. We do find out though what a slave was worth—a horse and saddle. Not cheap.

The heaviest traffic in Slavonic and Nordic slaves moved southward across Lyons to Spain. Spain alone could not use so many slaves, but traded them to the Eastern Caliphate, into the huge human mill of the Middle East. Arabic writers report thriving slave traffic between France and the Caliphate. Ibn

Khordadhbeh tells us that the Franks sold "eunuchs, male and female slaves, beaver pelts, martin skins and various other furs," and other merchandise to the Mohammedans. The accounts of various Arabic geographers corroborate this.

Slaves and furs France did not produce herself. The only conclusion is that the wares were brought by the Vikings from the Far North, and resold by Frank and Jewish merchants, via Spain, to the Caliphate. Ishtachri writes of "white eunuchs from Spain, and costly maidens." Ibn Hagal mentions "beaver from the land of the Slavs to Spain . . . from Spain to Egypt—Frankish and Gallic male and female slaves, and Slavonic eunuchs." Or the route stretches from the north Italian coast directly across the Mediterranean to the Orient.

Enormous distances, all Europe was circumnavigated to reach the farthermost customer—the Caliph in Baghdad. Ibn Khordadhbeh gives an exciting account of the trade routes followed, from which we quote this excerpt:

"The Jewish Raddamites speak Arabic, Persian, Roman, Frankish, Spanish, and Slavonic. They travel from east to west and from west to east. They disembark in the land of the Franks and travel overland to Al Kolzom [the Red Sea?] and from there, again by ship and land, to the holy cities of Medina and Mecca, to Sind, Hind and China. On their return, some of them go to Byzantium to sell their merchandise to the Romans. Others go to the homelands of the Frankish kings to dispose of their wares there. Sometimes the Jewish merchants sail from the land of the Franks across the Mediterranean to Antioch, and take the route over Baghdad to Oman, Sind, Hind and China. . . ."

Yes, but did the Northern goods have to traverse the whole of western Europe to reach the Caliphate? Such long trade routes must have considerably heightened the cost of transportation even according to the idea of travel-time prevalent in those days. So many middlemen. Constant peril. On top of that, the new decree forbidding the transport of heathen slaves across Christian lands and selling them to the Mohammedans (Meaux, 845).

There had to be a better solution. And it was pure genius that daringly contradicted traditional ideas. Since the Viking already dominated the Russian rivers, had even reached the Black Sea and encountered Arabic traders from the Caliphate in the Ukraine . . . why not shorten the whole laborious, immeasurably longer trade route through France and across the Mediterranean and sell one's furs directly to the Caliph in Bagdad, without any irritating middlemen at all?

So, shortly after 850, the entire trade route started to run in the opposite direction. Slaves and furs no longer sailed down the Southern Dvina and the Memel, but upstream. The ships were dragged across the Russian divides to sail down the Volga and Dnieper to the Black Sea. It wasn't necessary though to turn one's back entirely on one's good old partner, France. Frisian cloth, Frankish swords, Rhine wine, bronze, glass and wrought gold remained in demand, but the big new market opened in the East. To make safe the most important trade routes leading to it, to found colonies en route, to harness the manual power necessary, to negotiate with the Arabic merchants personally —for the enterprising Norsemen that was irresistible.

51. Map of the river lanes through Russia.

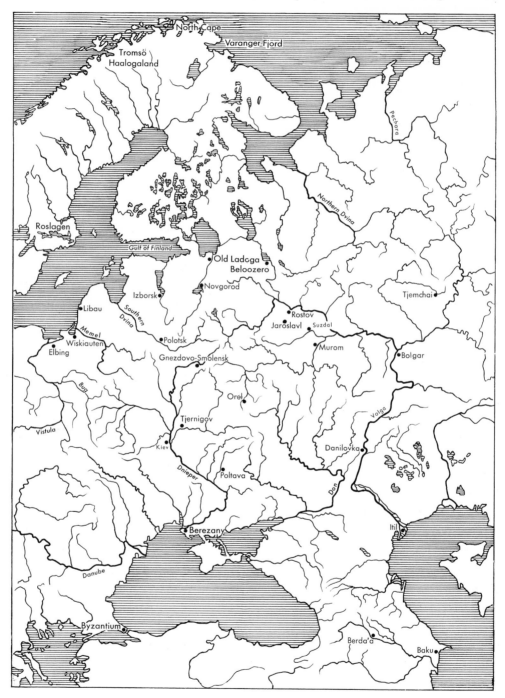

5

Was Russia Founded by the Swedes?

"THEY ISSUE FORTH from their land, anchor their ships in the Itil, which is a mighty river [the Volga] and build large wooden houses on its banks. Ten or twenty of them live in one house, but also less or more. Each one has a bench on which he sits with his beautiful slaves who are for sale. . . .

"They bring with them bread, meat, onions, milk and intoxicating drinks, and repair with them to a high upright wooden pillar which has something on it that looks like a human face and is surrounded by little statues behind which other wooden pillars stand upright. A man goes up to the high pillar and throws himself down on the ground and says, 'O my god, I come from far off and bring with me so and so many women and so and so many skins of martin. . . .

"And after he has enumerated all the wares he has brought with him, he goes on to say, 'And this present I have brought for you.' He lays it down before the high pillar and says, 'I wish that you should grant me a purchaser who has many gold and silver coins and buys everything from me that I want him to buy and is agreeable to all my demands.'

"After he has said this, he leaves. If his business does not go well, and his stay in the place is delayed for too long, he returns to the same spot with a second, and sometimes with a third gift. And if he still finds it difficult to achieve his aims, he brings a gift to each one of the little wooden statues, and beseeches them, saying, 'After all, you are the wives and daughters of our god.'

"Thus he moves constantly from one idol to the other, praying to them, begging them for help, bowing reverently before them. Often the sale of his wares is easy and good and he is able to sell all the merchandise he has brought with him. Then he says, 'My god has fulfilled my wishes. It is therefore my duty to reward him.'

"He then takes a number of oxen and sheep, slaughters them and gives away a part of the meat; the rest he lays under the high wooden pillar, and in front of the little ones; and he hangs the heads of the oxen and sheep on an upright wooden post. But at night the dogs come and eat up everything. Then he who laid the things there says, 'My god is pleased with me. He has eaten what I brought him.'

"I have never seen humans more nobly built. They are tall as palm trees, red blond, with light skins. They wear neither shirt nor coat with sleeves. The man wears a cape slung over one shoulder, so that one hand is free. Every man carries an ax, a dirk, and a sword. You never see them without these weapons. Their swords are wide and wavy and fluted, and have been manufactured in the land of the Franks. From the tips of their nails to their necks these men are tattooed with trees and various figures.

"The women wear a little box on their breasts of iron, copper, silver or gold, according to their wealth and the position of their man. (*See ill. 52.*) A ring

> 52. *Beads and a box brooch in silver and gold. The brooch is 2¾ inches in diameter. It is very similar to those found in Russia. State Historical Museum, Stockholm. Photo: E. Oxenstierna.*

is attached to the box, and a knife, which is also fastened to their breasts. Around their necks they wear chains of silver and gold. When a man possesses 10,000 Arabic silver coins, he has a chain made for his wife. If he has 20,000, she gets a second necklace. Thus his wife gets a necklace every time he is 10,000 dirhems richer. Many chains therefore hang around the neck of a Rus woman."

Thus wrote an alert-eyed brown-skinned diplomat about the blond, light-skinned traders whom he calls the "Rus." His name was Ibn Fadlan, and he was on his way to the city of Bolgar as legate of the Caliph of Bagdad in the year 922. He met up with the Swedes on the Volga, and has given us a more detailed and livelier report than any others we possess. Their appearance is accurately described, their apparel, armor—battle-ax and Frankish sword. We are familiar with the breast jewelry and necklaces of the women. The Scandinavians worshiped wooden idols throughout all antiquity, and with fine Oriental sarcasm the Arab makes fun of the superstitious heathen. His merchandise is well known to us too.

As roving traders in far-off lands, the Swedes installed themselves comfortably in eastern Europe. Archeological finds—graves and the remains of settlements—are infallible proof of this. Together with the often brief written sources, they give a graphic picture of life as it was lived a thousand years ago in the vast East. Let us follow what traces we have, beginning at the Baltic Sea.

For the dragon ships a crossing of the Baltic was nothing new. Then, once across the Gulf of Finland, all they had to do was sail a little more than 20 miles up the Neva, and Lake Ladoga opened up wide before them. On its eastern and southern shores we already come across many Viking findings, very logically at the mouths of the rivers that flow into the lake—the Svir, Pascha, Syas, and Volkhov. Groups of high barrows revealed charred remains but no metal objects that could be categorized precisely. We therefore have nothing to report on the origin of these graves. But other barrows are of the lower type found in central Sweden. They too appear in groups, contain cremation and inhumation graves, and many accessories, objects with which we are already familiar. Before World War I and after, Russian archeologists did some scrupulous investigating here. From among a wealth of finds, a few brooches attract our attention, some oval, others symmetrical, with two similar pieces on either side of an ornate round. One belongs to the ninth century, others to the tenth and eleventh. We also count chains of beads, one with an Arabian silver-coin pendant, minted in 922; horseshoe fibulae of the late Viking period; a ring fibula similar to ones found in Birka; combs, swords, battle-axes and spearheads. A rich assortment was found in a boat grave. Of the boat itself nothing was left but the rivets. It was about 33 feet long and 13 feet wide.

Women were often found buried beside the charred layer of a fireplace, furnished with kettle, chain, iron spade and clay vessels. This we don't find in Sweden, or anywhere else for that matter. It must be a local rite that developed on the shores of Lake Ladoga.

We have to keep in mind that now the Vikings were penetrating territory peopled by tribes that were alien to them. Here the Finns were at home, and we note the same procedure as took place earlier in Kurland. Gradually we find Finnish objects intermingled with Swedish finds. In this case, events moved quickly, since the Swedes were not just holding a bridgehead but were settling a large area. They were less dependent on the mother country and had therefore to rely more on the native population to help them form a communal way of life. Oval brooches probably always point to women from the Scandinavian mainland since they were rarely traded but were a part of the national costume. Gotlanders and Danes, for instance, never wore them. The Gotlanders wore only the round box brooches which are not found on the Swedish mainland. The amusing jingling small jewelry hanging from long chains is another matter. Here we find Finnish and Swedish pieces changing hands.

Old Ladoga on the River Volkhov was a trading center. The Vikings called it Aldeigjuborg. It did not lie in the river delta but, according to a principle we already know, about 7½ miles upstream. The wooden foundations excavated here are excellently preserved: at the bottom, a strata of large block houses, each with several rooms; directly above this, smaller houses with ovens in one corner, and at the top level, a poorly preserved settlement. Among the refuse in the black earth we find, as in Birka, many Viking pieces—a beautifully ornamented battle-ax, an oval brooch, combs, and also molds for Finnish jewelry.

Absolutely sensational though was the finding of an example of runic script in Old Ladoga, as published in a report of the Hermitage in Leningrad in 1957. A little wooden stave with fifty delicate letters inscribed on it was preserved most fortunately in the lowest layer of the black earth. The runologes easily recognized a verse in complicated cross-alliteration. The mysterious allusions have already led to very different translations, none of which we are going to favor here. In any case, it is an incantation about which we know nothing from the *Edda* or from any other written sources, and it certainly widens not only the sphere of Nordic poetry but also the geographic picture.

It is interesting to note that no Swedish findings of the eighth century exist in east Europe, not even in the Ladoga area. The great Viking push to the east did not begin before the ninth century. And this was probably when Old Ladoga was established as a base for all traffic inland. The Volkhov flowed south, the Pasha and Svir eastward. A fine network of small navigable rivers was spread across the great divide. Bundles of brush and wooden rolls made

53. *Swedish oval brooch found in Russia. State Historical Museum, Stockholm. Photo: ATA.*

it possible to drag the ships across it; smaller boats were carried. Such a portage area for boats is in Russian called *volok*.

Once across the divide, the route to the two big rivers ran swiftly along small tributaries. First the Vikings came to the upper reaches of the Volga. Immediately south of Lake Onega lay the famous city of Beloozero. Here we find oval, symmetrical and trefoil brooches of Nordic origin. There are innumerable small find sites and, south of the Volga, in the provinces of Vladimir and Yaroslavl, in a wide area northeast of Moscow, we find 167 burial grounds of the most colorful combination imaginable, unfortunately excavated in a horrible fashion. In the nineteenth century, 7,729 barrows were opened here so fast that up to 80 graves were uncovered in a day. As a result we can see Swedish, Finnish, Slavonic, Turkish, Permian and Oriental metal finds in the Moscow Museum, but so mixed up that it is quite impossible to tell which pieces once lay together; in fact there is no way of knowing now on what part of the huge exhumation site they were found. Finds were also made in Rostov, Suzdal, and Murom, which evidently belonged to this lively Viking settlement too. We can establish, however, that the Vikings were only a part of a population that was composed of various ethnic groups. (*See ills. 53, 54.*)

54. *Oval brooch from Yaroslavl Province, Russia.*

55. Viking finds from Gnezdovo-Smolensk. The ornamentation on these trinkets is typically Norse. The attachments to the ring are little Thor hammers.

On the great curve of the Volga we come across Swedish finds. Here the Vikings no longer met Finns, but Turkish-Bulgarians, whose capital was the goal of the Arabian legate previously mentioned. Farther east and north, and as isolated examples on the lower Volga, Viking objects have been raised—for instance, an ornamented chape, very similar to one in north Sweden.

If we press southward from Old Ladoga, we do best to accept the help of a trade route chartered in the year 1268, now in the Lübeck archives. In the Middle Ages, the Hanseatic merchants followed the trade routes discovered by the Vikings. They sailed through the Gulf of Finland past the islands of Berkö and Ketlingen (now Kronstadt), up the Neva, across Lake Ladoga to Volkhovminne and Old Ladoga (Aldeigjuborg). About six miles farther up the Volkhov, they had to change to a smaller boat, and *vorschkerle* gave them the necessary assistance through the rapids. In the word *vorschkerle* (German), or *vorsch*-men the Swedish word for rapids—*fors*—is still alive. Two custom-houses had to be passed, after which one finally arrived at the trading center of Novgorod on Lake Ilmen, called in Swedish Viking days—Holmgard.

Here the black earth is nearly 5 feet deep and has been assiduously dug in, but it seems to be very difficult to find the site of the oldest settlement. Most of the finds, also the frequently mentioned Slavonic inscriptions on bark, all belong to the Middle Ages. We shall be referring later to this city's importance in earlier periods.

We now sail from Lake Ilmen up the River Lovat to the west Russian divide. The traders could reach this divide via other river lanes too: the Southern Dvina, the Memel, Vistula, Bug. But to reach the Dnieper at Gnez-

dovo-Smolensk, all of them had to pass through a marshy area with a network of small, loamy rivers.

In Gnezdovo-Smolensk we find the largest Scandinavian burial ground in Russia. Still preserved are 3,850 mounds and work on them is going on constantly. To date 24 oval fibulae, 10 swords, and numerous other purely Swedish finds have been raised, among them Slavonic objects, the latter predominantly in graves with poor furnishings. The black earth demonstrates that Smolensk must have been situated on 3 different sites. (*See ill. 55.*)

Southward the Dnieper changes its face again and again. At one moment it is trying to squeeze through a narrow river bed; then it is suddenly flowing, wide and majestic, through primeval forests, like a water labyrinth. Not much can be left of the fearful dark areas of upright, water-undermined and finally toppled forest giants of those early days. The river does not become wide, calm and majestic again until Kiev. Here, too, we find black earth, the foundations of a fort, and many richly outfitted graves with Swedish accessories. In the past years important finds have been made and we may expect many more.

In summarizing the finds we can only say that, according to the last count made by Professor T. J. Arne, an expert on Russian antiquity in western Europe, 100 oval brooches from women's graves and 70 swords from men's graves are now preserved in Russia. Their existence is confirmed by rune stones in Sweden, of the same period. Close to a hundred such stones tell us that someone died "in the east," or at least was there. Sometimes a definite place is cited: Livland on the Dvina, Holmgard, or Gardarike, with which the land of the *gards* (Swedish for farmstead) is meant. In foreign lands they were nearly always fortified. Fortified farmsteads, therefore, or a Swedish fortified farm settlement in a foreign land, in this case Russia—that is the meaning of Gardarike.

A stone from the year 900 tells us, "Stig raised this stone for Öjvind, his son. He fell in the east."

The inscriptions are always short, the form concise. Most of the stones originated around and after the year 1000, a time when the incising of rune stones became general. One of them reports: "Ingefast had this stone inscribed for Sigvid, his father. He fell in Holmgard, as chieftain of his ship with his crew." Or, "Torsten raised this stone for Ärinmund, his son; bought this village [Veda, north of Stockholm] and acquired the money for it in Gardum [Gardarike]."

In all written sources, especially those by numerous Arabian geographers, the Vikings in eastern Europe were called the Rus. The origin of the word is clear and of exceptional interest. The coast north of Stockholm was called Roslagen, its inhabitants are called Rospiggar (pronounced Ruspiggar) to this day. Here the Swedish kings of the Middle Ages raised their armies; each locality had to contribute a fully armed ship with crew. This Nordic form of levy goes back to ancient times. It influenced the life of the Vikings and in all probability formed the military backbone of Svea rule when the Svea kings were founding the first colonies beyond the Baltic Sea. The word Rus probably developed as follows:

Rōðr   — oar-way (waterway, strand, bay, river, compare with the English word *road*).

Rōð(r)s   — the genitive of the word.

Rōðs-men   — the men of the oar-way. The men of this coastal area must have called themselves that.

Rōtsi   — a shortening of the same word in a typical Finnish way, originating when the Finns of the Ladoga area came in contact with these Swedes.

Ruotsi   — today's way of writing, and the Finnish name for Sweden, according to the custom of naming a race after the nearest tribe. Names similarly derived are Allemania, Swabia, Saxonia—all names for Germany.

Rūs   — in which form the Slavs took over the name from the Finns.

One may say therefore that the name traveled southward via the Finnish population around Lake Ladoga.

The Chronicle of Nestor, written in the Pechersky Monastery of Kiev toward the end of the eleventh century, tells about the arrival of the Rus among the Slavonic people on the Dnieper. It places the event in the year 862 and reports on the Slavonic tribes:

"Among them there was no law, and tribe rose up against tribe, and there were feuds among them, and they began to fight each other. And they spoke among themselves: 'We must find a prince who will rule justly over us.' And they crossed the sea to the Varangians, the Rus, for the Varangians were called Rus, as others are called Swedes, others Norwegians and Anglians, others Gotlanders, thus also these men. The Chudes, Slovenes, Krivichi and Vesses said to these Rus, 'Our land is great and rich, yet there is no order in it. Come therefore and rule over us.'

"And three brothers were chosen, with their tribes, and they took all the Rus with them and came. Rurik, the oldest, settled in Novgorod; the second, Sineus, in Beloozero; the third, Truvor, in Izborsk."

Now that is a pretty story, much too pretty to be true. People do not come to foreign lands and form colonies quite that way. And we grow even more skeptical when we hear what folklore has to say elsewhere, without ever having become part of a chronicle. In the Finnish *Österbotten,* an area around the Torne River which borders on Sweden, they tell of "three Swedish brothers who were the first to come to Lake Ytter. One was called Paul; he settled in a place now called Pavalsfolk . . . the second went to Göransfolk, beyond the river; the third to Bärklare." Or let us listen to the local saga around Abo: Three brothers came to Hitis Rosalaby [Abo], from Roslagen in Sweden. The one was named Nils, the second Tommas, the third Mans. Nissa, Tommossa and Manusa were named after them; and they are the oldest farmsteads. The village is called Rosala because the brothers came from Roslagen.

You will find innumerable variations of this saga in Finland and Estonia. Always three brothers come by ship across the Baltic Sea. They are as legendary as Grimm's Fairy Tales. It is the usual form in which the Swedish landfall in the east is described. But we are blessed with written sources.

To our astonishment, we find the subject dealt with similarly in the Guta Saga about the first settlement on the island of Gotland—and in Ireland! According to medieval historian Giraldus Cambrensis, a landfall in the ninth century took place in the following manner (Topographia Hibernica, compiled in 1185): "Three brothers called Amelavus, Sitaracus and Yvorus (Olaf, Sigtrygg and Ivar) came from Norway across the sea to Ireland. The one built the fortress of Dublin, the second the fortress of Waterford, the third the fortress of Limerick." In the same amiable way the Normans were asked to take the rich island of Sicily under their wing. Leo of Ostia tells us in the eleventh century: "And then Prince Waimar of Salerno had his ambassador bring to the Normans cedar, apples, almonds, gilded nuts as well as royal robes, harnesses ornamented in finest gold, and invited them, or rather urged them, to come to the land that could produce such treasure."

Only two brothers—Hengist and Horsa—were persuaded to come to England by the Anglo-Saxons, yet it is touching to read in Widukind's Saxon history how the old native Britons invited them:

"O magnificent Saxons! The poor Britons, exhausted by constant invasion of the enemy and nigh broken, have heard of the glorious victories you have won, and send us [the British legates] to you to implore you not to deny us your aid. They offer you a spacious land which includes an abundance of all things, that it may be subject to you. Until now we have lived under the rule and protection of the Roman. After the Romans, we know of no men better than you. We desire therefore to be taken under the wings of your valor. By your bravery, by your weapons alone, can we contain the enemy; and however you may wish to hold sway over us, we shall gladly bear it."

Has it not been ever thus, with all colonization, even during the Second World War? The powerful invader had to justify his aggression by producing some sort of request for aid.

And what followed the charming invitation described in the Nestor Chronicle? In the second half of the ninth century, the Rus crossed the sea in ever-increasing numbers, founded colonies, just as the western Scandinavians were doing in Ireland, Friesland and Normandy at the same time. They burst the narrow confines of their former sphere of power, sometimes as warriors, sometimes as traders. Cities that get special mention in the Nestor Chronicle are Novgorod, Smolensk, Beloozero, Izborsk, Polotsk, Rostov and Kiev, just the places where most of the Swedish grave finds are. Of Kiev the Chronicle says, "This is to be the mother of all Russian cities."

These events become dramatic when one realizes that the Rus, as the first state founders in eastern Europe, gave today's Russia its name. This fact was not very acceptable to the national pride of the Tsarist empire. The question often came up for discussion. There were many who spoke with disapproval of the so-called Norman school of thought. They wanted to derive the name Rus from other sources; they even evaluated the Swedish grave finds as evidence of nothing more than the thriving trade in those days. But it proved impossible to find a Slavonic word that came phonetically anywhere near the controversial word, and there is no evidence of any other culture on the Dnieper before the end of the ninth century. The anti-Normanists are still numerous; an index alone of literature on the subject is 150 pages thick. It offers various explanations, but a thorough analysis of the Swedish landfall in Russia still forms the backbone of any discussion on the subject. I summon, as first arbiter, Emperor Louis the Pious.

"Some men who called themselves and their people Rhos," came to Ingelheim in the year 839. Rhos is the correct Greek form of Rus. I have already mentioned that the Emperor felt harassed by the massive Viking raids in the west. He had conducted an investigation as to the reasons for the journey of these men who had turned up at his court, and discovered that they were Sveas. That was why he checked what they had to say very carefully before he let them go.

Another witness is the Italian historian, Liudprand (*circa* 922–972) who wrote in Byzantium of the military expeditions of the years 941–944. "There is a race living in the north whom the Greeks, because of a peculiarity [he is referring to their red-blond coloring] call Rusii, whereas we call them Normans, according to the location of their homeland."

Quite independent of such sources, al-Jaqub writes in Arabic: "In the year 844, the heathen men we call Rus attacked Seville, plundered, laid waste, burned and murdered." I have already mentioned this Viking raid. It becomes quite evident that, to people and writers of various nationalities, Normans, Vikings and Rus were the same Scandinavian people.

For more precise proof, let us include the results of excavation: first of all the 10 large wooden burial chambers in Kiev, 4 of them under the Decimal Church. In them rests a warrior with his armor, a woman at his side, a horse at his feet. To the north, in Chernigov, similar magnificently outfitted wooden chambers have been found, deeply buried. These are typical chieftain graves. We know of approximately 100 like them in Birka, among them several with woman and horse. The richest grave in Haithabu is also a wooden chamber; other west Scandinavian graves that are similar may be found in Mammen, Jellinge, Rolfsöy, Tune and Bygstad. The furnishings of the Dnieper graves are for the most part purely Swedish, although some foreign weapons and jewelry are intermingled with the accessories.

In a charred strata near Gnezdovo-Smolensk 234 rivets demonstrate as clearly as in many Scandinavian findings that here a chieftain was cremated with his boat. His wife was laid to rest with 4 oval brooches and other Nordic jewelry. The sword, however, is of eastern origin. A typical Thor hammer-ring is also one of the accessories. And we have a written source for the burial of a chieftain in his boat in a report by the Arabian Ibn Fadlan, who was the eyewitness of such an event. It took place apparently at a base camp of the Rus on the Volga. Here archeological findings and written sources complement each other excellently.

Ibn Fadlan writes: "I walked by the river where the ship [of the dead man] lay. But it had already been drawn on land. Four corner braces had been prepared; all around them stood big, human-like wooden statues. The boat was dragged to this site and set up between the supports. Meanwhile the men walked back and forth, speaking a language I could not understand. The dead man was lying on one side, in a trench out of which he had not yet been lifted. The men took a bench, placed it in the boat, and covered it with cushions, Greek silk brocade, and pillows made of the same material. . . .

"They then dressed the man, put on him trousers, socks, boots, coat and kaftan of gold weave with gold buttons, and a cap of silk brocade trimmed with martin. Then they laid him under the tent that was on the ship, supported him with the cushions, brought intoxicants, fruit and scented plants, and set all these things beside him. Bread also, meat and onions they put before him. Then they fetched a dog, cut him in two, and threw the pieces into the boat. Then they laid all the dead man's weapons at his side, led up two horses and chased them until they were dripping with sweat, then cut them to pieces with their swords and cast the pieces into the boat. Then they brought up two oxen, cut them up in a similar fashion and threw the pieces into the boat. Finally they came with a cock and a hen, killed them, and cast them into the boat."

All the details that we can corroborate are similar to the practices of boat-grave burials north of Stockholm. But the dead man on the Volga was supplied with more things:

"When the man mentioned above had died, they asked his slaves, 'Who is willing to die with him?' One said, 'I.' She was given to two other maidens who had to guard and accompany her wherever she went. Yes, sometimes they even washed her feet. . . . Meanwhile she drank every day, sang, was lively and content."

On the day of the burial, she visited the men in their tents, one after the other. Then she was borne to a framelike altar and elevated three times on the palms of the men's hands, during which, according to the interpreter, she said, "Lo, here I see my father and my mother." Then, "Lo, now I see all my dead kin seated together." And the third time, "Lo, I see my lord and master, seated in the hereafter, and it is so beautiful, so green. Men and servants are with him. He calls to me. Let me go to him."

Then the report continues: "They led her to the boat. She took off her two arm rings and gave them to the woman who was called the Angel of Death, who was to kill her. She also took off both anklets and gave them to the two maidens at her side, who were the daughters of the Angel of Death. Then they lifted her onto the boat, but did not yet let her enter the tent. Now the men came with shield and staff and handed her a goblet filled with an intoxicating drink. She took it, sang, and drained it. 'With this,' said the interpreter, 'she takes leave of her friends.'

"Then they gave her another goblet. She took it and sang a long song. Then the old woman bade her to hurry and empty the glass, and to enter the tent of her dead lord. But she had grown fearful and hesitant. She seemed to want to enter the tent, but all she did was stick in her head. At once the old woman grasped her head and led her into the tent at her side. Whereupon the men immediately began to beat with their staffs on their shields so that her screams might not be heard, for they might have startled the other women who would then be unwilling to die one day with their lords.

"Then six men entered the tent and had intercourse with her, one after the other, after which she was laid out beside her master. Two men grasped her feet, two her hands, and the old woman, who was called the Angel of Death, put a noose around her neck, gave the ends to two of the men; then she herself came forward with a big broad knife and ran it twice between the ribs of the maiden. And the two men choked her with a noose until she died.

"And now the next of kin of the dead man stepped forward, picked up a piece of wood, set fire to it and walked to the stern of the boat, the piece of wood in one hand, the other covering his buttocks—for he was naked—until the wood under the boat was burning. Then others came also with pieces of wood burning at the tip, and threw them on the funeral pile. Soon it was burning brightly—first the boat, then the tent and the man and the maiden and everything that was in the boat. . . . And it did not take long for boat, wood and maiden and the dead man to be reduced to ashes. On the spot where the boat that had been dragged out of the water had stood, they piled up a round mound in the middle of which they raised a pillar of beech-wood on which they inscribed the name of the dead man and the name of the king of the Rus. Then they went away."

Here the boat was not only buried but burned, a ritual we come across often in Sweden and five hundred times in Norway. Not only Ibn Fadlan but other Arabs also seemed to know of the custom that a woman sometimes joined a man in death. Ibn Dustah writes: "When one of their nobles dies, they bury him in a grave that looks like a roomy house [wooden burial chamber]. They lay him inside it and, beside him, his clothes, gold arm rings, a supply of food, vessels filled with beverages, coins and finally—his favorite wife, alive. The opening is sealed and the wife dies, entombed in the grave."

Al Massudi writes in a similar vein: "They cremate their dead, and on the same funeral pile they lay the weapons of the dead, their beasts of burden, and their jewelry. When a man dies, his wife is cremated with him. But when the wife dies, her husband does not share her fate. When an unmarried man dies, they let him celebrate his marriage after death. The women eagerly desire to be cremated with their husbands so that they may follow them to Paradise. This is customary also with the Hindus, who cremate a wife with her husband."

We frequently find proof of this sinister ritual in Birka, and in all Scandinavia. When weapons and oval brooches turn up in one and the same grave, the evidence is unmistakable. One could, of course, say that the wife may have died with her husband of a plague, or by the bloodshed of war, or simply of old age, except that we have so many finds of this sort. And the old Nordic sagas tell us how Jarl (Earl) Valgaut in Gotland went to war against Saint Olaf of Norway, and demanded that, if he fell in battle, his wife should drain the funeral beer, build a funeral pile, burn all their possessions, and cast herself into the fire.

It is almost impossible to grasp these ancient beliefs which produced such frightful ritual. All earthly life was preparation for the hereafter; all measures —even the most cruel—were intended to secure a continuation of marriage after death. In most cases the Viking wife came to a natural end and was given her own burial mound, yet the primitive urge to assure a continuation of a lifetime spent together when the husband dies, is something we come across frequently.

And what if the chieftain was unmarried? Al Massudi differentiates clearly between the obedience of wives and the weddings in death with slave girls. Until now we have come across nothing but married couples in our Scandinavian finds, recognizable by the jewelry of noble and married women, but since we have been able to analyze bone fragments, we are in a position to ascertain whether or not a young girl with no jewelry, therefore evidently a concubine, sometimes followed her lord to his death. According to pagan beliefs, a man had the same needs and rights after death as during his lifetime. But a slave had no formal rights; she had no hereafter coming to her. It must have been quite exceptional for her to be asked to follow her lord to his death like a good wife. What took place on that memorable day on the Volga, in the year 922, was apparently an actual wedding in the shadow of death. "She drank every day, sang, was lively and content." Beyond the framework of the altar—which was probably symbolic of a gate, the boundary between life and death—she heard him calling and wanted to be led to him. Her hesitation before the tent may not have been fear of death, but the hesitation of the bride. Wives were dragged by force into the bedchamber, sometimes even thrown on the marriage bed. And whose was the right to the wedding night? The groomsmen. Singly or communally—and in all respectability—they lay with the bride, and the groom sometimes had to wait three nights for the privilege.

These primeval beliefs reoccur in more enlightened times as amusing or symbolic fantasy. But the men Ibn Fadlan watched on the Volga were still practicing them realistically. They were giving their dead chieftain all the potency they had—via this maiden—just as the stallions had to be slaughtered at the height of their excitement.

In 1949, another boat grave was discovered in Gnezdovo-Smolensk; it, too, was furnished with weapons, and contained five Arabic coins, the most recent from the year 907. Among the woman's jewelry was a Slavonic temple band. Another item was an amphora of southern origin, made on a potter's wheel, with the word *gorouchtcha* engraved on it in Cyrillic letters, related perhaps to the modern word *gorkij* for "bitter." It could have been a vessel for Oriental spices, and since a majority of the people were Slavs, this Slavonic word—one of the earliest preserved for posterity—should not surprise us. The archeologist who found the grave wanted to identify it as Slavonic, but his Swedish colleagues didn't agree with him. Slavonic may have been spoken in the kitchen. The question as to whether or not the wife was Slavonic—because she wore a temple band—has to remain open.

A thorough treatment and discussion of archeological finds in Russia is woefully lacking. The results of similar Viking finds on the British Isles have been published recently in five magnificent volumes. We urgently need a comprehensive work, with modern illustrations, of the collective findings in Russia. As it is, we have to depend on obsolete and incomplete literature, augmented at best by notes from diaries and a few isolated publications. The barrier of language also poses considerable difficulties. And finally, we are much too cut off from each other, are not allowed to intertravel sufficiently, can visit one another only rarely, study museums much too cursorily, and cannot become familiar with the archeological milieu in Russia in any sort of communal effort.

Oval brooches have occasionally been interpreted in Russia as jewelry belonging to the bodyguard of the princes of Kiev. Whoever may have worn them—surely never men! We should be given the opportunity to study all this ornamentation systematically, to differentiate between Nordic pieces and those originating in the local cultural areas of the Dnieper. Innumerable other questions wait for accurate answers. It would be a blessing for the science of archeology if this gap could be closed. The "Norman question" might then be seen in a quite different light.

In the meantime, we can establish the fact that both Arabic scribes and Russian finds prove that the contents of double graves found in Russia seem to be Swedish. Wooden chamber graves and boat graves—with or without cremation—are definitely Swedish; for the most part the furnishings are, too. If, in a Finnish or Slavonic colony, isolated accessories of southern or eastern origin are found so far away from the Norseman's homeland, so close to the Orient, it is not contradictory or surprising. All the dead belong socially to the upper class. This fact is stressed also by Russian archeologists. In my opinion, immigrant Rus warriors and traders, who had founded new states in Kiev and surrounding areas, rest in these graves.

We find out more about how the Rus broadened their sphere of trade and power through another conscientious writer, the Byzantine Emperor Constantine

Porphyrogennetos, who in 950 wrote a manual for his son, telling the boy what was worthy of note for a future ruler. We may therefore expect it to be reliable. In Chapter 9, he writes: "In the winter, the life of the Rus is hard. At the beginning of the winter, their chieftains and all the Rus leave Kiev at the same time and set out on *poliudie,* which means 'circuit,' into the territory of the Slavonic Vervians, Drugovichi, Krivichi, and Severians, and to the other Slavonic tribes who pay tribute to the Rus. There they spend the winter, but in the month of April, when the ice on the Dnieper has melted, they return to Kiev. . . . They may come from Novgorod, Smolensk, Ljubec, Chernigov or Visgorod. In the spring, after the thaw, they assemble in Kiev, which is called Samvatas. Here they destroy their old boats, which are hollowed out of a single tree, and buy new ones from the Slavs who have felled the trees during the winter. They take dippers, thole pins and other gear from their old boats and equip the new ones with them. In spring the voyagers to Greece set forth. For a few days the fleet lies assembled near Vytechev. This is a tax collector's fortress, just below Kiev [fortified for the Rus who were to collect taxes and therefore had to count on the hatred of those being taxed]. When the whole fleet is assembled, all the boats sail down the river to face the hazards of the voyage together."

Dragon ships belong on the open sea. On these eastern rivers, streams, rapids, and inland stretches, smaller boats had to be used. This the Emperor

56. *The rapids of Dnjepropetrovsk, before the building of the dams. Photo: T. J. Arne.*

corroborates for us in a very vivid way. Quite large and durable boats, or dugouts, could be fashioned out of felled primeval forest giants. It was up to the Slavs to shape them with fire and hatchet and prepare them for launching. In the winter the Rus spread out in the vast reaches of the forests around the divide, lived on the tribute they had collected, rounded up pelts and other merchandise for the summer voyage. We should study the Emperor's words more closely, after having seen how trading in Sweden had been co-operatively organized. For this was accomplished in a similar fashion in the winter preparations north of Kiev, and in the summer drive south of that city. And all this was very necessary because south of Poltova the wide river had to force its way through a 50-mile-wide granite hill, a spur of the Carpathian Mountains. Today the wild waters are tamed in the powerful plant of Dnjepropetrovsk, but in those days they tumbled as rapids over countless rocks and could be ridden by boats only in early summer when the greatest force of the high water had eased somewhat and drought had not yet set in. Seven falls posed a special hazard. (*See ill. 56.*) Only when the water level is low do the underwater rocks and reefs become visible on the old photographs. The Emperor writes about it and must have received his information from a reliable source.

"They come to the first waterfall, which is called Essupi, which means 'don't sleep,' in the Rus as well as the Slavonic language. It is as narrow as Tzykanisterion (a place in Byzantium). High steep rocks that look like islands are in the middle of it. When the water washes over them, it creates a great and frightful noise as it falls. That is why the Rus do not dare to sail between these rocks but stop their boats first, let the crew go on land, but leave the cargo in the boats. Then they walk into the water naked, feeling their way with their feet so as not to stumble over the rocks. All the while they are pushing their boats forward with staffs, some at the prow, some in the middle, some at the stern. With all these precautions, they manage to traverse the first fall along edge and bank. As soon as they are through, they take the rest of the crew on again and sail off in their boats."

The Emperor's description is so detailed, he even gives us the names of the seven waterfalls in both languages.

	Russian	*Slavonic*
1	Essupi	—
2	Ulvorsi	Ostrovuniprach
3	Gelandi	—
4	Aifor	Neasit
5	Baruforos	Vulniprach
6	Leanti	Verutzi
7	Strukun	Naprezi

The interesting thing is that all seven Rus names are of north-Germanic origin and show various parallels with the Swedish word for rapids. Three even end in *fors*.

> Ulvorsi—Holmfors—a rapid with a little island.
> Aifor—Edfors—a narrow rapid.
> Baruforos—B(V)arufors—a wavy or rocky rapid.

Two are present-participle formations:

> Gelandi—Gaellandi—a shrill or loud rapid.
> Leanti—Leandi—a smiling, bubbling rapid.

Two are vowel variations of strong verbs:

> Essupi, from *supa*—a drinking rapid, or one that figuratively drinks itself up.
> Strukun, from *stryka*—a fleetly passing rapid.

Here we have an example of the dual language of the Dnieper. Most of the remaining rapids were conquered like the first one, but the fourth posed a special hazard. As late as 1916, an author writes, "Already from far off, one hears the dreadful roaring of the biggest of all the rapids, the Djid, the Nenasytek. White masses of foam cover the rocks at all times, and the water shoots with sinister speed, quick as an arrow, across the twelve boulders."

In the Emperor's manual we read about it too. "At the fourth great rapid, which in Rus is called Aifor, in Slavonic—Neasit, pelicans nest on the rocks. Here everyone brings their ship to land and those who are to stand watch disembark. These sentinels are necessary because of the Pechenegs who lie constantly in ambush. The rest take their belongings out of the dugouts and lead the slaves across land for six miles, until they are past the rapids. After that they transport their skiffs, sometimes by hauling them, sometimes by carrying them on their shoulders past the rapids. Then they put them in the water again, reload their cargoes, get in themselves, and travel onward."

Here, at the worst spot, the Turkish Pechenegs were still waylaying the Rus when he was most absorbed. Sometimes this ended badly for the voyager. The Nestor Chronicle in the year 972 reports on Rurik's grandson, Svyatoslav: "Svyatoslav approached the rapids, whereupon Kurya, the prince of the Pechenegs, fell upon him. And they killed Svyatoslav, and took his head and made a beaker of his skull by mounting it; and they drank out of it."

It must have been tempting sometimes to deceive the treacherous enemy, and risk the boat trip across the dread rapids between rock and reef. Such daring adventure appealed to the courageous Vikings. Tersely a bold venture

57. *Rune stone on Gotland, raised for a man who died on the Dnieper. Gotlands Fornsal, Wisby. Photo: ATA.*

in the white foam of Aifor is described on the Gotland rune stone of Pilgards: "Hegbjörn, and his brothers, Rodvisl, Östen and Emund, had this stone painted in colors and raised. They also raised stones in memory of Ravn, south of Rufstein. They went afar into Aifor. Vivil gave the order." (*See ill. 57.*) And that is all. "They went far into Aifor." They had almost ridden the fearful rapid when their boat capsized. One of them lost his life. Just the same, the deed was considered worthy of commemoration on a rune stone.

After overcoming the seven waterfalls, a pause and thanksgiving are in order. The Emperor writes: "Then they reach an island which is called St. Gregor, on which they make their sacrifices because a giant oak tree stands there. They sacrifice living birds. All around the tree they plant spears in the ground. Others sacrifice bread and meat as well, and anything else they may have, as is customary with them. They also cast lots for the birds, whether they should slaughter or eat them or let them live."

This rite was probably customary also on the island of Gotland where we know of a sacrificial site. Circles of spearheads, as well as hundreds of other objects, have been found on the so-called Gudingsakrarna. It is to be hoped that we soon discover another such place of sacrifice which can be more thoroughly investigated.

At last the Rus came to the end of their river journey—the island of Berezany at the mouth of the Dnieper. Berezany means Birch Island; in Nordic—Birka. It couldn't possibly have been named after anything but the trading center on Lake Mälar; just as we find marts called Birka on the great rivers of north Sweden and near Helsinki in Finland. The Vikings settled similarly on islands in Frankish and Frisian rivers, at points located strategically for war and trade, and easily defensible. The Emperor in the East didn't like this any better than the Emperor in the West. In the peace treaty of 944 between Byzantium and the Rus, we therefore find a clause: "And the Rus shall not be permitted to spend the winter at the mouth of the Dnieper, neither in Beloberezye nor with the Holy Elentherios (Berezany), but when autumn comes they are to return to Rusland."

Just the same, they stayed long enough on the island of Berezany to erect a rune stone there, the only one known in Russia. It was discovered in 1905, on a hillside—not its original location—and is now in the Odessa Museum. The text reads, "Grane raised this memorial for his comrade Karl." (*See ill. 58.*) The word for memorial, *half,* equivalent to *valv,* or arch, is Gotlandic, and the shape of the stone conforms with that of Gotlandic stones. The rune stones of Pilgards and Berezany stand at either end of a frequently traveled Gotlandic trade route. A typical Finnish horseshoe brooch, now in Odessa, indicates that Finns were wont to accompany the Swedes on these long treks.

But their goal lay beyond the Black Sea—the imperial capital itself, Byzantium, in its immeasurable east-Roman, Oriental glory. Should they attack the

58. Rune stone found on the island of Berezany. Museum, Odessa.

city with a vast military force? According to the Nestor Chronicle, this was attempted in 865. It gives a more detailed account though of a raid in the year 907:

"Oleg set out to fight the Greeks and left Igor [Rurik's son] in Kiev. . . . And the boats numbered 2,200. He arrived before Byzantium, and the Greeks blockaded the sound and sealed the city. And Oleg went on land and began to ravage the surroundings of the city and killed many Greeks. . . . And Oleg commanded his soldiers to make wheels and to place the boats on these wheels. And when a favorable wind arose, they hoisted their sails and advanced upon the city from the open countryside. When the Greeks saw this, they were afraid and sent messengers to Oleg, who said, 'Do not destroy the city. We are willing to pay whatever tribute you ask.' "

No. We don't believe Nestor. To set boats on wheels and let them "sail" across the fields surrounding Byzantium wasn't such a simple matter, and we have every reason not to believe this tall tale because the Roman scribe Frontinus tells a similar story in a different connection: "When the Lacedaemonian, Lysander, was locked in the harbor of Athens with his entire fleet, because the enemy had sunk ships at the narrows in the harbor's entry, he sent his soldiers on land secretly, had them set their boats on wheels and steer them across the countryside to the nearby harbor of Munychia."

This is the sort of yarn soldiers and seafarers like to tell when they want to outdo each other in heroic deeds. There isn't a word of truth in it. But the peace treaty is probably reliably notated, for Nestor mentions it explicitly as a "Copy of the treaty of friendship which was agreed upon under the Emperors Leon and Alexandros." "We, of the race of the Rus: Karly, Inegeld, Farlof, Veremud, Rulav, Gudy, Ruald, Karn, Frelav, Rual, Aktevu, Truan, Lidul, Fost, Stemid, sent by Oleg, the Rusian Grand Duke, and all the illustrious and mighty princes subject to him and his great boyars, to you, Leon and Alexandros and Constantinos, the great and sole rulers in God, the Greek emperors, to the preservation and strengthening of the friendship existing for many years between Christians and Rus . . . we have recognized as right that this friendship should not be confirmed by words alone, but in writing, and by an oath sworn on the sword according to the [Christian] faith and according to our [pagan] custom. . . . Toward this affirmation and the inviolability of our agreement, we have had the peace treaty between you Christians and us Rus drawn up in cinnabar script, in two copies, on parchment."

This is obviously a state charter, a reliable diplomatic document, which fortunately was preserved because it was copied and inserted in the Nestor Chronicle. Now, as we know only too well, peace treaties can be of short duration. In 944 war broke out again between the Rus and the Greeks. The new peace treaty is also inserted in the Chronicle. In all, one hundred names of Rusian legates and merchants are mentioned in the two documents, and these are of the greatest interest to us. Taking only the names mentioned in the first agreement, and putting them back into their original form, they read as follows: "Karli, Ingjaldr, Farulfr, Vermundr, Hrolleifr, Goði, Hróaldr, Karni, Friðleifr, Hróarr, —, Þrondr, —, Fasti, —, Helgi." Only three are of unclear origin, the others are correctly transcribed from the Nordic.

The same observation may be made with all the names. They are for the most part Nordic; about one third are predominantly east Swedish; none are Gotlandic; a few are unclear. This confirms the fact that east Swedish Vikings held leading positions in the nobility of Kiev. Only a few controversial names can be derived from Slavonic or Finnish forms. This list of officials and diplomats therefore has an absolutely stunning testimonial value.

In both treaties there are quite a few civil rights clauses that are concerned with murder, theft, wreckage, plunder, serfdom, and so on; most important to us though are the trade regulations for the Rus traders visiting Byzantium. Before the year 945, ambassadors from Kiev wore gold seals, the merchants wore silver ones. From then on they had to show a document of identification from their ruling prince.

"And they are to enter the city with an imperial overseer, through a certain gate, unarmed, fifty men at a time, and to trade. . . . And they are not to buy silk worth more than 50 aurei. And whoever buys silk is to show it to the imperial overseer who shall seal it and hand it to them. And when the Rus leave the city, they shall receive from us the food necessary for the journey, and whatever their boats may require, as has been previously established, and they are to return safely to their own country. But they are not permitted to spend the winter in the suburbs of the Holy Mamas [an ancient fertility saint]."

The document shows great respect for the warriors who had fought the Greek Emperors in previous years. Only 50 Rus were to be permitted within the gates of Byzantium at a time, unarmed! As traders they were faced with a strict guild system, price controls and rigorous monopoly regulations. This was especially valid for the trade in silk. The material was rationed and the Emperor protected himself against black marketeers by a seal. The merchandise of the Rus is not mentioned, but Prince Igor gave the Greek diplomats gifts of "furs, slaves and wax." These are the wares we come upon again and again in the vast territory covered by the eastern Vikings.

Thus the entire Dnieper line from Kiev was under their control, and the Rus began to eye the neighboring big rivers. The upper reaches of the Bug and Vistula brought them to Cracow and across the divides of these rivers, by tried and trusty methods, to the sources of the Oder and Elbe. Across the Sudeten Mountains they probably used pack animals and horses. Ibn Jaqub writes in 965: "The city of Prague is built of stone and chalk. It is the largest trading center of the Slavonic lands. Rus and Slavs come from Cracow with their wares; Mussulmen, Jews and Turks appear with their merchandise, and Byzantine Mithquals from the Turkish territories; they receive in return, slaves, beaver, and other pelts." To complete the list, it is reported: "Rus merchants come from Kiev to Regensburg to buy horses and slaves."

Meanwhile the Vikings reached the Volga. To get there they didn't have to go back across the swamps of the divide; there was a shorter way. From the mouth of the Dnieper they sailed around the fruitful Crimean peninsula and pushed on across the Sea of Azov, up the Don, to a point where the Volga flowed not very far away. If this last land obstacle could be overcome, then the way to the East lay open. At this point we find a *volok*, or tow path, that was already mentioned in 59 B.C. by the scribes of antiquity. Today the site is called Stalingrad. Here, on the sandy banks of the Volga, the Rus came in contact with alien tribes who gave them an inkling of the vastness of the Asiatic continent.

During the era of the Mussulmanic and Christian conversions, the Turkish Khazars had oddly enough embraced the Mosaic religion. In their capital, Itil, in the Volga delta—today Astrakhan—there was a bustling conglomeration of peoples of every race and language. Merchants from the Frank Empire and the Caliphate traded their wares with dealers from the Upper Volga. The latter came for the most part from Bolgar in the great Volga curve, named after the Bulgarians, who, however, had already wandered on to the Balkan peninsula. Various tribes moved into the abandoned settlements. The remains of the town have been found on the left bank of the Volga, south of the mouth of the Kama River where the village of Bolgary is situated today. Walls, towers, houses and baths for 10,000 once stood there, allegedly even actual Finnish saunas, and the Arabian influence was so strong that the king put himself under the protection of the Caliph during Ibn Fadlan's visit in 922, embraced Islam, took religious instruction according to the Koran, and sent to Baghdad for a court tailor.

In Bolgar we find the true fur Eldorado of Russia. Al-Masudi writes: "Big ships travel on this river [the Volga] with merchandise from Kharezm [east of the Caspian Sea]. Other ships from the land on the right side of the Volga bring black fox pelts and these are the most highly valued and precious furs. . . . The black kind is found only in this region and in districts bordering on it. The kings of the barbarians live luxuriously in that they clothe themselves in these skins and wear caps and coats made of fur."

Muqqadasi recounts: "Sable, squirrel, ermine, corsac, martin, foxes, beaver pelts, colorful hare, goatskin, wax, arrows, birchbark, caps, fish-lime, fish-teeth, beaver-gall, amber, horny leather, honey, hazel nuts, hawks, swords, armor, acorns, Slavonic slaves, small cattle and oxen—all this from Bolgar to Kharezm."

The Rus trader of course could not be missing in Bolgar. Arabian geographers outdo one another in a profusion of reports. Ibn Hauqual: "Beaver pelts are found only on the northern rivers, which lie in the vicinity of Bolgar and the Rus in Kiev. And what is found in Spain in the way of beaver also comes from the rivers of the Slavonic lands. The greater part of these furs, or I should say all of them, are to be found in the land of the Rus. They then sell them in Bolgar."

Ibn Rustah: "The Rus bring their merchandise to Bolgar. All those who live on both banks of the river come to them with wares such as sable, ermine, squirrel and other pelts."

Gradually we get a rounded-out picture of the Rus in eastern Europe, especially when we include the words of the Arab Abulfeda, that the Rus obtained sable, fox, lynx and similar furs from the northern people in what was called "mute trading."

This is undoubtedly one of the strangest manifestations of human communal life in ethnographic history. Eerie and apparently conflicting is the information we glean from the Arabian geographers. One had to travel for three months northward from Bolgar to reach a land called Visu, and it was necessary to take along provender for the entire trip. Ibn Fadlan says the night there was shorter than an hour; others speak of a land of constant darkness. How were the southlanders to grasp such descriptions?

The inhabitants of Visu were not allowed to come to Bolgar, for they brought a sinister coldness with them, so that all growing things congealed, even in summer. Had anyone ever seen them? Traders shook their heads and spoke in great fear of giants and snow specters, for trading with these people took place mutely and blindly. We do best to let Abulfeda tell us about it:

"Still farther north there live a people who trade without seeing the traveler with whom they are dealing. Someone who visited this region reports that the homeland of these natives borders on the Arctic Ocean. He goes on to say that caravans arriving in these lands first announce their arrival. Then they repair to the place appointed for buying and selling. There each trader lays down his merchandise with a note, and returns to his camping ground. The natives draw near, deposit their merchandise—weasel fur, fox and other pelts—and withdraw. The traders return. Whoever is satisfied with what has been offered him for barter, takes it. Those who are not satisfied leave the goods untouched, and the negotiations are continued in the same way until both parties have reached an agreement."

This primitive form of trading existed in other parts of the world. The

writers of antiquity tell the same story of northwest Africa; similar reports
come to us from Ceylon, the Himalayas and Somaliland. Explorers of later
years have tales like this to tell of the Senegalese, Moroccans, Circassians and
the neighbors of the Chinese. German naturalist Alexander von Humboldt
(1769–1859) names tribes of Indians with whom the Spanish in New Mexico
traded in the same manner, and his contemporary Otto von Kotzebue writes in
1821 about the Chibocks in northern Siberia:

"First the stranger lays down his wares on the bank of the river and withdraws. The Chibock comes, looks at what is there, then lays down as many
pelts beside it as he wants to give, and goes away. Whereupon the stranger
approaches again, sees what is being offered and if he is satisfied, takes the
pelts with him. His wares remain where he laid them. If the opposite prevails,
he leaves everything as it is, withdraws again, and waits for the buyer to prof-
fer more. Thus the entire transaction takes place mutely."

Modern merchandising is also very often mute and blind, in that the partners in trade have never seen or spoken to each other, in some cases they
haven't even seen the wares! But the mute trading described here always took
place between a superior partner and a primitive, mistrustful native population, which chose to deal this way out of fear and a constant expectancy of
bloodshed. The risk of theft was as good as nil, for if it occurred, the other
partner would never return, and, after all, both desired that the barter take
place. The strangers brought with them practical things, the savage offered
the warm furs of the icy North.

The Rus probably participated in such mute trading only in exceptional cases,
but reports like this serve to demonstrate the wide scope of the trading between
Bolgar, Birka and Byzantium. Distances should be kept in mind. From Bolgar
to Kiev, as the crow flies, was about 870 miles, to Birka 1,900. We would like
to know more about the organization of the winter journeys of the Rus mentioned by Emperor Constantine, but our Eastern written sources are brief, and
we cannot help regretting that the burial fields northeast of Moscow were so
hastily dismantled. Meticulous excavations according to the most modern
methods would certainly have resulted in rich disclosures of the social and
economic life of these communities. We can only hope that there are enough
undisturbed graves left to permit further and more precise research.

We may conclude though, from the sources at hand, that there were solidly
united communal forms of life, guilds, settlements, some even with religious
ties, forerunners of the German Hanseatic League in the Russian Middle Ages!
And we may assume that there were dissimilarities between the Rus who had
settled in Kiev and the traders who came from Sweden and went back to that
country with their wares. Because human behavior is unpredictable, those who

traveled back and forth had to be armed, and we know that the Vikings were not shy when it came to the use of weapons. They had to stand by each other in every respect, above all when it was a question of selling favorably in the summer what they had acquired during the winter. They were also confronted with problems of a quite different nature. They had to create what might well be called a convoy system through the rapids of the Dnieper and past the Pechenegs lying in ambush. Like members of a guild, they arrived in Byzantium with their silver seals from the chancellery in Kiev, but when they got there, they had to cope with cartels and the nuisance of a silk monopoly. Now we understand better Ibn Fadlan's Rus traders in their encampment on the Volga. They had apparently just finished buying, and had assembled to pray to their gods for purchasers with much gold and silver coin, who would in turn buy all they had and be agreeable to their terms. The Arab could afford to be ironical about it because he knew what the Rus were up against, what shrewd bargainers his compatriots were.

The high cultural level, the worldliness and diplomatic skill of the Oriental again brought the Rus face to face with new problems. But both partners were offering merchandise that the other desired. They learned quickly from each other, and could come to an agreement in a friendly spirit. In spite of the monopolistic aspirations of Byzantium, the Arabs had silk to offer, and above all, that simplest of trade media—coins, jingling silver, well-filled purses. A certain cultural level is undoubtedly prerequisite to the acceptance of a commodity—in this case money—which a man does not intend to use directly, but can exchange for merchandise whenever he feels like it. The people who practiced mute trading had of course no appreciation of this; for the peasants in Scandinavia it was also a new concept.

The Rus traders quickly caught on to the usefulness of Arabian silver, if only because it was so easy to transport. We follow them from far-away Russia, back to Sweden, where, in graves and hoards we shall find the reflection of their eastern voyages, and witness the cultural flowering of their homeland as a result of colonization and overseas trading.

6

What the Vikings Brought Home from the Orient

THE TRADERS returned to Sweden laden with souvenirs, which we find *en masse* in Birka graves and scattered fanwise inland. Especially popular were richly ornamented belts with palmettes and figuration originating from the Sassanide art of Persia, and developed by the Khazars in the Volga delta. (*See ill. 59.*) The belt mountings and strap tags in silver and bronze must have looked strange to the Norsemen, so different from the Frankish accouterments with floral decoration. The men who had come back from the East probably

59. East European belt mountings from Birka.

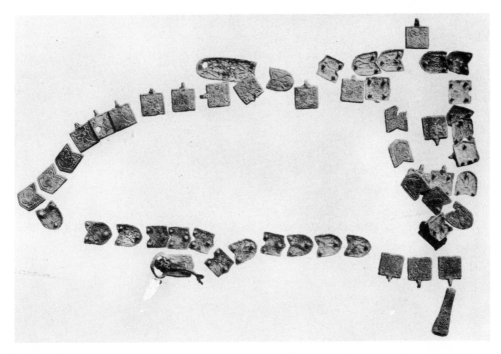

60. *East European fittings from Birka, with animal ornamentation.*

strutted around like the cowboys in the Wild West during the last century. Some wore colored purses with fittings like those used by the Tartars in the region of Omsk not so long ago. Sometimes the fittings had loops and were incorporated in the bead jewelry of the women, perhaps by the very men who had returned to their homeland via Ingelheim in 839. Other appurtenances bear the head of a wolf, owl, fox, griffon, animal masks that were popular as amulets in Mongolia and brought a breath of the Asiatic continent to Scandinavia. (*See ill. 60.*)

The homecomers brought back all sorts of vessels, even Arabian glass. In contrast to the many Frankish pieces, we find only two examples of Eastern glass. It is almost incredible that these fragile pieces should have survived such endless and complicated voyages. One is practically undamaged. It has a geometric design with birds that have been painted over with a silver-white paste. Fragments of numerous glasses were found in a dig north of Stockholm, also with bird figures on them, multi-colored, with Coptic or Greek inscriptions. Just as astonishing is a small baked-clay cup with handle which was found on the island of Gotland. It is undeniably alien because it is glazed. The form is

61. *Arabic finds in Sweden. A Persian bronze flask and a glazed Persian cup with handle, copied from a Chinese original. State Historical Museum, Stockholm. Photo: ATA.*

originally Chinese, developed later by the Persians. Similar finds in Suzdal and Livonia show the transition from Persia to Gotland. (*See ill. 61.*)

More frequent finds are cylindrical bronze bottles with narrow necks. Three were found on Baltic Sea islands, two on the mainland. They were probably traded in Kharezm, east of the Caspian Sea, via the Khazar kingdom on the Volga. Perhaps the Vikings found out that the ornamentation on the neck of the bottle consisted of Arabic letters that said: "There is no god beside Allah; there is none like him."

A few verses from the Koran have been found on Swedish soil. In Roslagen, on the coast north of Stockholm, a round silver disc with pendant attached turned up; on it the inscription: "In the name of Allah, the Merciful, O Allah, O Redeemer, mayest thou protect the bearer, O Allah who doth forgive all sins." (*See ill. 62.*)

62. *Silver disc with Arabic inscription, found in Sweden. 2¾ inches in diameter. State Historical Museum, Stockholm. Photo: ATA.*

63. *Brazier shaped like an Arabic mosque, found in Sweden. 16 inches high.*
    Gävle Museum. Photo: ATA.

64. *Sassanide-Russian silver bowls found in Sweden. State Historical Museum, Stockholm. Photo: Iwar Anderson.*

During World War II an extraordinary rumor was circulated by the Swedish press: An entire mosque had been found in a rocky gorge! True. But its measurements were modest. It turned out to be a brazier on carved legs about 16 inches high, crenelated, with parapet and capital, operable on a hinge. (*See ill. 63.*) Under the crown of the shaft is the inscription: "In the name of Allah, the Merciful."

Some people believe that a modern-day sea captain brought back this souvenir with him and hid it not far from the harbor town of Gävle, but it was more customary for the Vikings to entrust their treasures to the earth, and if the date given to the brazier by historians of art may be considered binding—out of the time of Harun-al-Raschid—then the little mosque may well have traveled north on Russian rivers one thousand years ago. Even the tongs and candelabra lay beside it.

Eastern silver bowls were valued highly. (*See ill. 64.*) One was found near

65. Pattern of Chinese silk found in a Viking grave in Birka.

Danish Haraldsborg-Castle; five near the king barrows of Old Uppsala. Most of them are fluted, with a smooth rim, along which runs a Persian floral ornamentation that was popular in the Khazar kingdom. A silver plate had been attached to the bottom of one of the bowls, showing a lion with floral decoration as well as a definitely Eastern motif, recognizable as such by comparison with numerous finds on Lake Aral, and east of the Volga. A similar lion bowl from Augst, near Basel, was probably brought to Switzerland as the result of a Magyar incursion.

Perhaps, though, we should be most delighted that we can identify Oriental silk forty-five times in Birka graves. In these cases, as with the Frisian cloth and Northern fur findings, all that remains are infinitesimal fragments—probably not parts of a whole silk garment but scraps from the bands and strips used as ornamentation on clothing. They are of uniform quality, often patterned. (*See ill. 65.*) We know of similar traces of silk from findings in the Mediterranean countries, and we obviously have here silk that was traded by the Rus in Byzantium.

Six finds must be differentiated from all the others, because the natural gum has not been removed from the taffeta or raw silk. The weaving method used in one of them gives a patterned sheen, and may be classified as an attractive forerunner of a later material—damask. We know of such quality material with the silk gum preserved and with very similar patterns from Turkestan and Mongolia. Our material was probably traded from China westward across the famous "silk road," and northward through Arabian middlemen.

Swedish rune stones mention persons who were in "Särkland," by which they could hardly have meant the land of the Saracens (Syria) but Silkland. The name wandered with the material, as we have already noted where furs were concerned. The Romans took over from Asia the word *sericum,* and handed it on via Byzantium to the Vikings almost unchanged, in a shortened version, as *serk* or *särk.*

For centuries, the rough undershirt of the Swedish peasant was called *särk,* but in our day and age the expression is no longer considered refined by an underwear industry that has become very style-conscious. But for the Vikings, a *särk* must have been the finest type shirt, namely a silk shirt. And Särkland was the land below Kiev and beyond the Black Sea, where the silk came from. In the English word *silk,* the "a" and "r" has become an "i" and "l."

The most vital import of all from the East is not found in graves but in excavated hoards—namely silver. Buried hoards of the ninth century are still relatively rare. Now and then, here and there, we come across a few pieces of jewelry and coins, but they don't begin to tell what still lies in store for us. The hoard of Hon in Norway is unique. As already mentioned, it weighed 2,548 grams and consisted for the most part of gold, with only a little silver.

The great stream of silver from the East is introduced with the hoard of Asarve, on Gotland. It was found in 1903, approximately a thousand years after the former owner buried it beside a stone fence, already abandoned in his day. Undoubtedly he thought he would easily find it again, but perhaps death summoned him before his time.

66. Silver hoard of Arabic coins, found in Gotland. Photo: ATA.

There are 47 arm rings, 19 fragments of arm rings, and 19 bars, weighing in all 7,060 grams. The spiral arm rings which terminate in a rectangular faceted button and loop are the most noteworthy items, for they come from the district of Perm, east of Bolgar, east of the Volga, and their weight is quite obviously standardized. The undamaged pieces have an average weight of either 202.58 grams or 101.07 grams, with inaccuracies of at most 2.65 grams. Since the Persian pound was 408 grams, these 20 arm spirals weigh approximately one half and one quarter Persian pounds respectively, and if at all, are only very slightly underweight. They are certainly not to be evaluated as jewelry but as currency that could be worn easily on the arm.

Here we have the treasure of a successful trader who returned home from the Volga district. (*See ills. 66, 67.*) Similar spiral arm rings were traded all the way to Denmark, England and Ireland. Only 2 Arabic coins were included in the find, though Arabic silver usually predominates in the hoards of the tenth century. This is evident in the second largest hoard found in Scandinavia, again on the island of Gotland. In 1936, two bright boys caught sight of it while

67. *Silver hoard of east European arm rings, found in Gotland. State Historical Museum, Stockholm. Photo: E. Oxenstierna.*

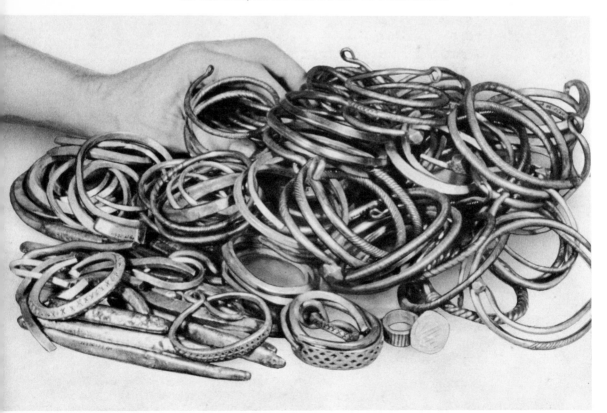

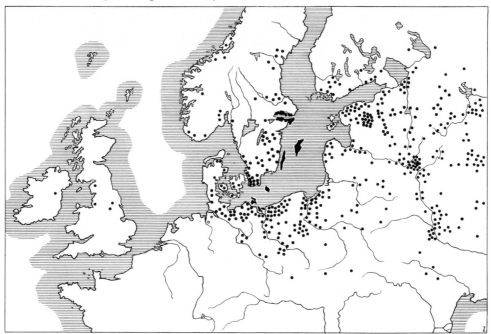

68. *Map showing Arabic coin finds in Europe and on the British Isles. Coins have also been found on Iceland.*

playing in a quarry. Their pockets full, their faces radiant, they ran to fetch the grownups to see it. A single arm band lay among 2,673 Arabic silver coins struck in 55 different Caliphate mints. Several go back to the year 708, though most of them were minted in the ninth century. The five most recent ones were issued in 910. They are the freshly minted coins with which a Gotland trader was paid before he set out for home and therefore of decisive importance to us. Arabic coins are fortunately marked with the name of the mint site and the year they were struck; that is why they lend themselves exceptionally well to research. The oldest coins still in circulation are, of course, sparsely represented and often very worn. Determinable coins are usually of a time period shortly before the most recent coin. In large hoards the year on the most recent coin may be considered as binding for a date of the treasure.

The Viking era is the Silver Age of the North; the stream of silver that poured across Scandinavia during that time was gigantic. A fortunate amount remained buried in the ground. From the Baltic Sea island of Gotland come 40,000 Arabic coins, and new finds are being added to this number yearly. In the rest of Sweden and Denmark we have registered to date about 17,000 coins, whereas Norway can come up with only 400 examples of this Eastern standard of value. To this must be added the silver jewelry which constitutes the greater part of the hoards found. The Gold Age of the North ended *circa*

600. As we have already noted, gold existed in Viking days, but only in limited quantities, as a modest adjunct to the silver that predominated. As a result, the Historical Museum in Stockholm has been able to establish a Silver Room of the Viking era as counterpart to the Gold Room of the Great Migration of Peoples period, similarly safeguarded by heavy armored doors and the most modern burglar-alarm equipment.

The silver of the tenth century came from the eastern regions of the Caliphate. There silver was being mined. Ibn-Jaqub reports: "Penjir's people [in Afganistan] are a polyglot race. There violence and wickedness predominate. Murder is a frequent crime. The dirhems [silver coins] are large and numerous. No one will sell anything for less than a dirhem, even if it is only a bundle of greens. The silver is found on the summit of a mountain which, because of the many pitholes, looks like a sieve. A man may make a profit of 300,000 dirhems in digging. Often he finds enough to make himself and his heirs wealthy. Frequently he can at least cover his expenses, but sometimes he may be impoverished, namely when the water and other hindrances gain the upper hand. It may happen that he who is rich in the morning is poor at night, and he who is poor in the morning, is rich at night."

Here we have the Klondike of the "Wild East," with inflation, brawling, adventure, opportunism and human catastrophes.

In the year A.D. 800, the Caliph in Baghdad had a yearly income of 1,200 tons of silver, [approximately twenty-five times the world production of silver in the year 1500], of which the governor of Chorasan contributed about one tenth. A vast stream of Arabic mint silver could therefore flow northward. Numerous silver finds and coin hoards have also been raised on the Volga, the Dnieper, the rivers of Central Europe that were Slavonic, and on the Baltic sea coast, the largest allegedly weighing 230 pounds.

Silver treasure was buried for a variety of reasons. In his *Heimskringla,* Snorri mentions the fact that Queen Gunnhild's sons were so miserly they buried their treasure in the ground. According to Snorri, the heroes were to enjoy in Valhalla what they themselves had buried. This seems to be a strangely timeless custom, deeply rooted in the human soul, for a man in Funäsdalen, in north Sweden, kept shiny talers in a tarred wooden canister and buried them in an unknown spot according to ancient faith in the year 1840! His intention was to dig it up again after his resurrection so as not to have to start all over again at the bottom. In Viking days, quite a few men must have had the same idea.

When he was a blind old man, Egil Skallagrimsson had his own views on the subject. He wanted to ride to the *thing* with two chests of silver. "I want to

bring them to the *thing*-mountain when most of the people are already assembled there. I want to empty out the silver, and it would be surprising if
those present were to divide it peacefully among themselves. Perhaps we would
see blows and fisticuffs, and it could come about that the entire *thing*-commu-
nity would fight among themselves. . . . This is a priceless idea, of which people
will speak as long as the country remains settled." Here Egil shows himself
to be a modern individualist and a sarcastic observer of human nature, in a
way we ordinarily do not expect at such an early stage in the development of
human culture.

Actually, he did something quite different. "One evening he left his house,
carrying his chest of silver. He got on his horse and, with two slaves, rode
into the fields until he disappeared behind a rise of land. Next morning, when
his servants got up, they saw Egil feeling his way along the woodland east of
the courtyard, leading his horse behind him. They followed him and brought
him home. But slaves and chest had disappeared and were never seen again, and
many have tried to guess where Egil buried his silver. East of the fence surrounding the meadow on Mossfjäll, there is a gorge in the rocks. It was observed that when there was a big thaw, much water would flow through it.
After which one could find English silver in the gorge. Some believe that Egil
buried his treasure there. South of the brook there are warm springs, and not
far off, deep caverns. And some believe that Egil's silver lies in these caverns,
for a nocturnal fire has often been observed flickering there. Egil said that he
killed the slaves and buried the chest, but he told no one where he buried it.
In the autumn Egil was stricken by a sickness which ended his life."

Now by a peculiar coincidence, a silver hoard was found in Mossfjäll in the
eighteenth century; all we know of it is that it contained, among other things,
coins with the inscription ANSLAFR. Anslaf ruled in England 941–952, and Egil
Skallagrimsson died in 990. All our silver hoards are anonymous. Here lay
the rare possibility of being able to connect a treasure with a historic personality. Unfortunately it was raised with the haphazard methods of those days,
thereby sinking forever into anonymity. We wouldn't have found out anyway
why Egil buried it. At best we may suspect that, as a wise old man, he knew
human avarice and rapaciousness only too well and did not want to encourage
these vices.

But all these are isolated cases. Many treasures bear witness to prosperity
and active and successful trade. In the year 1930, however, there was serious
disagreement in the scientific camp. Professor Sture Bolin, in his introductory
lecture at Lund University and in several publications, defended the theory
that buried hoards were first and foremost proof of warfare, valuables en-
trusted to the earth in times of military disturbance, which had never been

raised because the owner had met with sudden violent death. Seen historically, an aggregation of hoard findings usually coincided with demonstrable warfare. The situation probably was no different in antiquity.

> Just think: in those so frightful times
> When hordes the land o'erflooded, and its people,
> How this man, that man—as it frightened him
> Did hide his treasure, hither and yon.
> Thus 'twas in powerful Roman days,
> And on to yesterday, e'en till today;
> And all this lieth buried in the earth.
>
> (Goethe's *Faust*, Part II)

After much heated discussion, a majority of prehistory professors agreed that Mephistopheles and Professor Bolin were right. We may also call in twelfth-century historian Helmold's Slavonic Chronicle (1170) as witness:

"As soon as there is a threat of war, the Wends bury their barley, after having threshed it, and all gold and silver articles of value, but they lead the women and children to fortified places or at least into the forest, so that nothing is left behind for the enemy to plunder but the huts themselves."

The silver hoards speak to us directly without having to say a word. Most of them lie close to a large stone, or to one side in old graves, beside old country roads or under former houses. A few have been lowered in peat bogs. On a meadow, an old oak tree may have offered an easily recognizable indication. Quite frequently we find twin hoards of the same age and nature buried a few yards away from each other. The lucky finder was supposed to go away satisfied with half the treasure! On some treasures we find a fire stick, intended to exorcise evil spirits. Everything we can prove, points to the fact that the owner had every intention of raising his treasure again. Burying it was a precautionary measure when there was a threat of war.

The 525 silver hoards found on the Baltic island of Gotland deserved the most thorough research. Professor Marten Sternberger devoted himself to them, and the second volume of his work on them appeared recently. In comparison we have only 340 hoards for all the rest of Scandinavia. Is such a preponderance on Gotland surprising?

For two or three centuries, the unprotected island was the target of Viking raiders. The Norsemen were aware of the trade that flourished there; the freebooters of the Baltic found it simpler to get hold of treasure on Gotland, rather than in far-away Russia. It was the tragic tribute the Gotlanders had to pay for the favorable geographic position of their island—surprise attack of no historic importance yet no less painful for the victim. There are a few reports, one from the late period, in the *Bandadrapa,* an epic that tells of Earl Eric:

> The famous prince had,
> After that, still many battles.
> This we have truly heard.
> Eric subjugated the land,
> A shield-protected warrior,
> He laid waste far and wide
> To the green coast of Gotland.
> The prince fought boldly.

Gotland commerce with the East is a puzzling thing. Women's jewelry, such as we found in the settlements on the Baltic coast, is missing in Russia. Not a single round box-brooch, such as worn by Gotlandic women, among a hundred oval brooches once worn by Svea women. And only a few graves on Gotland contain souvenirs from the East. Judging by the grave finds, Gotlandic participation in the eastern Viking voyages must have been as good as nil. And Gotlandic names are missing among those of the hundred delegates to the peace negotiations between Kiev and Byzantium. And yet, a rune stone speaks of Raon who perished on the Dnieper. Other stones speak of men in Holmgard and Ventspils. A rune stone was raised for a Gotlander on the island of Berezany at the mouth of the Dnieper, and the treasure found on Gotland constitutes three fifths of all Scandinavian findings. The answer to the riddle may well be that the Gotlanders were active as state founders only in the Baltic, not in the East. The colonies on Lake Ladoga and on the Dnieper were settled exclusively by the Svea. The Gotlanders probably didn't take their women with them, but after the voyage was over, returned to their homes. Their Guta Saga (written *circa* 1200) tells us a little about their social structure:

"Thus the Gutars [Gotars] put themselves under the command of the King of the Svea of their own free will, so that they may be permitted to visit any point in Sweden freely, without having to pay tithe or tribute of any kind. The Svea too have the right to visit Gotland freely, without corn-tax or other prohibitions. The Svea king is to offer the Gotlanders protection and aid when they need or ask for it. The king and the Jarl [Earl] are to send delegates to the *thing* of the Gotlanders, and levy their taxes at that time. The delegates are to ratify the *peace [freedom] to travel across the sea to all places subject to the king at Uppsala,* and in like manner to endorse the peace of those who have the right to come here."

That the Svea levied taxes on Gotland is corroborated on a rune stone near

69. *Balance, weights and fake silver belonging to Viking traders. The bar in the center and the spiral to the left are silver-plated bronze, apparently counterfeits.*

Torsatra in Uppland: "Skule and Folke had this stone raised after their brother Husbjörn. He fell ill abroad, while they were collecting money on Gotland." But the tribute the Gotlanders had to pay was light when compared with the advantages they derived from being able to trade in the East and in this way bring home an enormous amount of silver treasure.

In those days, the silver was weighed; coins were too, because their weight could differ. That was why the trader needed a scale. (*See ill. 69.*) In innumerable finds, we come across small balances with two scalepans. Balances in graves clearly indicate the professional merchant. A small bronze box for keep-

70. *Arm rings from a silver hoard found in Gotland. State Historical Museum, Stockholm. Photo: ATA.*

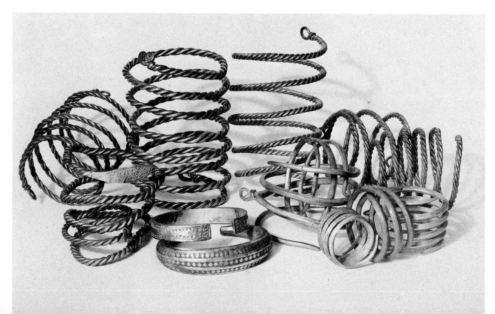

ing the pans of a balance bears in runic letters the inscription: "Djärv received these pans from a man in Samland. Vermund carved the runes."

For a balance you needed weights. These we also find, and very sensibly made—of lead. A thin bronze veneer, makes it impossible to scratch a little something off the weight and thereby make it lighter. Well-preserved weights seem to be derived from the eastern and western Mediterranean systems, with 24.5 grams as the norm.

The buyer, of course, had to be sure of the quality of the silver, and here he could draw on old and trusted methods for testing the metal. He scratched it to check its white sheen, and he bent the coins to see how flexible they were. There is evidence of this in many finds. Still he sometimes got cheated. At

71. *Ring fibulae from a silver hoard found in Gotland. State Historical Museum, Stockholm. Photo: ATA.*

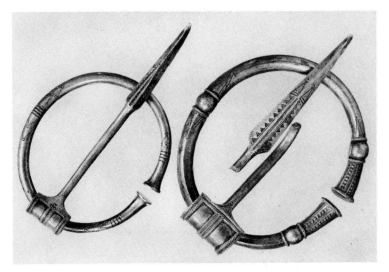

least five finds include silver-plated bronze bars which were undoubtedly intended to pass as silver. In a typical trader's treasure with scale and weights, this makes a poor impression. On the Krinkberg near Schenefeld, not far from Haithabu, several pieces of a large silver hoard contain a core of iron.

Since, in the course of a business transaction, all silver pieces were weighed anyway, the trader was not wholly dependent on coins. Any piece of silver could be put on the scale. If it was too heavy, as much could be cut off as the transaction of the moment demanded. Small change could thus be obtained at any time by the simplest methods and we begin to understand how it could happen that in the course of the tenth century, the silver hoards began to consist of hundreds and thousands of fragmentary pieces of silver. We call it hack-silber. (*See ill. 70, 71, 72.*) Dreadful—granted—to show today's modern

72. *Hack-silber, part of the silver hoard of Botels, Gotland. State Historical Museum, Stockholm. Photo: ATA.*

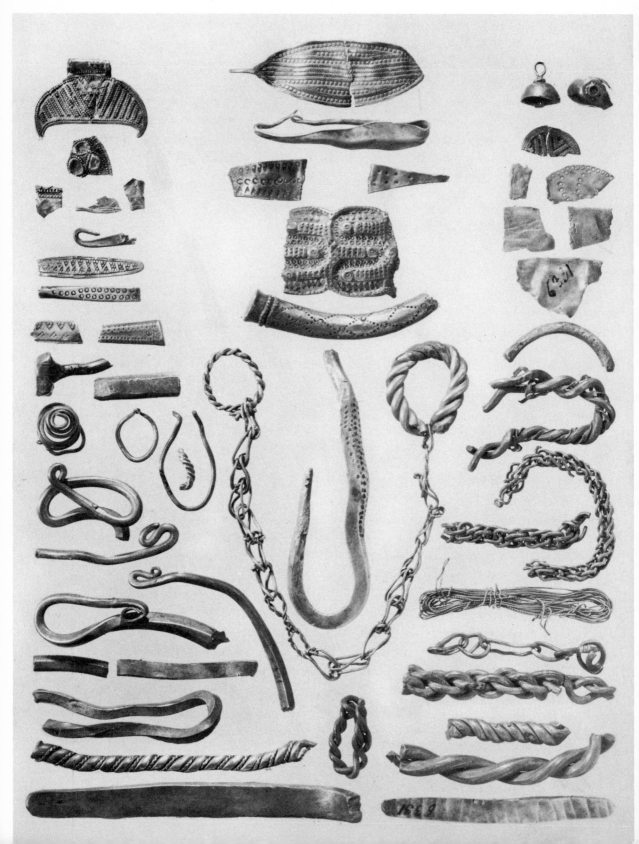

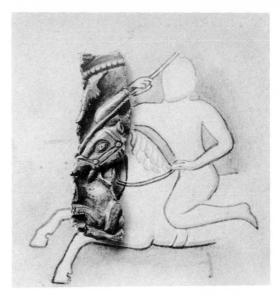

73. A piece of Arabic hack-silber, part of a riding figure, found in Gotland. State Historical Museum, Stockholm. Photo: ATA.

man, thirsting for beauty, these scrap heaps in our museums. And what a tremendous piece of work to determine the origin of every fragment, and arrange all of them systematically. But how welcome the knowledge we gain from this profusion of objects. We recognize 27 Arabic or Khazar silver bowls of the type already mentioned through as many of these fragments, some of them not bigger than coins. We see a little of the palmette ornamentation, a piece of a galloping rider, his lance raised. (*See ill. 73.*) We read in Arabic letters, "Allah be praised." For a long time many-faceted knobs of arm rings from the district of Perm were used like coins, and turn up here and there in our finds as hack-silber.

Let us examine a hack-silber board found in Botels, on Gotland, under a tree. (*See ill. 72.*) The treasure was hidden in two clay vessels and a box made of birch bark. Twelve twisted or smooth silver arm rings were completely or almost undamaged, also a half-moon-shaped pendant from Russia. All the rest was scrap. We believe that the pointed elliptical object was once an all-too-fragile belt slide of Slavonic origin. Under it lies a dented finger ring, then the clasp of a necklet. The wide ornamented object was once part of a handsome arm ring, typical of its period. Nine undamaged arm bands similar to it were found in the rich moor find of Malms Myr. (*See ill. 74.*) Here we have a Gotlandic form found solely in localities within reach of Gotlandic trade.

The carved piece of silver below is again part of a ring-pin and may be compared with a pair of undamaged, richly ornamented ring brooches—fibulae,

74. *Silver arm bands from the Malms Myr hoard, Gotland. State Historical Museum, Stockholm. Photo: ATA.*

as we call them—from the find of Sigsarve previously illustrated. (*See ill. 71.*) The completely bent little rod was also once part of such a handsome piece of jewelry. On the left side of the picture we find mainly pieces of arm rings, necklets and fibulae; on the right, fragments of silver plate, a few bars, silver wire and twisted silver.

The latter was the great love and art of the tenth- and eleventh-century silver smiths. They would twist doubled silver thread to the right, then braid it to the left, which was especially effective when interwoven with thin threaded wire. The technique had endless possibilities and reached the acme of perfection in the loose, openwork intertwining, in which as many as eight threads were woven to the right around a supporting core, as we can see in the necklet of Unsarve. This silver twining process originated in Russia and the Orient, but achieved its most beautiful and greatest variations in what are certainly authentic Northern pieces. (*See ills. 75, 76.*)

Let us look finally at the coins in the hack-silber hoard of Botels, where we find 217 Arabic coins undamaged, 2,046 fragmentary pieces, all struck in the years 715 to 969, excellently complemented by 21 Byzantine coins (945–959). The most recent coins are 11 so-called Wend pennies and 15 German coins, minted by Otto III, who ruled 983–1002. Since we find no earlier coins, we may presume that they come from the early years of his reign, and that this treasure was buried at the close of the tenth century.

75. *A Nordic gold necklace, plaque and pendants, found on the German island of Hiddensee. Historical Museum, Stralsund.*

76. *Woven silver necklets found in Medebys and Unsarve, Gotland. State Historical Museum, Stockholm. Photo: ATA.*

Gradually we come upon the first delicate objects from a Slavonic smithy. (*See ill.* 77.) Exceptional evidence of Viking expeditions to the South is a fine type of ear pendant similar to those found in several Swedish silver hoards.

The whole world of the Vikings is conjured up before our eyes in this hack-silber hoard, even if only after a laborious investigation of the fragments. One thing must certainly have come to the reader's attention by now—the fact that again and again we are able to compare the fragments we find with undamaged pieces from other silver findings. For this there is an explanation—and a story.

We have seen that many silver hoards consist entirely of magnificent jewelry. In the year 1739, on a day when the butcher had been slaughtering, Farmer Wible's dog wanted to bury a bone. Out of the hole he dug, he scratched not only sand but also some coins, and 6 fibulae and arm bands. The museum bought three of the pieces and had the other three copied, "and from them two mugs were made which are to belong to the owner of Wible's farm for all time." And they were inscribed with a pretty verse.

In shrewd peasant opinion, silver mugs and spoons were status symbols. In the sixteenth century, a German traveler, Samuel Kiechel, mentions that a peasant in Sweden would sometimes possess as many as fifty silver spoons. Unlike the corn fields waving in the wind, they constituted capital that could be used at any time. Even if they paid no interest, they were sure-fire security against such disasters as sickness or famine. But the finder of the Wible treasure could have added the three arm bands and fibulae to his farmstead's treasure in their original form without a qualm, for their usage in Viking days had been no different. Rings of various shape were the unfrozen assets of the peasant in those silver-rich times. If an undesirable Viking fleet appeared on the horizon to devastate the coast, the ring silver was quickly buried, while the peasant militia defended their homes. Some died a hero's death, and their treasure remained where it was to the present day.

We hardly ever find silver in graves. For a long time this was puzzling, but seen from the point of view here explained, it becomes understandable. *Undamaged* silver jewelry was *farm* property—just like the silver spoons and mugs of later days—tribal riches, bridal jewelry if necessary, and feast-day ornamentation, *not* personal property that might follow its owner to his grave. And this fact again demonstrates that the frightfully bent and hacked fragments from all over the world were the buried *capital* of the professional traveling salesman. What would these businessmen have done in their graves with silver scrap? Silver had work to do, had to be traded, passed on. Silver fulfilled its purpose only as permanent capital and currency. Its use as jewelry was secondary. First and foremost it was money; regular, valid currency.

77. *Slavonic silver earrings and pendants found in Sweden. State Historical Museum, Stockholm. Photo: ATA.*

And how much did things cost in this silver currency? We have only isolated information on the subject. For instance, Kormak says in one of his songs (*Kormak's Saga*):

> Some things are dear for man to buy.
> This boat cost Torveig 3 öre to hire.

That would mean 600 grams of silver, and sounds plausible, even if we don't know whether the Viking ship was hired for an overseas voyage, for the summer, or for a longer time.

A merchant named Gilli, the Russian, demanded a silver mark (400 grams) for a beautiful slave girl. He wanted 3 marks for his loveliest slave, but that was a pretty fancy price. Rimbert paid a saddled horse for a slave, the afore-· mentioned nun. A saddled horse must therefore have cost 400 grams of silver; according to old peasant practice, a cow would have cost only half as much. Or to put it a little differently—a Perm arm band for a cow, 2 Perm arm bands for a horse or a slave girl. Such information and conclusions don't permit us to set up a price list for the Viking era, however, especially since there were two periods when silver was scarce; in between there were probably local inflationary tendencies.

If, for instance, a Gotlander came to a west Swedish peasant province, would his currency be worth more because silver was rare in the rural areas and therefore very much sought after? Or did it lose value because old-fashioned peasants had little understanding of the metal? We cannot answer such questions. All we can do is establish the fact that in the coastal areas where there was trading, especially on Gotland and in the large trading centers, people were prone to deny themselves some wares in order to be able to hoard silver rings. To build up capital for a rainy day seemed more important than the immediate procuring of cattle, furnishing or clothing.

These silver hoards are reliable sources for tracing the economy, the prosperity, the crafts, traffic and Viking expeditions, even if only a fraction of the silver has found its way to us in the hoards we have found. We find some gold and a little Western silver mixed in with this massive stream of Arabian silver, but all in all there is no denying that the Vikings acquired an astonishing amount of the valuable metal from the Arabs on their trading voyages in Russia. The true dimensions of the Viking achievement in the East become visible in their silver and its importance to their life at home.

7

We Know No Master — All of Us Are Equal

OCEAN VOYAGES. . . . They offered grandiose new vistas to the dragon ships. After crossing the Baltic Sea, the Swedes had had to be satisfied with the rivers of a continent. The Norwegians opened up unknown reaches of the Atlantic Ocean with its dread storms. In his saga, Kormak's sharp eyes saw them clearly:

> The sea's thunder rumbles
> The mountainous waves are high as rocky walls;
> Out of them bursts the whole roaring mass of sea. . . .

Countless such sea pictures breathe fascination with the salty sea air and wide horizons, familiarity with moody winds and tides. By them the durability of the Viking ships was tested, their miraculous ability to speed across agitated waters, to withstand the fury and howling powers of nature.

The Norwegians did not have to take to the high seas. The Gulf Stream flows along Norway's coast, making it habitable far beyond the Arctic Circle. The ice-free harbor of Narvik and the rugged fissured world of the Lofoten Islands were already thickly settled in the Roman Iron Age. The number of finds dating back to the Great Migration of Peoples increases constantly. Hundreds of Viking findings and twenty-one silver hoards demonstrate that we are on true Norwegian soil all the way to Tromsö, in the northernmost province of Scandinavia: Haalogaland. We needn't picture the men on the Lofoten Islands as poor fishermen. The heights may have been icy and barren, but the narrow strip of coast offered rich pastureland and a mild sea climate. In this rocky world, there were many protected areas. Sickles, scythes and spades in graves testify that the inhabitants considered themselves first and foremost peasants. Hammers, tongs and iron ingots prove that they made their own the wealth of bog-iron the countryside had to offer. And not the least of their fame in an era of ocean voyages rested on their wharves. Raud in Ramme, on the Salt Fjord, in Haalogaland, owned the best of all "northland ships"; it served as model for the most renowned king-boats.

Ottar was a native of Haalogaland. We have already met him in connection with King Alfred's translation of Orosius. His encounter with the English king in the 880's was a stroke of good fortune. Wasn't King Alfred the great humanist of the early Middle Ages, a glowing soul in an ailing body? In the midst of violent warfare, he had succeeded in collecting the literary works of his day, and had learned Latin in order to understand them because he recognized their cultural value. "In the midst of the diverse duties which this realm imposes, I began to translate a few of the books, which are of paramount importance to all persons, into the English language, into a language all of us can understand." And he commissioned his scribes in North and South to make as many copies as possible. "All those who today are young and free in England shall learn how to read English books; boys of lowly origin as well as aristocrats."

He was striving for an amazing, absolutely modern cultural ideal. The purpose of life was "to grasp more and more." This astonishing man, in founding his university library in Oxford, did not select only religious works but also philosophy, history and geography. To the Orosius *History against the Pagans* he added—as already mentioned—two accounts of voyages of discovery: Wulfstan's voyage from Haithabu to Truso (page 45) and Ottar's voyage across the Arctic Ocean.

Ottar was a rich peasant. On his farm in Haalogaland (perhaps in Lenvik, southwest of Tromsö) he could count 20 cows, 20 sheep, 20 pigs. He ploughed with horses, and owned a herd of 600 reindeer. A brief look into his animal kingdom shows us how much prosperity could be developed north of the Arctic Circle. We quote an excerpt from Ottar's report on his voyage:

"Ottar told his sire, King Alfred [in whose service he apparently was], that of all Normans, he lived farthest north. Once he had the desire to explore how far the land went northward, and to see if anyone was living in that part of the wilderness. So he traveled along the coast in a northerly direction. Throughout the entire voyage, he kept the wild land to the starboard side and the open sea abaft. After three days, he was as far north as the whale hunters go. Then he sailed northward as far as he could travel in the next three days [apparently to North Cape]. Here the land curved in an easterly direction, or the sea into the land—he did not know which of the two—but he knew that here he had to wait for a west wind, and a light northwest wind, and from here he sailed along the coast eastward as far as he could go in four days. Then he had to wait for a direct north wind, for here the land curved to the south, or the sea into the land—he did not know which of the two. From here he sailed south along the coast as far as he could get in five days. There a great river flowed upward into the land (the Northern Dvina!). He had come upon no more habitable land since he had left his homeland, but had seen only wilderness on the starboard side, except for fishermen, bird catchers and hunters, and all of them were Finns; and to backboard he had constantly had the open sea. Now he navigated his ship up the river, for he did not dare to sail past it for fear of hostile attack. For the land beyond the river was thickly settled. Here the Bjarmians had cultivated the land, and the Norsemen did not dare to settle down. The Bjarmians told Ottar many things about their own land as well as about the lands surrounding them (*See map, ill. 51.*) but he did not know how much of it was true, since he himself had not seen it. The Finns—so it seemed to him—and the Bjarmians, spoke almost the same language. His main reason for undertaking the voyage was to explore the land."

And this was exactly what Alfred, the humanist, wanted, and what Ottar had to offer: the discovery of unknown territory. Only one can't believe that Ottar was the first Norman to travel so far north, because 408 grams of gold, from as far back as the Great Migration Period, have been found on Lakse Fjord, east of North Cape. Among the dozen Viking graves, two women in a double grave in Ekkeröy, on the Varanger Fjord, is exceptional. It lies opposite today's Soviet Russian border and contains two of the most beautiful oval buckles ever unearthed, a trefoil buckle, and other jewelry of Ottar's period. (*See ill. 78.*)

Why did Ottar describe his voyage as one of the first and a unique discovery? Surely not to impress King Alfred. No. He had important trading interests to protect, and a monopoly to maintain for Haalogaland. In a direct continuation of his account, he speaks cautiously of a second reason for the trip:

". . . but then also because of the walrus; for they have very costly ivory in their tusks. Of these he brought back a few for the king. Their skin was also valuable for ship rope. These walrus were much smaller than other types of the species. They were not more than seven ells long. Ottar said that he slew 66 animals in two days."

Ottar and his countrymen found the entire, still-virgin hunting grounds of the northern ocean at their disposal. In those days, the coveted walrus, the elephant of the North, still swam and cavorted along the North Cape littoral. The strongest of all ship hawsers was woven from their thick hide; their blubber was in great demand, but Ottar was right—the most valuable part of their anatomy was the ivory of their tusks. We find sword handles, game counters, dice and first-rate artifacts made of this magnificent material. Many

78. *Jewelry from Ekkeröy, east of North Cape.*

were found in Birka. Among the objects made out of whalebone, we would like to mention especially the hundred loom-rods in the Tromsö museum, and some beautifully carved boards, one of which was found in Birka, together with an ironing stone of Frankish glass. These were apparently used for the pressing of fine linen. (*See ill. 79.*)

All in all, there were enough tangible reasons for Ottar and his crew to explore this Nordic ice-and-fog land. Casually, but most revealingly, there is mention that Ottar's revenue came for the most part from taxes levied on the Finns:

"Each man pays according to his position. The noblest must deliver 15 martin pelts, 5 reindeer skins, 1 bearskin, 10 buckets of feathers, 1 coat of bear or otter fur, and 2 ship ropes, each 60 ells long, the one made of walrus, the other of sealskin."

He who had the power, extorted heavy tribute from alien peoples yearly, in one way or another, or there would have been bloodshed. Right was seated in the spearhead. And this "Finn-tax" was to become an especially important source of revenue for the Norwegian kings.

Today Finland's borders run southward from the region around Petsamo; but in those days the Finns moved freely along the entire Arctic Ocean littoral. The aggressive Vikings found Finnish tribes in northern Scandinavia as well as in the upper reaches of the Volga. We find this corroborated in infallible archeological findings. Just as happened in the East—a fascinating Germanic-Finnish mixed territory emerged in the Far North. Here, among the Finnish objects we find horseshoe fibulae with rods like the fibulae from the island of Berezany at the mouth of the Dnieper as well as other similarly shaped brooches, animal-shaped jewelry, chain clasps, and metal pendants grouped

79. *Ironing board made from the shoulder blade of a whale and green Frankish ironing glass. The board is 14 inches long. State Historical Museum, Stockholm. Photo: ATA.*

together so that they jingled to attract attention. (A forerunner of today's "charm" bracelet?) The Varanger Fjord is fringed with exceptionally numerous and revealing finds.

Westward, across the open sea. . . . The Norwegian mariner could already navigate in the high seas at the beginning of the Viking era. The Shetland Islands were reached easily from the thickly settled areas on the Norwegian west coast. They form a green, friendly group in the middle of the Gulf Stream, with rich cattle-pasture land, protected harbors and good sites for a journey's pause. Their existence constituted a deadly danger for Ireland and England; from them, rested and with fresh provender, the Vikings could push forward. It is significant, and in the spirit of the aggressor, that they called this group of islands *Hjaltland. Hjalt* is a sword hilt or cross bar. From the Vikings' standpoint, their drawn, shining, striking sword lay west of the Shetland Islands, its blade directed against an alien people; fortified homeland and deployment area lay east of Hjaltland.

Mucklebister and Helgabister are typical farmstead names on the Shetland Islands. The rich farms on Sogn and Möre, on the west coast of Norway, are called Mycklebost(ad) and Helgebost(ad). Rocks that rise out of the water, on the Shetland Islands and in Hordaland, are called *drang;* for instance Drangsholt, Drangsland, Drange. But the strangest conformity, perhaps, is the following:

Fedeland, Meland, Haland and so on are the names of numerous farmsteads on the Shetland Islands, while on the Norwegian southwest bulge, facing the Shetlands, there have been unearthed farms bearing the same names which were abandoned at the beginning of the ninth century. Here we are dealing with the heritage of emigrants who named their new farms in Hjaltland after places in their homeland. From farm to farm and from year to year, we can see a human stream leaving the Norwegian littoral, emigrating and settling on the Shetlands. The procedure was repeated in the emigrations of the nineteenth century. A few Viking grave and treasure finds complete the picture of this island group where a Norwegian dialect was still spoken in the year 1800 and heroic lays were sung *ex tempore.*

From the Shetlands quite a few seafarers found their way northward to the lonely Faroe Islands, a small world rising sharply out of the sea, uninviting and barren. (*See ill. 80.*) They were not the discoverers, however, or the first settlers, for the Irish monk, Dicuil, writes in 825:

"Already a hundred years ago, the urge to live a hermit's life brought some Irish monks to the many islands in the northern British Sea, which, with a good wind, may be reached from the British Isles in two days. These islands, unsettled and nameless since creation, were abandoned by the hermits as a

80. *The Faroe Islands. Photo: Föroya Ferdmannafelag, Torshavn.*

result of the arrival of Norse pirates. There you may find many sheep and a great variety of sea birds."

On the Faroe Islands (the name means Sheep Islands) there was little a warrior could do. Here the Vikings settled down as cattle-raisers, fishermen and bird-catchers. They took collective possession of all sheep and cattle-pasture lands, but the cows that had to be milked daily remained private property. They set out on fish, sea lion and whale-hunting expeditions together, and shared what they caught. In the ninth century theirs was the outermost post in the Atlantic Ocean. Later they were to make still farther voyages of discovery and landfall.

But the main route of the Viking discoverers and warriors flowed southward. First they came upon the Orkney Islands, directly north of Scotland. Place names there were formed like those on the Shetland Islands, giving clear evidence of the same migratory stream. Near Pierowall on Westray, the north-ernmost island, lies a burial field with sword, shield and spear for the soldiers, and oval brooches for the women from Norway. Farther south, near Sweindrow, on the island of Rousay, a magnificent sword of the 850's was raised. Near Skaill, not far from Scapa Flow, the largest silver hoard of the Western islands was unearthed. Weighing almost 15 pounds, it consists of 9 fibulae, 14 woven necklets and arm bands, 27 arm hoops, all sorts of fragments, silver bars, and approximately 18 coins, with a dirhem struck in 945 as the most recent. (*See ill. 81.*) We already know that the large silver hoards are of a relatively later date. As usual, these finds augment the written sources that bring us the com-plementary personal data we need.

The enemies of the Vikings had to admit: "The Normans are comely and of noble stature, skillful and bold. They live on the high seas and reside in their ships."

There could be no doubt about their superiority on the high seas where they felt more secure than on land. That was why they preferred to continue to use a sea route—southwestward now—and made the Hebrides and the rugged islands on Scotland's west coast their next basis of operation. On the southern-most island of Arran, a shield boss and dagger of the year 750 were found. Had it not definitely been a warrior's grave, we would have taken it for that of a solitary traveler. On the other hand, one such find does not suffice to establish organized Norwegian colonization of the western seas similar to that of the Svea beyond the Baltic. For the present it means only—but quite clearly —that this sea route was already familiar to the Norwegians in the eighth century. A typical trader's grave, with balance, scalepans and weights, was unearthed on the nearby tiny island of Gigha. Along this Scottish littoral, piece by piece, we find a whole anthology of Nordic customs. On Islay, a grave rich in weapons was found, with sledge hammer and tongs. A woman was buried

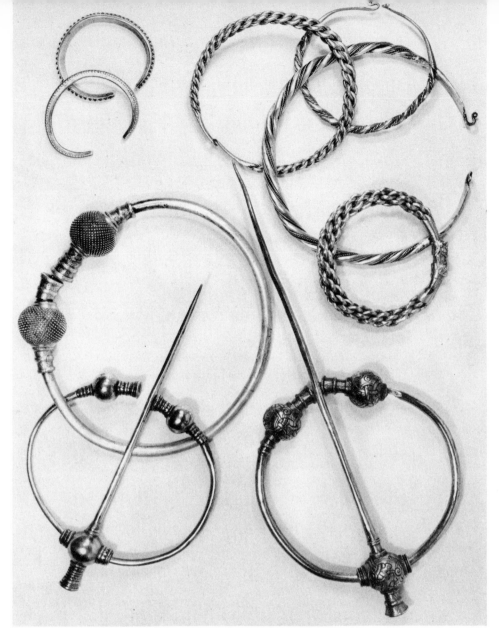

81. *Part of a silver hoard found on the Orkney Islands, near Scapa Flow. National Museum of Antiquities of Scotland, Edinburgh.*

in a boat on Oronsay, a rare but authenticated custom in the North. Is it possible that she enjoyed a position akin to a male chieftain in her lifetime? At any rate, such graves demonstrate the native equality of the Nordic woman. On Colonsay, in the Firth of Lorne, we find boat graves, among them the richest of all Western finds with complete weapon equipment, harness parts (quite likely for a saddle horse), bronze kettles, balance with weights in Celtic style and many more artifacts. Three Anglo-Saxon coins unfortunately are not

82. *Tynwald Hill on the Isle of Man.*
Originally a Thing-*hill for Viking assemblies, the mound lies opposite St. John's Chapel at the end of a processional route. The English king who presided here for the last time in 1945 was titled "Lord of Man." Since then he (sometimes she) has been represented by a lieutenant governor who presides at the top of the hill, facing east. The next three tiers are filled according to rank. In similar fashion, the Nordic petty kings of Viking days gave up their positions at the summit of the* Thing-*hill, took seats on the lower tiers, called themselves "Jarls" (Earls) thus recognizing Harald Fairhair as ruler over them all. Photographs courtesy of the Manx Museum.*

dated, but they were certainly struck before 854, and the burial of the chieftain probably took place in the second half of the ninth century. Finally let us list the island of Skye. In a stone barrow of the Bronze Age, the Vikings later embedded a cremation grave: ax and ring-pin are male accessories; a pearl is part of the woman's equipment. These and other double burials in the West corroborate what we have learned in the East, and in the Viking homelands.

From this chain of islands, the sea route leads directly through the North Channel into the Irish Sea, with its centrally situated Isle of Man, which the Vikings naturally found very attractive. A numerically small Celtic native population was unable to defend itself against the invaders. Here a Viking colony was founded, and what is exceptional about the event—even unique—is the fact that its laws have remained practically unchanged to the present day. Such things are possible only with the traditionally minded English. The island had broken all ties with Norway long ago, but when it put itself under

the protection of the English king (Henry IV) in 1405, it did so with the express condition that its autonomy be guaranteed. Thus five-hundred-year-old laws were fixed in 1405, to remain unalterable forever after.

The island has a *thing*-hill, 82 feet in diameter and about 10 feet high called Tynwald Hill. It is exactly like the *thing*-hill beside the three king-barrows in Old Uppsala, and like innumerable *thing*-mounds in the rest of Scandinavia. On them all public debate took place in Viking days. They formed the focal point for administration and politics. King Gustave Vasa of Sweden was the last to speak to the peasants in Old Uppsala in 1531. The northern *thing*-hill of the Orkney Island of Rousay was still used in the fifteenth century for a *Vapnastefna*. Lawting Court (Judgment Day) was held for the last time near the Loch of Tingwall on the Shetland Islands in the year 1691. But on Tynwald Hill on the Isle of Man, laws are still read aloud today before they become valid, and rulers are still proclaimed there, as was Queen Elizabeth II in 1952.

The island administration is in the hands of six high officials and the

Bishop of Sodor and Man. By Sodor, the "southern islands" are meant, the Hebrides, which of course lie in the northern waters of the British Isles. From a Viking perspective, however, they were the most southerly. And only from a Viking perspective can the Isle of Man be considered part of the Hebrides. The lower house of the island administration consists of twenty-four members of the House of Keys. *Keys* is equivalent to the Nordic-Icelandic *kuidir,* meaning landowning peasant.

And most curious of all, the Isle of Man is still divided into six sheadings as it was in Viking days, when a sheading consisted of 78 families, divided in 3 to form 26 *treens.* Now, according to an old Nordic conscription law, a *sheid* is the smallest warship, with 13 oars on each side, a ship with 13 benches, a 13-seater. Since 26 is the exact number required to man a 13-seater, every three families was called upon to man a warship. The Vikings who settled on the Isle of Man therefore had to provide six such dragon ships, a fact brilliantly paralleled by the precise organization of the sheadings, and corroborated in the Middle Ages by Robert of Scotland ("the Bruce"), who, in 1313, demanded that the Isle of Man provide six ships with 26 oarsmen each.

The old Scandinavian military classifications are well known to us through all sorts of documents; conscription laws of the early Middle Ages mention them, and on the coast north of Stockholm, in Roslagen, the smallest administrative unit was a *skeppslag,* or ship's crew. Nowhere, however, has the old order been so precisely preserved to the present day as on the Isle of Man, which is so small that it only had to provide 6 *sheidar,* or 13-seaters.

And while we are on the Isle of Man, let us take a look at the stone carving. A stone richly incised with plated band tells us in runes: "Gaut cut these and all (stone crosses) on Man." We know of two signed and seven other picture stones by this professional stonecutter who called himself Gaut. His style intimates that he came from Scotland, or from the islands off the Scottish west coast, where we find predecessors for his method of stone carving. But the way the bands are interwoven is Scandinavian, and betrays a definite influence of the Viking homeland. With Gaut, the Isle of Man received a school of stonecutting which various artists of the tenth century were able to develop further. Gaut's somewhat younger contemporary, Sandulv, left us the first picture stone on which animals and scenes from Nordic mythology are incised. (*See ill. 83.*) Master and basic style are Scotch, but the runes, motifs and pictorial themes are Scandinavian—a characteristic combination of these Western islands. We can follow anonymous and known masters for generations and write an exact history of their styles. The rune stones of the West are richly ornamented when compared with the native Scandinavian ones, which had to be cut in much harder granite. The inscriptions, though, are in a similar vein: "Odd raised

83. *Rune stones from the Isle of Man.* (LEFT) *Gaut's stone cross.* (RIGHT)
Sandulv's stone cross. Photo: Manx Museum.

this cross after Frakki, his father, but Tho(rbjörn)...." or "Druian, Dubgall's son, raised this stone after Athmiul his wife."

But there is one difference clearly evident in both stones. Odd, Frakki and Thorbjörn are Nordic names, found often in Scandinavia. Druian, Dubgall and Athmiul belong to a Celtic family, even though they had their gravestone cut in runes. Thus a mingling of indigenous population and new arrivals unfolds before our eyes in the works of art of the Scotch stonemasons they called in. And when a certain Thorleiv has a stone raised in memory of his son, who bears the Celtic name Fiac, we may assume that Thorleiv's wife was a Celt.

Now we understand why the first major attacks of the Vikings were made on Ireland. To the Norwegians, the island seemed not very far away. Of all the larger countries, it was the easiest to reach. As early as 820, the Irish coast was swarming with Vikings. They probably knew very well that church treasures could be wrested from the religious Irish more easily than from anyone else; that the Irish chieftains were fighting among themselves and would therefore be easy prey for any mass attack. And the expected success didn't fail to materialize. Ireland was occupied by the Vikings, and the annals tell of endless bloodshed.

"Lochlann [Scandinavia] with its dark ships . . ." In a few graphic words the Irish describe Norway as they saw it, a land of constantly threatening danger. In an Irish manuscript now in St. Gallen, Switzerland, we find a short poem:

> Grimly howls the storm tonight,
> Fomenting the white spume of the ocean.
> Now I need not fear that the wild Lochlann fighters
> Sail forth on the Irish Sea.

Who has not rejoiced in time of war over a nocturnal storm that protected against sudden surprise attack? We can understand the inhabitants of Erin, but also the tactics of their superior adversary.

We have already mentioned the eternal warfare between feudal lords and royal brothers that made the Viking victories possible on the European continent. In this respect, the Vikings were no better. They jeopardized their extraordinary chances by the same internal schisms. The policy of the balance of power is the age-old evil heritage of the European, whether Christian or heathen. Envy, betrayal, desertion to the enemy, are its symptoms. In the year 849, we note an edifying event: the Danes hastened to help the Irish with 104 ships. With a certain amount of satisfaction, the account records that "the Danes carried off the women of the men of Lochlann, their gold and their possessions. Thus God robbed them of all they had stolen from churches, altars and from the holy men of Erin." The Irish even had a chest full of gold and silver returned to them, and add, with something akin to admiration, "The Danes at any rate had a certain piety; out of piety they were capable for a while of abstaining from food and drink."

"Amlaib Conung, son of the kings of Lochlann, came to Erin . . . the stranger in Erin obeyed him and the Irish paid him tribute."

Here the annals are referring to King Olaf the White who ruled 853–871, not exactly mildly but more or less unchallenged. The mighty royal house of Ivar's sons, which continued to rule, for the most part from Dublin, was founded by Olaf's brother Ivar. Ivar's sons were Amelavus, Sitaracus and Yvorus (Olaf, Sigtrygg and Ivar). In Chapter Five, we read about their immigration.

It does not surprise us to hear that a large Nordic burial ground was found not far from Dublin. Unfortunately only single pieces from it, with no visible connection to each other, found their way into museums. All in all, we have 35 swords, 32 spearheads, 27 shield bosses, 7 oval brooches and a few other items. (*See ill. 84.*) Some good pieces were found in other Irish Viking areas, also some buried silver—and something surprising, although we should have counted on it—Celtic silver, which was probably buried hastily when the aggressor arrived.

The Viking hordes sailed along a well-established route, from Norway across the northernmost British islands and around Scotland into the Irish Sea, then, from England's southwesternmost point, the short distance to Brit-

84. *Oval fibulae and sword hilt from Viking graves near Dublin.*

tany. This route had considerable advantages over the stormy North Sea and the narrow English Channel. The few early written sources we have often mention it. In the year 609, a trading ship with full cargo arrived from Ireland in Nantes on the Loire, and brought Saint Columba back to his Irish homeland after his banishment from France. In the year 677, an Irish freighter bearing shoes and clothing for a cloister took the same route and returned from Nantes with wine and salt as cargo.

We have already mentioned the gruesome feast of John the Baptist in the year 843, when the citizens of Nantes were overpowered by Vikings who were called more precisely *Vestfaldingi*. Vestfold is the coastal landscape on the west bank of the Oslo Fjord. Soon after that, we see them landing in Africa.

In 859 Danish Ragnar Lodbrok's son, Björn Ironsides, set out with another Viking called Hasting in 62 ships to penetrate the Mediterranean, an excursion that lasted three years. In the Rhone delta they found a suitable island for wintering, and successfully plundered Nîmes and Arles. They got as far as Valence, west of Grenoble, and continued their travels to Italy. There, in quick succession, they took Pisa and Fiesole and the harbor town of Luna, which has ceased to exist.

Some chroniclers declare that Hasting and Björn got as far as Byzantium, but this must be a confusion with the Rus Vikings who, a little later, in 865, were threatening the Bosphorus from the Dnieper. Danes and Swedes almost met in the Mediterranean, but the time for a complete circumnavigation of Europe had not yet arrived.

Although 40 ships foundered in a storm off Gibraltar, and Arabs confiscated 4 more, the remaining 18 ships pushed on to Pamplona on the southwest slope of the Pyrenees, where the Prince of Navarre fell into their hands. They let him go for a very high ransom, and were hugely satisfied when they got back to the familiar surroundings of Nantes.

After this a few of them took off for Ireland again, probably taking Arabian slaves with them. Six years later, when the Irish won back Limerick (in one of their numerous military successes which, however, led to nothing in the end), they gained as booty a magnificent Moorish saddle and colored silk garments from Arabia. Repeatedly we hear of "blue men," with dark skins. This too must be a heritage of the Mediterranean voyagers.

Hasting continued to make a name for himself. For three decades he was leader of the Loire Vikings, and actually was like a Norman king ruling over them. In between we know of peaceful trading, *i.e.,* when the Vikings settled with their wives and children in Angers on the Loire. "They were given permission to stay there and open a market." They sold back to the Franks what they had robbed them of only a short while before. We come upon such transitory trade agreements in every part of Europe. But in the documents preserved, the chronicling of wars always outweighs all other data, and because accounts of cruelty tend to predominate, we still cannot form a satisfactory picture of social and economic conditions in the Viking occupied territories.

Danish "piety" in Ireland was an interlude. On the continent the Danes turned up yearly in a hostile fashion. It would be impossible to enumerate all the battles, but their encampment on the Seine island of Oiselle (today Jeufosse) deserves mention. From it the Vikings plundered Paris in 856. Charles the Bald wanted nothing so much as to be rid of them. When, in 861, 200 Norse ships were announced, he agreed to give their chief, Veland, a reward of cattle, grain and 5,000 pounds of silver if he would drive out the Oiselle Vikings.

In those days everyone participated with the same enthusiasm in the policy of compensation. Veland was an honest man. He carried out his end of the bargain, encircled the Oiselle Vikings, and granted them free departure from the river island if they paid him 6,000 pounds of silver—whereupon the two forces took up winter quarters together in the heart of France! Veland was interested in future co-operation with the king, so he let himself be baptized. Shortly after this, however, two other baptized Vikings in the king's service accused Veland of treason—apparently this had nothing to do with the Oiselle affair—and in a fight with them, he was stabbed and died.

Lothair had already begun to appoint Vikings as vassals or feudal lords. They could be used to protect the borders of the realm; at the same time, this policy was to lure them little by little into the camp of the Carolingian kings. The Dane, Rorik, actually did reign for twenty years over Friesland (856–876) and was followed by his relative, Godfred (876–885). But Godfred permitted Viking hordes to sail up the Rhine to Duisburg. He demanded Coblenz, Andernach and Sinzig from Charles the Fat, "because the land he had received through the Emperor's gracious benevolence produced no wine!" Godfred knew only too well which were the desirable regions. The Emperor naturally didn't like the idea of handing the center of his realm over to his vassal; so he had him and his followers slaughtered. The matter was attended to by Count Gerolf, who with this became a founding father of the Dutch nobility, and there could be no more thought of a Viking fief in Friesland.

The aforementioned Rorik had sailed in the year 850, with 35 ships, across the English Channel, plundered Canterbury, London and Surrey, but in the end was thoroughly beaten. He took up winter quarters, as usual on an island in a river delta—this time Sheppey on the Thames. Thus England was spared for a relatively long time from major occupation.

In 866, the Vikings returned to England under the leadership of Lodbrok's sons, Halfdan, Ivar and Ubbe. They provided themselves—peacefully at first —with horses, then proceeded to conquer London, York and all East Anglia. A decade later they were able to found a regular colony with Danish laws. They divided the land into five districts and chose five fortresses as administrative areas: Lincoln, Stamford, Leicester, Derby and Nottingham. That is why this fruitful strip of England has ever since been called collectively *Five Boroughs,* borough in its original sense of fortress.

The Annals report, "Anno 876. Halfdan divided up the land of the Northumbrians, and his men tilled the earth and cultivated it."

The Vikings wanted to spread their might across the rest of England as well, especially over the southwest region of Wessex, where a very young regent ruled. But his name was King Alfred the Great. He knew how to deploy his small army cleverly and to disperse the Vikings until he finally won a decisive victory in 878 at Ethandun. Although the Five Boroughs remained a state founded by the Vikings, the Norman danger was lifted, for the moment at any rate, but only for England.

On April 12, 879, the Viking hordes, on the loose because of King Alfred's successful action against them, landed at the mouth of the Schelde River and assembled all their armed forces on the continent. With this Great Army they ravaged the continent of Europe for thirteen years. Their wars, rapine and incendiarism surpassed by far all the comparatively modest operations of earlier decades. From every river delta, this roving, sailing kingdom shifted its battle-grounds inland. A powerful army was raised and set out against them, a brilliant achievement in itself. For twelve days the Normans were surrounded in Elsloo near Maastricht. Then they were given 2,800 pounds of silver and permitted to leave. The superior attackers' fear of Norman armed power was incredible.

Towns, whole countrysides, went up in flames—Liège, Mecheln, Coblenz, Trier, Cologne, Aix, and with it the palace of Charlemagne. The Octagon, sumptuous chapel of the Imperial Palace, became a stable for Viking horses. The Viking armies encamped for a while in Flanders, Brabant, Picardy. "You cannot see a place where the dead don't lie."

Paris was threatened again, this time by 700 ships and 40,000 men. Because of Count Odo's heroic defense of the city for eleven months, the Vikings were able to take only one of the south towers. The Count's action was decisive for the city's fate as future capital of France, and he became the founding father of the Capetian royal house of the Middle Ages. In his way, Carl the Fat helped to relieve Odo. He offered the Vikings 700 pounds of silver and a free hand to plunder the Upper Seine region. His true goal, however, was less altruistic. Actually he was availing himself of their power to subdue the feudal lords in that area.

At last, in the famine year of 892, the Vikings left a continent to which they had laid waste. "And since God in His mercy decided to take pity on us, He calmed the fury of their fire, suppressed the raging of the heathen, brought peace and unity, and gave richly again of the fruits of the earth."

The Great Army moved on to England, this time with women and horses aboard ship. But Alfred had made good use of this rest period, recaptured London, and devoted all his energies to rearming. He had had an idea that hadn't occurred to any landlubber on the continent:

"King Alfred had long ships built to go out against the Vikings. They were almost twice as long as the Norsemen's boats. Some had 60 oarsmen, some even more. His ships were faster than those of the Vikings, were more seaworthy and higher. They were built neither like the Frisian ships nor like those of the Danes, but according to his specifications, so as to be of the greatest practicality."

But he lacked experienced crews for his "navy," and had to hire Frisians. The English were still a far cry from being sailors, and Alfred scored his greatest successes with his old proven tactic of exhausting the enemy. Only today can we really evaluate what this ailing monarch achieved, in the way of folk-education, the study of Latin and the humanities, while his own kingdom was indeed giving him "plenty of trouble." It must have been the most profound satisfaction of his life when, in 846, he saw what was left of the Great Army sail away from England, back to the continent. There they continued to rage as professional soldiers—no longer able to practice any other profession, knowing no home but a military encampment, no values but trickery and force. For this band of straggling mercenaries there was no way into the tenth century. Soon they were "a very small army," the fate of which isn't worth recording.

Historic sources from the years 900–910 are unfortunately scant. We see fresh forces leaving Norway and Denmark in search of land in true emigration spirit. One man among them stands out; soon he was to be leader of all the Vikings on the continent—Rollo Gånge-Rolf. That was his Nordic name, and he was so tall that no horse could carry him. Some say he was a Dane; according to other sources his brother was the second Earl of the Orkney Islands and came from Möre in west Norway. Charles the Simple at once wanted to negotiate with the Vikings and bade their ruler appear before him.

The reply came just as promptly, "We know no master. All of us are equal." This one sentence reveals the nature of all Vikingdom—freedom, absolute independence for the individual, a superior value put on personality.

In the year 911, Normandy became a Norse kingdom on the continent by the treaty of St. Clair-sur-Epte in which Gånge-Rolf swore fealty to the Frank king "for the protection of the realm," and accepted baptism. But he didn't feel like a vassal; he felt like the ruler of a newly founded kingdom. Eight days after his baptism he began to measure the land and divide it among his chieftains, just as Halfdan had done thirty-five years before in the "Five Boroughs" land. In Normandy, therefore, the names of localities also immortalize the Nordic colonizer through word suffixes such as -gard, -torp, and -tot, or by direct Nordic names for places: Osmundiville, Toberville, Regnetot and Ulveville. Yvetot is probably derived from the Scanian *Ivetofta*. As in the Nordic homeland, the peasant population was free; very different from the pronounced feudalism prevailing in the rest of France.

Brittany and the dukedom of Nantes were for a long time a part of Normandy, and the dukes of Rollo's lineage made noteworthy contributions to the history of the continent in the days that lay ahead.

How many spears must have hummed through the air in the ninth century, how many swords must have smote hard and cleaved their target. Yet only isolated pieces of both types of weapon have been preserved for us, and astonishingly few graves—a few dozen in England, among them boat graves; on the continent only three; one of them the richly furnished boat grave on Ile de Croix, on the south coast of Brittany, dated 900. In the charred layer, 20 iron shield bosses, a richly ornamented sword, a gold finger ring, caldrons of iron and bronze, attract our attention, and here too are the puzzling tools—hammer and tongs. A sea captain from Norway must have been given his last resting place here, with a magnificent view of the sea. From Pîtres near Rouen come 2 oval brooches; from Holland a grave with armor, and that is all. The sparseness of graves in comparison with the documentary evidence of warfare is surprising. In the tenth century, after the conversion to Christianity, we can, of course, expect to find no more pagan graves.

Frequently a weapon fell into the water and turns up today in river slime where the Normans once fought. The possibilities of finding and raising weapons and Viking ships in mud three or four feet deep is limited, even for the archeologist, and we have to depend on occasional chance findings. To complete the count we must mention the innumerable silver hoards from England, akin in their composition to the finds we already know.

And finally we must ask ourselves: What was brought home by the Vikings from England and Ireland? The catalogue for Norway in 1940 lists 114 orna-

85. *Irish bronze bucket found in Birka.*
State Historical Museum, Stockholm. Photo: Iwar Anderson.

mented objects, 35 vessels (for the most part bronze), 11 silver fibulae and other objects; also a few pieces found in Swedish soil, and in some sparse Danish graves. Among the vessels, the most beautiful is perhaps the richly ornamented bucket found in Birka grave No. 507. (*See ill. 85.*)

One can't help but note that the Vikings seemed to prefer plundering the more easily accessible monasteries. A richly decorated incense burner was found in a woman's grave and we frequently come across house-shaped reliquaries, or the metal fittings that belonged to them. (*See ill. 86.*)

"Rannveig owns this casket," is inscribed in runes on a small reliquary which was certainly never made for Rannveig! (*See ill. 87.*)

The trading center on Helgö, as already mentioned, surprised us by producing a beautiful bishop's crozier from Ireland. (*See ill. 36.*) The crook forms the head of a monster with its mouth wide open, biting a human head. Enamel, glass and gilt were used by the artist. The symbolism is familiar from examples of early Christian art—Death devours a man in order to vomit him up again, as in the case of Jonah and the big fish. The crozier is the oldest Irish example we know.

86. Irish incense holder found in a woman's grave in Norway. 4¼ inches in diameter. Bergen Museum, Bergen.

87. *Irish reliquary, probably found in Norway. National Museum, Copenhagen.*

Western silver found its way into Viking pockets even before the big stream of Arabic silver began to flow in the direction of the eastern traders. In the years 845–883, Charles the Bald and his successors paid ransom eight times to get rid of the Vikings "for all time"—or anyway for twelve years! If we add up all this money gained by "legal" means, we reach the sum of 45,347 pounds of silver, with some gold included. And when we consider the fact that the Oiselle Vikings had accumulated 6,000 pounds of silver—with which they bought their freedom from Veland—we may surmise that the amount of silver not registered in our written sources was also considerable.

From a colorful mosaic of documentary reports, legends, name places, archeological grave and hoard findings, we have followed the Vikings eastward and westward. Out of all this profusion of clues, one realization that cannot be overlooked comes clear: Their activity on the continent in the east parallels that on the western seas, and vice versa—what we learn of them in western Europe we find repeated in Russia.

The Scandinavians pressed forward in both directions, first and foremost as emigrants who could not nourish themselves adequately in their own meager, overpopulated country. They called the state they founded in Russia, Gardarike,

or Land of the Fortified Homesteads; in England they named it Five Boroughs.
Ireland and the small group of North Sea islands were incorporated in the
Nordic sphere of power, but on the continent the Vikings encountered bitter
resistance, which was why they were able to get a grim hold in the ninth century only as savagely fighting army units. They also penetrated the icy north
of Europe, but here had to be satisfied with levying taxes on primitive natives.

In the ninth century, the grave finds of the West are richer than those in
the East. But in the tenth century, the state founders were converted to Christianity, and the customs of Christian burial do not include grave furnishings.
With this, Viking artifacts disappear from the archeology of the West as the
Russian finds become more and more numerous.

Most of the Irish relics found in Scandinavian earth originated in the eighth
century and lie in graves of the ninth century; early pieces are almost completely lacking. This is no coincidence. The monasteries had been plundered
so thoroughly by the first Viking generation that nothing more could be sought
there. Love of art decreased, savagery was on the rise. The study of Latin,
once practiced so assiduously in Ireland, was neglected; orderly teaching methods were lost. The chroniclers complained, "Pupils no longer want to show
the necessary respect and stand up when their teachers are present."

The teachers themselves left their homes as starving, freezing, mendicant
refugees. "The north wind rages among us learned Latin scholars, among us
pious priests."

And it was ever thus in prolonged times of war. We must not forget, however, that the exploring immigrant intruders were above all founders of states
in foreign lands and introduced Scandinavian laws, administration and customs
there. The Five Boroughs in England were also called Danelagen, a word
very similar in construction to the east Swedish Roslagen. The military conscription order of Scandinavia has been preserved on the Isle of Man to the
present day. *Thing*-hills are situated at all central administration sites. The
landowning peasants assemble and resolve their problems according to their
own laws, just as the English King Edgar promised them in 970: "I want such
good laws to prevail among the Danes as they themselves deem right; just as
I have permitted it to them and shall continue to permit it to them in return
for the loyalty they have always shown me."

In similar fashion, a form of communal life with the native population had
to be created wherever the Vikings chose to go, whether among the Finns,
Slavs, Celts, Anglo-Saxons, Frisians or Franks. We have seen Celtic and
Nordic names turn up separately on rune stones on the Isle of Man, but very
soon they begin to merge.

Viking Olaf the White of Ireland married Aud the Deepminded, daughter
of Ketil Flatnose, who had come from Sogn to the Norwegian west coast and

ruled over the Hebrides—Norwegian royal houses intermarried apparently in their new homelands—but he also married the daughter of the great Irish king, Aedh. Olaf's successor in Dublin, Olaf Cuaran, conferred rewards for heroic Irish lays that a bard sang to him. Similarly we find Finnish and Slavonic names in the list of Rus ambassadors in Kiev. Slavonic words appear on spice jars in Smolensk and on tree bark in Novgorod. The western Nordic princely houses became Celticized, those in the East fell under Slavonic influence. All of them alienated themselves from their homeland and settled down to an existence of their own.

Finally we studied the objects brought home: from the East—metal fittings, souvenirs of the voyage, silk and silver; from the West—relics, Celtic and Frank jewelry, bronze caldrons, glass and cloth. Some we feel were war booty, other objects, according to circumstances, could only have been merchandise, for there was constant fluctuation between war and peace. The Vikings brought a profusion of luxury goods home to Scandinavia; they came back with stories of wild adventure; they took their wares to Birka, Haithabu and Skiringssal. Scandinavia had become a European great power, one could say a world power. And what was it like meanwhile in the old peasant homeland?

8

The King Ships

SOMEHOW KINGS always manage to get themselves talked about. They see to it that songs are sung in their honor; they glorify their own heroic deeds; they build graves for themselves to last into all eternity. But the researchers of posterity seem to be most concerned with the royal art heritage, unjustly sometimes, for only the cultural history of *all* social classes can truly familiarize us with the peoples of any epoch.

On the west coast of the Oslo Fjord, there reigned a dynasty of petty kings who understood marvelously how to get the right publicity for themselves. They ruled in Vest(West)fold; their soldiers were the Vestfaldings who fought in France. The names of six generations have been handed down to us:

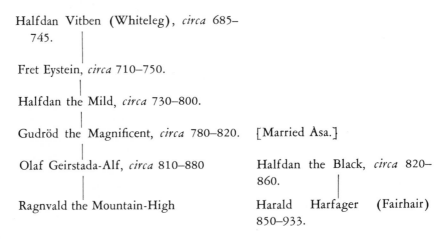

Halfdan Vitben (Whiteleg), *circa* 685–
745.

Fret Eystein, *circa* 710–750.

Halfdan the Mild, *circa* 730–800.

Gudröd the Magnificent, *circa* 780–820.   [Married Åsa.]

Olaf Geirstada-Alf, *circa* 810–880   Halfdan the Black, *circa* 820–
860.

Ragnvald the Mountain-High   Harald Harfager (Fairhair)
850–933.

A list of ancestors going back six generations was not enough for Ragnvald the Mountain-High. He attached his family tree to that of the most famous royal house of his time: the Ynglinga dynasty in Old Uppsala. He also summoned a poet and singer to his court, the scald Tjodolf of Hvin, to compose a lay about his twenty-seven new ancestors.

All we can do is shake our heads. Things like this can happen in life—the mighty monarchs of Old Uppsala are transformed into petty kings on the Oslo Fjord, but it isn't very likely. And we really can't give the story much credit for another reason: the kings of Old Uppsala were cremated, whereas the Vestfold kings were buried in their ships.

Yet Tjodolf sang of the death and graves of Ragnvald's twenty-seven new ancestors. This was his most important theme, for in a pagan state there were no other ties than those to the clan. The living family, together with those who had gone before, constituted an inextinguishable community. The ancestors resided in the grave mounds, could receive visitors and give advice. Until into the Middle Ages, landowning peasants could trace their ancestors *til Hangs ok til Heidni* . . . "back to the ancestral barrow and heathendom." And this was especially valid for royal houses.

Snorri Sturluson was in Vestfold in 1218, and probably collected word-of-mouth traditions on the spot. Tjodolf's poems and Snorri's *Heimskringla* are therefore important sources.

Halfdan Whiteleg is supposed to have his mound in a place called Skereid, near Skiringssal. We have been unable to find it, but its alleged proximity to the trading center pleases us, since we have already noted that the important trading cities must have had royal patronage to thank for their existence. Of Eystein, Snorri writes: "His body was brought to Borro and a mound was raised over him on a height beside the sea near Vadla."

Halfdan the Mild also "received a mound on Borro," or, as Tjodolf puts it:

> And on Borro   victorious warriors
> The chieftain   later buried.

Halfdan the Black was given a "Halfdan's Mound" in Vestfold. We have no information about his father, but we may take for granted that he also lies in Borro—today Borre—because only under very exceptional circumstances was a man buried away from his clan.

In the heart of Vestfold, directly on the important waterway of the Oslo Fjord, lies an entire burial field of 9 king graves, approximately 108 to 150 feet in diameter and originally 16½ to 24 feet high. Here we looked for the Vestfold dynasty and have already found some of them.

In 1852, when scrupulous methods of investigation were still unknown, a few laborers, loading sand, came upon a ship in the northernmost hill. In it they found all sorts of precious things: a dark brown Rhenish glass goblet, richly ornamented fittings for the bridle of a saddle horse, saddle, stirrups, the reins for a cart horse, caldrons, iron chain and ax; valuable objects of a more personal nature were lacking. The burial coincided with the dates of Halfdan the Black.

This is the Halfdan who divided Vestfold with his half brother Olaf Geierstada-Alf. The latter received the southernmost part of the little country; we therefore cannot expect to find him in Borre. But near Gokstad, about 16 miles southwest of Borre, a splendidly preserved ship turned up in a king barrow in 1880 and since the next farmstead, to which the mound once belonged, is called Gjekstad, the buried man must be Olaf Gjekstada-Alf or Geirstada-Alf. Snorri corroborates this:

"He was the most comely and strongest, and tall of stature. . . . King Olaf's seat was in Geirstader. He was afflicted by a pain in his foot and died of it and received his grave mound on Geirstader. . . ."

> Now the belligerent   king of armies
> Lies on Geirstader   covered by his mound.

An examination of the bones resulted in the revelation that the buried man was of extraordinary stature and suffering from rheumatism!

Other objects of the greatest interest to us were contained in the blue clay: a tent with ornamented gable, beds, a sleigh, vats, pails, wooden jars, torches, spades, a copper caldron with iron chains, a gaming board, twelve horses, six dogs and a peacock! Again we are reminded of the fact that the Vestfaldings took active part in the Viking raids on France. But most surprising of all is the ship itself—a 16-seater, about 78 feet long, and 3 smaller boats. (See ill. 88.)

Truly a royal find! It is surpassed to date only by the ship grave in Öseberg [south of Borre] of Olaf Geirstada's stepmother, Queen Asa, wife of Gudröd the Magnificent. The Öseberg ship is $5\frac{1}{2}$ feet shorter than the Gokstad ship, a 15-seater, a little more heavily built, with a mast which is really quite weak. Some think the ship was a coastal sailing vessel, others believe it was an older and technically not so noble ship, but what carving! All along stem- and sternpost, the most glorious animal ornamentation forms loops into each of which the head of the next animal is thrust. They follow a rising rhythm, a crescendo like symmetrical waves, yet none of them alike.

The Öseberg mound was made up of sod. That is why this find—incomparably richer in artifacts than any other—was so flawlessly preserved. The works of six different wood carvers and three simple artisans from the court of Queen Asa are easy to tell apart. Each has his own personality. Haakon Shetelig, who published an anthology on the Vestfold School, named the artists of Öseberg after their approach to their work and their style.

The "Conservative Academician" worked, for instance, with much more finesse than did the "Shipmaster," or ship constructor. On the shaft of a sled, carved by the former, pairs of birds face each other, elegantly and artfully interwoven, the necks curved like scrolls, the feathers intertwined; a ceaseless,

88. *The richly ornamented prow of the Öseberg ship.*

restless interplay of patterns. Similar is the ornamentation by the same hand around a wildly grinning dragon head. (*See ill. 89, 90.*)

The "Master of the Carolingian Dragon Head" worked in a quite different manner, in whorls of little, fat, "gripping" animals with snub noses and protruding eyes. (*See ill. 91.*) They hang on to each other frantically, they claw and paw each other and just about dislocate their clumsy bodies in their grotesque efforts to make room for themselves within the framework of the design. A grip on the throat; six fists grasping crisscross. They tousle the next animal's back hair, snuffle along the edges, bite each other in the rump. And in the end there is room for them all. Not an interstice of tranquility, nothing but tenseness, motion and writhing life. And all this contained within the confines of a grinning dragon head with fangs. And such different master craftsmen could receive commissions at the same royal court. Some of the objects in the find may

89. *Dragon head of the "Academician" from Öseberg.*

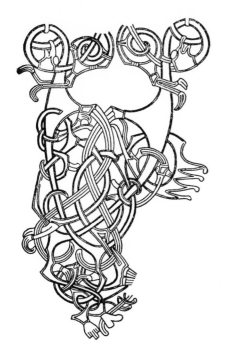

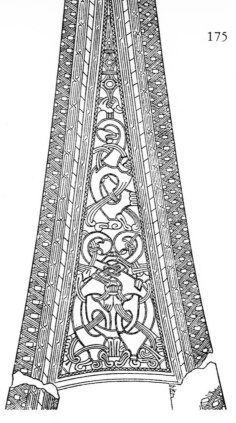

90. *Wood carving by the "Academician" of Öseberg, from the dragon head and the shafts of the sled.*

have come from the parental home of Queen Asa's husband, King Gudröd, and therefore been over fifty years old when everything was buried, *circa* 850. The works are of very different temperament, yet they stood side by side in the same royal household.

And a rural wood carver also was summoned. Let him show what he could do! Did he carve after ancient models or according to peasant custom, as he

91. *Carving by the "Master of the Carolingian Dragon Head."*

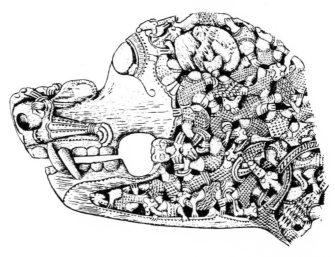

had been taught at home? Be that as it may, "The Wagonmaster," as he was
called, produced the most peculiar and rare pieces of the entire Öseberg find:
the heavy, four-wheeled cart. (*See ill. 92.*) Strange, long, snakelike animals
are interwoven with grinning cat heads, and on the gable end a man is being
tortured in a snake pit. (*See ill. 93, 94.*) We know him: Gunnar, or Gunther,
from the legend of the Nibelungs—Niflungs in the *Edda,* meaning warriors.
In the *Atlakvida* (Lay of Atli) Atli tells us:

> Living the Huns laid   in loathsome dungeon
> Alive with adders   the lordly Niflung. . . .

We even see a toad biting Gunnar in the waist, and this too we find in the
Edda, in The Plaint of Oddrun:

> Then out did crawl   Atli's mother,
> The evil wretch,   may she rot foully!
> Into Gunnar's heart   she hewed her teeth . . .
> That I (Oddrun) might not save   the matchless king.

92. *The Öseberg cart.*

93. *Figure head on the Öseberg cart.*

94. *Gunnar in the snake pit on the Öseberg cart.*

95. *Gunnar in the snake pit, strumming the lute with his feet, as depicted on a medieval drinking horn from Norway.*

96. *Gunnar in the snake pit, depicted on a baptismal stone in the church of Norum, western Sweden. State Historical Museum, Stockholm. Photo: ATA.*

It is extremely interesting to see certain events of the saga—written so many years later—illustrated in such detail, even before 850. The lute is missing which Gunnar, in chains, strums with his feet to exorcise the snakes. This motif appears later. We find it on Norwegian stave churches, even on a baptismal stone and on a drinking horn of the Middle Ages. (*See ill. 95, 96, 97.*) Haakon Shetelig believes "Wagonmaster" and "Shipmaster" to be one and the same man; stylistic details betray it. No one has come forward to contradict his conclusions. The talented country artist may have learned courtly styles in Öseberg, and been commissioned to build the state ship—a noteworthy career.

97. *Gunnar in the snake pit, depicted in wood carving from the portal of the stave church of Hylestad, Norway. Universitetets Oldsakssamling, Oslo.*

But the greatest carver of them all was the "Baroque Master." We call him that because his two sled shafts and dragon head have the power and magnificence of the baroque spirit. He works in medallions, with which the pictorial surface is firmly constructed, but he has carved droll, puffy "gripping" animals into all his rondels. They, too, try to burst the confines of their bodies; they snap at each other, rub beaks, bite each other and get entangled with each other in every conceivable fashion. On the dragon head itself every rondel is

98. *Two dragon heads from Öseberg. The one on the right was carved by the "Baroque Master."*

99. *Ornament on a dragon head by the "Baroque Master."*

composed of two snapping interlocked animals with heads and legs, and another little animal is staring at us out of the center of the rondel with enormous eyes. (*See ills. 98, 99, 100.*)

Such profusion of wood carving, such seething vitality in every motif, run-

100. *Bands of interwoven animal ornamentation on the dragon head of the "Baroque Master."*

ning the whole artful gamut from measured classicism to excessive yet fully controlled baroque—the same characteristics which the Ancient Greek, Gothic and Renaissance arts display from time to time. And this in the Viking era which we thoughtlessly called barbaric and savage!

Unfortunately, robbers got to the three king barrows ahead of the archeologists. All personal jewelry, all objects of monetary value such as table silver, swords, brooches, buckles, clasps and rings are missing. Only 7 unimportant glass beads, 3 combs, and 2 pairs of shoes were left behind. The prow and the queen's bed were badly damaged. In the Gokstad ship the whole dragon post was removed, evidently also by thieves.

Such thefts are extraordinary undertakings and a great deal more puzzling than the Egyptian grave robberies. In Scandinavia one was proud of one's clan. These huge mounds could not have been opened by night, or in secret; it could have been done only in co-operation with the native population. The intruders quite evidently were "killing" the ship and resting place of the royal personages, removing their strength and spirit, leaving nothing behind but worthless wood. They must have taken place after the conversion to Christianity, for the buried bodies were already decayed, something we *were* able to ascertain from the disorderly scattered skeleton parts. And the intruders evidently knew exactly where the shaft had to be dug in order to hit upon the royal treasure. Was it their intention to "kill" the heathen living in the grave mound? How could the clan stand by and let it happen? What was the motivation of the plundering that followed? We don't see the answers clearly yet; we can only hope that future finds will give us deeper insight into the beliefs of these people.

Most exciting though, in every case and in spite of what is lost, is the ship itself—for its size if for nothing else. Gokstad and Öseberg ships are now housed in the ship room on Bygdöy, near Oslo, together with the remains of a third ship from Tune in Öst(East)fold. Thus three coastal or overseas vessels of the Viking era are united again, a world sensation, which is corroborated by the number of visitors.

One has to stand in front of the originals to grasp the noble curves of their outlines. (*See ill. 101.*) The towering prow is startling in itself, powerful and high, capable of cutting through the waves, yet only the thinnest of dividers in the turbulent oceanic element. Above all, one has to see for oneself how wide these Viking ships are; how the sides bulge out amidships, yet how flat they are! One feels they must have been awash with every wave, yet this was just why they rested so lightly on the water, always gliding atop the wave's force. Just the same, it took courage to cross the ocean in such a wide-open boat.

Since 1880, we have been subjected to a plethora of old wooden tubs, out-

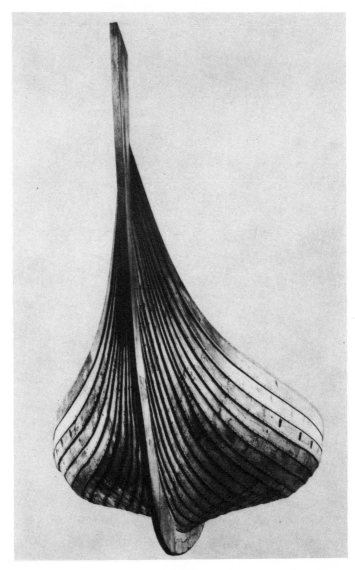

101. *The Gokstad ship, Vestfold, Norway. Exhibited in the ship museum in Bygdöy, near Oslo. Universitetets Oldsakssamling, Oslo.*

fitted with dragon posts and sails, which have been passed off as copies of Viking ships. With their false proportions they confuse our vision, so that we no longer recognize the true lines right away. A faithful copy of the Gokstad ship crossed the Atlantic in 1893, manned by a crew of experienced sailors who were still available in those days. The effort demonstrated how smooth the sailing was in such a ship, and how easily the huge side rudder on starboard could be manipulated by the cross tiller. With a good wind, the ship could reach a speed of 10 to 11 knots an hour.

102. *Viking ship dragon post, raised from the Schelde River. National Scheep-vaartmuseum, Antwerp.*

As already mentioned, the dragon posts on the Gokstad ship are missing. The coiled-snakehead posts of the Öseberg ship were found lying on its fore-deck. This has a special significance, for the sagas tell us that these animal-head posts served to frighten away evil spirits. When land was sighted, they were taken down so as not to startle the good land spirits. Perhaps this was also valid when the hereafter was in sight? In these animal-head posts was housed the very life of the ship which the grave robbers of the Gokstad ship "killed" and chopped up.

When were we going to find a grinning dragon post? The dragon heads of the Öseberg ship were too small to count as such and were probably used for unknown cult purposes. The Schelde River came to our assistance. A dragon post was raised out of its slime. It is nearly 5 feet high and exudes a wild, eerie power, equal to the best woodcarving in Öseberg. To this we must add four more dragon heads from the Schelde, the last one found in 1953. Only one is large enough to have been part of a post. The others may have been attached to chairs, tents, or implements of ritual. They are simple yet brutal, and primitively pagan in their ferocious expression. Surely they came from Viking ships that sank there. (*See ill. 102, 103.*)

We envy the Norwegians their many ship findings. In Sweden and Denmark, we come across little more than neat rows of rivets, all that is left of a completely rotted ship. We can measure and remeasure and reconstruct theoretically, but always only at a desk. We have no material for a ship room.

Suddenly Germany surprised us with the next—the fourth—Viking ship, in —of all places—the harbor of old Haithabu! In 1950 and in 1953, Professor K. Kersten, director of the Schleswig Museum, decided to do some underwater exploring. Just for the fun of it, and with no compensation other than his daily bread, the diver Schwendt, who happened to be out of work at the time, put himself at the professor's disposal. They felt their way across the slimy harbor bed where it was pitch-dark about 5 feet down. They found that the palisades, which had once stood on the semicircular wall, ran on down into the water in the form of stakes that were rammed into the ground close to each other. Their complete course, and the harbor entry itself, have not yet been fully mapped out, but it is already possible to establish the fact that the typical semicircular wall is an optical illusion. This Baltic Sea town was *surrounded* by a wall, just like the fortified inland towns of the Middle Ages. Innumerable millstones, whetstones, clay shards, soapstone, deer horn, and other debris, have been

103. *Viking dragon heads.*
Small heads from the Schelde River.

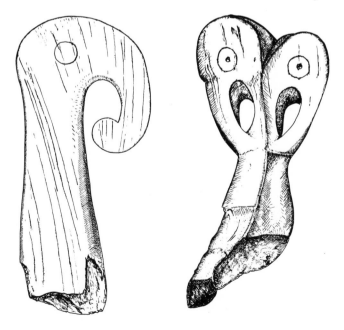

raised. As in all harbors, iron weapons lay close to the palisades and in what was surmised to be the harbor entry, the divers found the Viking ship. The oak railing of one side of the riveted ship proved to be more than 50 feet long; the ribs are of ash, the planks calked with animal hair. Next to it lies part of a smaller boat. In the big ship lay the skeleton of a man with serious injuries to the cheekbones. Naturally all of us hope that the considerable sums of money required to raise the vessel will soon be forthcoming, because here, in the harbor of Haithabu, lies a ship that can lead us straight into the life of a world harbor of a thousand years ago. The thought of being able to recover individual pieces of the cargo and utensils of everyday usage seems even more important and fascinating than the raising of the ship itself.

The Swedes of course had to match this. In the seventeenth century, one of Birka's governors had several oak posts pulled out of the water and sold them to a carpenter. So Birka, too, had harbor palisades, of which remnants are left to this day. The water bed is just as slimy, but the water level has sunk more than 15 feet in the last thousand years, so that its depth in the harbor is negligible. Frogmen should get busy in this harbor. There must be ships in it too!

104. *A sunken ship recently discovered in the slime of the Baltic sea, some 20 miles south of Stockholm. It is possible that the ship dates back to the battle of 1007. Underwater photo: Bengt Börjesson.*

Meanwhile lay divers announced on July 22, 1959, the finding of three sunk ships in the Baltic Sea bay of Landfjärden, about 22 miles south of Stockholm. The ship most clearly visible is open, has riveted sides of pine (not oak), mast and gear. The site fits in with an account in the *Heimskringla,* according to which Norwegian King Olaf II (Saint Olaf) waged war in the Baltic Sea in 1007, but whether these ships were originally Viking vessels is doubtful. (*See ill. 104.*)

Most successful during the past years were the Danes who, in 1962, managed to raise no less than 5 ships. With the C-14 dating method, it was possible to tell that they originated in the first half of the year 1000. They lay near Skuldelev and blocked the Roskilde Fjord on the island of Seeland. Due to some danger or other, of which we know nothing, the inhabitants of Roskilde must have barricaded their harbor by sinking the ships. All movable objects and parts that could be used elsewhere were removed and the ships were filled with heavy stones.

For the excavation a shaft of steel girders had to be rammed into the water bed and pumped free of water. The wooden ship parts were vacuum packed in plastic bags to protect them against air and dryness until they could be preserved. All in all, about 545 square yards of timber were salvaged. Although damaged and incomplete, we were able to ascertain—to our joy—that here we had 5 different ship types and an invaluable source of research material. One ship, which is preserved almost in its entirety, is 17 yards 24 inches long, light, elegantly constructed, with a prow like the ones on the Gokstad and Öseberg ships, but with no possibility of attaching a dragon head, for it was quite obviously a trading vessel, intended for a small cargo and speed. Another ship is 21 yards 31.4 inches long, broad, solid, with all its timbers very strong. It was apparently used for heavier loads.

Until now we knew the Viking trader only from written sources. On the rune stone of Mervalla it is called a "knarr."

> Siegrid had this stone raised for her husband Sven:
> Oft he sailed   to Semgallen
> With costly knarr   around Domesnas.

So Sven traveled the more or less regular trade route to Lettland. The word "costly" refers of course to the cargo, and only indirectly to the "knarr."

On the Roskilde ships the cargo space or hold is amidship and there are few oarholes. They must have sailed with the wind and a small crew. One, though, has quite a few oarholes and a low railing, and was evidently intended for swift passenger service. Only one is a warship and was probably reconstructed for cargo transport when it had outlived its usefulness as a fighting ship.

At present we don't know of a single ship of a later period, but we know through written sources that they were larger, more impressive and seaworthy than the ships in the mounds of Öseberg and Gokstad. Olaf Trygvasson sailed to Haalogaland in 999 in a magnificent 30-seater, the *Crane*. He was received by the powerful native freeholder Raud in Ramme on the Salt Fjord in his *Short Snake*. The *Heimskringla* reports: "It was a much larger and more beautiful ship than the *Crane*."

This left the king no peace. That autumn, with Raud's ship for a model, Olaf Trygvasson built the most famous of all Viking ships, the *Ormen Lange* or *Long Snake*, a magnificent 34-seater, approximately 164 feet long. It is difficult to grasp such length and envision it in the shape of a Viking ship on the open sea or to imagine the difficulty of finding the oak with which to build it. For the replica of the Gokstad ship, built in 1893, a suitable keel couldn't be found in all Norway, and a Canadian oak had to be imported. For the mast block, which gives the decisive balance amidship and supports mast and sail ($39\frac{1}{2}$ inches by $15\frac{3}{4}$ inches in diameter), an isolated oak was found in Norway. In Viking days, Norway was rich in oak and it was prepared by experts. When a king gave the order for a ship to be built—mostly in shipyards in the Trondheim area—it would be completed in one great winter effort. In the year 1000, Olaf Trygvasson was able to sail forth proudly in his *Long Snake* against the combined Nordic armed forces. Olaf Skötkonung of Sweden and Sven Forkbeard of Denmark had forced him to arms; Haakon Ladejarl was also his enemy. The aid Trygvasson had been expecting failed to materialize. In the famous battle of Svolder, somewhere in the neighborhood of Öresund, his fate was sealed. When he saw that defeat was inevitable, he jumped into the water from his long ship, in the full splendor of his war regalia.

His *Long Snake* lived on by word-of-mouth tradition, mentioned always with awe and admiration. On his travels in the thirteenth century, Snorri found out that the shipbuilders in Trondheim still knew its measurements by heart. It became the model for the 12 "admiral ships" that were built between the years 1000 and 1263, all more or less the same size, down to the last one, *Kristsuden*, a 37-seater. The king sagas are full of fine phrases for their elegance: "O King, thou canst sail a ship on the stormy seas, and live for a long time under its water-sprayed tent. *Visunden* shall carry thee, majestic friend, like a keen hawk on the quarterdeck. Ne'er did a more beautiful ship sail with a more magnificent king."

The sagas, however, give us little information as to its construction, unless we resort to Harald Hardruler's dissatisfaction with his ship, and his demand that it be nearly 20 feet longer. The criticism is at least honest: "*Mariasuden* was not a beautiful ship. In prow and stern everything was smaller than amidships."

For ocean voyages or a heavy cargo, these ships of state were unsuitable; nor were they of any use in sea battles. Here the 20- and 25-seaters were preferred. They were faster, easier to maneuver, and more durable.

Battles were never fought on the open sea. For that the Viking ship lay too lightly on the water. A sheltered bay was found for the conflict; the point being to maneuver one's ships into a favorable position, "to take the wind out of the sails" of one's enemy and encircle him in closed formation. That was why all decisive strategy fell to the helmsman. He was the admiral. Olaf Trygvasson himself stood at the helm of his *Long Snake,* trying to make the best of his hopeless position.

The Viking ships demanded a high degree of navigation. They were obedient instruments in their element. Coastal dwellers, sailors and seafaring peoples were justified in doing honor to these masterworks. They are the glorious trade mark of the seafaring Nordic world; their equal has never been found.

9

"And the Men Spoke
of How Commanding
the Woman Was."

THE SUITOR came back, unsuccessful. The father had said, "No." Was it because he didn't want to give his daughter to a man who was already married? Or did he object to the suitor's arrogance, which was notorious? We find out nothing about such personal motives. The suitor was King Gudröd the Magnificent of Vestfold, mentioned in the previous chapter. Didn't he think a good deal more of himself than of the other petty kings in Norway? Was he going to let an insignificant regent in the neighboring land of Agder behave like this to him? He was not. Snorri writes:

"He set out for Agder with a large army. He arrived unexpectedly and landed there. At night he drew up his forces before King Harald's homestead. When the latter became aware that an army stood outside ready to attack, he went out against them with his men, but the difference in their forces was great. Harald was killed, and Gyrd, his son."

But Gudröd continued to use force to press his suit. He overpowered the girl and made her marry him, the arrogant one, now doubly hated. This was Asa, the queen with whose ship grave in Öseberg we became familiar in the last chapter. Literally overnight, she was abducted from the sanctuary of her home, bereft of parental protection, bound to a man of whom her father had spoken only in derogatory terms. Gudröd had ruthlessly murdered her closest relatives, reviled her clan and weakened it—how was she to endure life at his side? How could she be expected to respect and love him? Was there no way but to endure this hateful marriage and share bed and board with him?

105. *Hild the avenger, between her husband Hedin, and her father, the Viking sea king Hogni.* (TOP) *Picture stone from Gotland.* (CENTER) *Picture stone from Lärbrö Hammars.* (BOTTOM) *Cloth fragment from Östfold.*

106. *The "triangle" drama on the Öseberg cart.*

Suddenly Asa had matured from sheltered girl to Queen of Vestfold. She was expecting his child. A year after her son's birth, her pride turned against Gudröd:

"There was a big drinking feast and the king was drunk." In the darkness on his ship, "A man came up to him and ran his spear through Gudröd. That was how he died. The man was a servant of Queen Asa. She did not deny having ordered the deed." Tjodolf says:

> Lusting for vengeance   wife craftily prepares
> For her drunken lord   perilous ambush.

After which Asa ruled alone in Vestfold until her stepson Olaf Geirstader and her son Halfdan the Black were grown and divided the land between them.

Can these dramatic human conflicts be corroborated in any archeological finds? Indeed they can. The Vikings, who took passionate part in all human strife, must have had full understanding of Asa's action. But it would not have been suitable for someone who had weakened the Vestfold clan to be buried in that clan's cemetery. That is why Asa does not lie on Borre itself but 6 miles away, next to her royal court in Öseberg.

Poet and historian have depicted for us in sharp outlines the sudden death of her father and brother, her unhappy marriage, and the vengeance she took. Let us also have a look at the pictures on the curiously splendid cart in her grave. Between the snakelike animals on the one side, a man brandishing a sword is being attacked by a rider. The exceptional thing about it is that a woman stands behind them, not holding the swordsman back, but egging him on. The event reminds us of Queen Asa's fate as a woman in the drama between her father and husband. The Vikings liked allusions such as these, but only a heroic saga could be immortalized pictorially.

If we turn to sagas, we are reminded of Hild, the avenger, who stood between her husband, Hedin, and her father, Hogni, who had arrived by ship. Because she had been abducted and raped, she demanded battle and revenge. She appears like this in four Nordic pictorial scenes. On the Öseberg cart, however, the avenger arrives on horseback. Since, in those days, pictorial art was very precise in its formulation, we do better to draw on the Nibelung legend for an interpretation of the pictures on the cart. In this legend, Gudrun stands between two hate-filled men, Atli and Hogni. Queen Asa must have studied the old Nordic heroic lays and recognized her own fate in these tragic figures. (*See ills. 105, 106.*)

Shortly after 850, Asa died, a lonely queen-widow, whose household was dissolved after her death. In her grave—as already mentioned—we found exceptionally splendid artifacts of a caliber rarely seen. They prove that she was

107. *Queen Asa's sleigh, as it was found in Öseberg.*

an energetic, art-loving woman with a luxurious court. As a reigning monarch she had herself buried in a ship, like the woman on Oronsay, in the Hebrides, whose name we don't know. But Asa was also given three richly carved sleighs and a baggage sled for winter travel. (*See ills. 107, 108.*) Her clumsy cart is unique. In spite of its splendid carving, it could not have made the summer trips on bumpy roads much pleasure. For the most part people rode horseback.

108. *Queen Asa's sleigh, after restoration.*

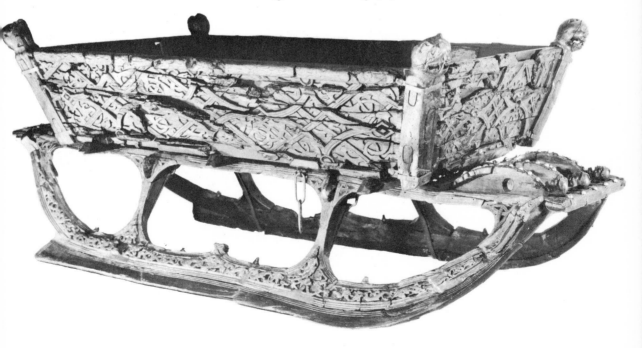

109. *Household objects found in Queen Asa's ship burial: a lamp, a wooden plate, a pestle, a wooden iron, a chair, a bed, a small trough, a chest.*

A saddle, and the metal fittings of reins were also found, a few of them Irish imports. It looks as if all the stable animals—thirteen horses and six dogs— had been slaughtered.

On a long journey—and who could tell how long the journey into the here-after was going to be?—one sometimes had to rest. On Asa's ship two tents could be raised, the largest having almost 19½ by 16½ feet of floor space, and a beautiful dragon gable. Much more than the usual necessary tent equip-ment was packed aboard, a lot of furniture in fact and many implements from the royal court. (*See ill. 109.*) Three beds, one of them magnificently built as befitted a monarch, with down cushions and costly materials; a chair, three chests, a standing whale-oil lamp of iron, a brass-bound wooden bucket that could hold more than 133 quarts, and a more simple one, the handle of which

110. *Carts and horses. Woven design from Öseberg.*

was fastened to crouching figures in enamel inlay. Both pieces were from Ireland and are not unique among the Norse booty or merchandise from the West.

Equipment for an entire kitchen was dragged aboard Asa's ship: an iron caldron with stand and chain, a skillet, a few wooden troughs, ladles, plates, bowls, vats, kitchen hatchet, carving knife, millstones, a young ox and an ox's head. Some wheat and oats were still preserved, cress, wild apples, hazel nuts, and—surprisingly—a walnut. It couldn't possibly have ripened in Scandinavia; the Nordic summer is too cool and short. Like the peacock on the Gokstad ship, it must have been brought north by traders or voyaging Vikings.

A woman's homemaking energies were naturally well provided for: four standing looms, spools, distaff, linen roll, stool, wooden pressing iron, scissors, sewing awl, whetstone, boxes, basins and many other articles; also the requisite raw materials—linen, hemp and woad dye. Woven cloth and fabric were packed in bales, unfortunately so crushed and damaged that our hopes of salvaging the enchanting pictorial designs on them today—half a century after the find—are dwindling. We have pieced together fragments showing festive pageantry on wall hangings, with which the royal hall was decorated on feast days—warriors, women, riders, wagoners, ships, tents, worshipers—all torn out of continuity, yet incredibly intriguing in their mobility. (*See ill. 110.*) We have reconstructed innumerable geometric patterns, timeless motifs of the loom in a clearly Viking epoch style. (*See ills. 111, 112.*) There is also quite a lot of silk—in narrow strips, as in Birka—but with the colors well preserved. We can only hope that more will be salvaged for posterity than the publications offered to date have to report.

The bones of the queen were badly damaged when robbers tore her jewelry from her. Not even the shape of the skull can be reconstructed. The teeth tell us most. They are free of decay and were kept thoroughly clean with toothpicks. Signs of erosion at the top of the tooth betray this. The lower jaw is gracefully constructed, and the masticating areas are not very worn. Anthropologists evaluate her age as between thirty and forty, but historic data comes closer to fifty.

And—a special surprise—also found were the bones of a second person, an old woman with definitely foreshortened skull, with rheumatism and a back stiffened by many years of hard physical labor. She was not a queen. We haven't a moment's doubt about who she was—a slave who was strangled so that she might follow her lady; probably the Queen's most faithful old retainer at court, she remained in the service of her queen even after death.

We are reminded of Ibn Fadlan's dead chieftain on the Volga, with his strangled slave, and of Siegfried's burial in *The Short Lay of Sigurd* (his name in the Icelandic *Edda*):

111. *Woven cloth from Öseberg.*

For he is followed (into his grave)   by five handmaidens
And eight attendants   of noble kin,
His companions   from his father's estate.

Such numbers are undoubtedly poetic exaggerations.

In the Öseberg grave, little was done to provide for the cultivation of land. Eighteen spades were found, but they were quite evidently lost by the men who were raising the mound. The same can probably be said of the pitchfork and barrows. As a noblewoman, Asa was to concern herself only with household tasks, and her slave could resume her work, which had been temporarily interrupted by death: baking, cooking, spinning, weaving, cleaning. When we compare the luxury of Asa's court with the written inventory of Queen Blanche of France in 1365, the latter is poor in comparison. From the grave of Queen Asa, we gain valuable insight into the high living standard of the upper classes in Viking days, and can find this corroborated in other ways.

112. *Woven cloth from Öseberg.*

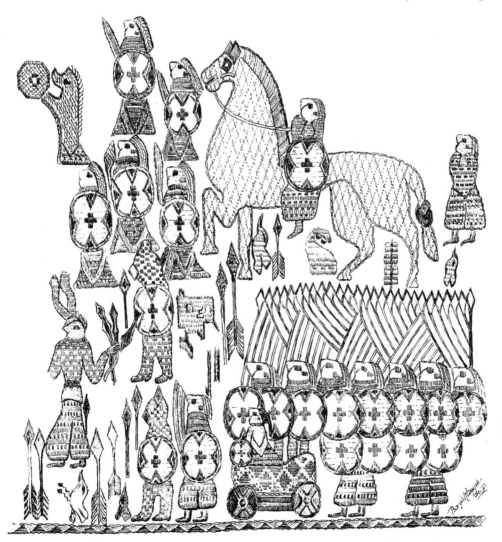

Among the *Edda* lays, there is an especially charming one in which princely customs are depicted. In *The Lay of Rig,* that god wanders on the earth:

With his staff, Rig strode   steadfastly onward;
A hall he saw   was southward the door,
The portal was wide,   with a ring in the doorpost.

He strode in straightway   the floor was strewn.
Sat there the spouses,   gazed at each other,
Father and Mother,   their fingers moving.

The master sat   a bowstring twining;
Made taut the bow   shafted the arrows;
Whilst his good wife   toyed with her dress,
Stroked the cloth   straightened the sleeves

Wise counsel then   gave to them Rig.
Now he was sitting   in middle of bench
'Twixt the twain of   the spouses he benched himself.

A broidered cloth   of fine bleached linen
Did Mother take   covered the table.
Loaves of thin bread   light, made of wheat
She then carried in   laid them down on the cloth.

Then she brought trenchers   filled to the brim,
Plated with silver   put them on the table,
Meat well browned   and fully cooked birds.
There was wine in a crock   bright were the goblets.
They drank and chatted.   Thus passed the day.

Queen Asa probably lived in similar style. A table set festively with a linen cloth; thin, light wheat bread; meat and wine plentiful. Her personal silver was unfortunately stolen. At table, one conversed at length and cleaned one's teeth with toothpicks. The god shared the nocturnal marital bed:

Wise counsel then   gave to them Rig.
Rose to his feet   ready for bed.
In the middle of bedstead   his berth he made,
'Twixt the twain   of the spouses he laid himself.

And there he stayed   three days altogether;
Then walked unwearied   in Middleways.*

Full nine months   meanwhile went by.
A son bore Mother   in silk she swathed him,
Sprinkled water on him   and called him Jarl [Earl].
His hair was flaxen   and fair-hued his cheek,
Sharp were his eyes   like those of a snake.

Jarl's exploits are recounted and praised: he wore a buckler, carved bows, hunted with hounds, wielded a lance, sat well in the saddle, brandished his sword, swam in the sea, interpreted runes, married, sired sons, among them a young king who went and did likewise.

But before that, Rig had paid a very different call, and it gives the verses that follow a special flavor:

To a dwelling he came   the door was bolted.
In he went   on the ground was fire,
At the hearth, hoary   sat husband and wife,
Ai and Edda,   in an old bonnet. . . .

Coarse bread   brought to them Edda,
Thick and heavy   and full of husks.
Brought on the repast   put it on the table.
In the middle of board   in the bowl was broth.

Here the one-pot dinner is *en vogue.* The bread we know from two separate Swedish finds of blackened bread that were examined microscopically. The one was of coarsely ground barley flour mixed with a lot of grit or stone dust from a hand mortar. The other consisted of coarsely ground dried peas, pine bark and also a lot of grit. Both were in all probability baked in hot ashes. In times of famine, the Scandinavians mixed the inner layer of pine bark with their dough, and actually it does contain a lot of vitamin C and therefore protects from scurvy, but is "so bitter and indigestible that, for those who have not eaten bark since childhood, it is almost inedible." The short Nordic summer, and the cultivation of all acreage year after year with the same mixture of grain resulted in the end in barley being raised almost exclusively in the North. Day after day, the barley was ground in primitive hand mills or mortars, and since it is practically impossible to get dough made of barley flour to rise without leavening, the unleavened daily bread had to be eaten at once, when hot; otherwise it became hard as a stone. In the barren North we have a history

* *Mitgarth,* which may mean "on this earth," or "the world of men."

of extreme poverty that lasted until 1870, which is why we are so well versed in these pitiful food customs.

And what were these people like to whom Rig had come? He stayed three nights with them, and nine months later came the answer:

> A swarthy boy   was born to Edda.
> She sprinkled water on him   called him Träl (Slave)
> Black were his nails   his face was ugly
> Gnarled were his joints   crooked his back,
> Thick were his fingers   and his feet were long.

Träl meets a girl, but there is no mention of marriage.

> They chattered and whispered   the livelong day,
> Boy and wench   and lay together. . . .
> Content in their hut   they had a brood.

> The boys were called: Cattle-boy, Blusterer,
> Lout, Hunchback,   Concubine-keeper, Sluggard,
> Clod, Knockknees,   Squarehead, Brat,
> Horse-fly, Paunchy.   They laid fences,
> Herded the goats,   dug for peat. . . .

> The daughters were called: Clumsy-girl, Fat-One,
> Spindly-legs,   Kitchen-maid,
> Slattern   and Fat-legs,
> Servant-girl, Hasty,   and Beanpole.
> From them are sprung   the class of thralls.

The scald had a lot of fun with the names and the drastic exaggerations, and with them aptly portrayed the miserable milieu of the lowest social group of which we find no trace in the archeological heritage of antiquity. Asa's *trälinna* and the female slaves who were bartered happily in Viking days led a very different life from these poor wretches in their cottages, who enjoyed no rights whatsoever. Only very rarely was it possible for them to work their way up out of thralldom; most of them had to resign themselves to their fate. A life with no rights to a grave mound or a life after death was bitter enough, but they had no civil rights in their lifetime, no clan, no officially recognized family ties, no protection against manslaughter or murder. They lacked the pride and self-respect with which the life of a free Viking was so strongly impregnated.

The third house visited by Rig looked like this:

> To a dwelling he came   the door was ajar.
> In he went,   on the ground was a fire,
> At their work busy   sat husband and wife.
>
> A weaver's beam   out of wood he was shaping,
> His shirt was tight-fitting,   o'er his brow was a lock,
> Trimmed was his beard   on the floor stood a chest.
>
> At her work weaving   sat the woman.
> She turned the distaff   stretched wide her arms
> Ati and Amma owned this house.

For Rig there was a veal roast, but it is very annoying to find the line about the bread missing. What could we expect? Certainly not dark leavened rye bread, because it wasn't introduced in Scandinavia until the Middle Ages, and then from Mecklenburg and Pomerania. The cultivation of rye remained a risky undertaking for a long time, and was tried only on the big east Swedish feudal farms. In the West and North, oats and barley were adhered to doggedly until, in the nineteenth century, a hard thin bread was baked of rye which kept well. This is the modest predecessor of today's *knäcke*bread, which has achieved world-wide popularity; in the United States under the trade name "Rye Krisps." Such thin bread, to be used either oven fresh and soft, or well stored and hard, must have been baked on hundreds of the baking pans we have found in Viking graves, also in Queen Asa's kitchen; it is baked in peasant ovens to this day. This is probably the bread that was described in the missing line. In our museums we have about sixty preserved fragments of bread that go back to Viking days. For lack of funds they have not yet been chemically analyzed, but they could broaden our agricultural and culinary knowledge of those days considerably.

With this third couple Rig also exerted his godly right to three nights:

> Amma gave birth to a child   swathed it in linen
> Sprinkled it with water   called the boy Karl,
> The fresh, the rosy one.   He opened his eyes
> Began to grow   also to thrive.
> He tempered plough-shares   built barns,
> Tamed oxen   raised houses,
> Fashioned carts   guided the plough.
>
> They brought home   a bride for Karl,
> In goatskin dressed,   keys at her waist.

Her name was Snoer [daughter-in-law]   she wore the veil
They lived as man and wife   and exchanged rings.
They lay in linen   and built a house.

Their sons were called Fair-of-face, Freeholder, Smith, Husbandman, Farmer, Crofter, Steep-beard, Broad-shoulders, Bound-beard, Swain, Dirk, Man. And the daughters: Maiden, Bride, Sprightly, Girl, Proud-one, Dame, Woman, Daughter, Capable and Chaste.

From these came   the class of freeholders.

This lay, known as the *Rigdula,* is particularly illuminating in its three repeats that illustrate the three social classes of the Viking era as personified in the short names: Träl, Karl and Jarl.

No poet or scald functions entirely without inspiration. There are stories from the Christian Middle Ages about Noah and his sons, in which we can read: "From Japhet come the knights, from Shem the lesser freeman, from Ham those who are not free." The scald who gave us the *Rigdula* may have picked up a story like this—which is neither here nor there. Essential is the freshness with which he sees the three folk classes and places them in apposition to each other. Among the freeholders there was a great deal of interclass gradation. One could own a lot of land or be reduced to almost complete poverty and still retain one's status as a free man. We have come across professional traders, smiths, trappers, wood carvers, ship builders and other specialists. In the *Rigdula* we miss the warring Viking, but we must bear in mind that daring men were recruited from every social strata. The fact remains that for a long time the North was almost purely peasant and farming land.

Everything that grew and thrived on the farm was of value—cattle and grain, slaves to work the land, sons to inherit it, and daughters to provide the possibility for a more widely ramified kinship with other families. In those days this meant incomparably more than it does today, since the state consisted of nothing but clans. Blood ties were sacred, imposed obligations, were appealed to. And marriage was the only way of widening the clan and renewing it. That was why the marriage of a daughter was such an important and decisive event, connected with lavish gifts, and a dowry that was decided on with peasant shrewdness.

We read for instance in the Njals Saga of proud Hallgärd: "Hallgärd was very beautiful and grand of stature; that was why she was called Longlegs. Her hair was thick, and so long that she could wrap herself in it. She was extravagant and defiant."

A man called Thorvald wanted to marry her, and set out with his father to make the arrangements with her family. They were well received, and at once began to discuss their business. Hallgärd's father, Höskuld, told them, "Your circumstances are known to me, but I must not keep from you the fact that my daughter is a stubborn creature. Her appearance and her arrogant manner you can see for yourselves."

Thorvald replied, "Name your terms, for her nature is not going to keep me from my intention."

After this they discussed the terms, but Höskuld didn't consult his daughter; and Hallgärd became enraged. "Now I know what I have dreaded for a long time—that you do not love me as you have always professed, since you didn't even consider it worth the trouble to discuss this matter with me. What is more, I don't see this marriage as something as grand as you promised me."

To which Höskuld replied, "I don't pay so much attention to your arrogance that I would let it stand in the way of my business. I give the orders, not you, whenever we happen to be of different opinion." This patriarchal attitude prevailed in the North until the first World War.

Young people would have liked to know each other before they married, perhaps love each other, but in the day of the Viking, this was not considered desirable, since the girl's virginity was supposed to be unquestionable. The main thing was to be married according to rank. The marriage had to be useful to the father of the bride; let love come later. That was the couple's private business and concerned no one else.

Today we hold different views. Love is the decisive factor. But our times seem to be no happier for it. Perhaps we should see with less prejudiced eyes how the Vikings managed their arranged marriages; how man and wife lived together in those days.

Love was rarely mentioned. Love songs were punishable, and the law was strictly enforced. It was probably considered unwise to publicize a woman's emotions in such a way. Not even her beauty was lauded unless it was a source of misfortune or threatening danger. The sober Nordic peasants valued energy, wealth and lineage. With these attributes, a good marriage was assured. When Gisle Sursson's brother died, he asked for his sister-in-law, Ingeborg's, hand in marriage, since "he did not want to see such a good woman leave the clan." This is a typical attitude. Widows were masters of their own fortunes and future life. Ingeborg said yes, and through her Gisle Sursson "gained many possessions and became a respected man." The social position of the husband could also be influenced by that of his wife.

In the *Lay of Rig,* a bridal veil is mentioned, but more detailed is the prank through which the god Thor got back his hammer which the *thurses* or giants had stolen. For its return they demanded the goddess Freya as wife for their king, Thrym. Freya didn't like the idea, so bearded, blustering red-blond Thor was dressed up as a bride.

> They arrayed Thor   in bridal veil,
> And with the ornate   Brising's necklace.
> Let housewife's keys   from his waist dangle,
> A woman's kirtle   fall to his knees.
> Wound many large beads   on his breast,
> And a pretty cap   to crown his head.

Charley's Aunt a thousand years ago! Thor's voracious appetite is just as farcically dealt with:

> An ox he ate   also eight salmon,
> And all the dainties   spread for the women.
> And then Sif's mate [Thor]   drank three tuns of mead.

> Then said Thrym   the thurses' king,
> "Didst e'er see bride   could sharper bite?
> Ne'er saw I woman   so frightfully eat,
> Nor maiden drinking   so much mead."

> Fleet answer came   to giant's speech,
> "Naught ate Freya   for eight full nights.
> So eager she   to see Thrym's halls."

After a few more such japes, comes the apotheosis of the ceremony:

> Then said Thrym   the thurses' king,
> "Bring the hammer   the bride to bless.
> Lay Mjölnir   in the maiden's lap.
> With the hand of Vor [a goddess]   our wedlock hallow."

We see the marriage consecrated by a hammer ritual. We can read elsewhere that the first wedding toast was drunk to Thor, and the bridal bed was called the "Hammer-bed." In a great many parts of Scandinavia, it was still the custom, as late as the last century, to hide a hammer, preferably a large sledge hammer, in the bridal bed. This was a traditional prank that quite obviously originated in pagan times.

And it gives the witty solution, the humorous victory, over the stupid giants:

> His heart within him   laughed the god Thor,
> The stern one,   when saw he the hammer.
> First he smote Thrym   the thurses' king,
> Then he slew all   the race of giants.

Wedding ceremonies were simple; the feasts, however, were opulent and lasted several days. The maiden was transformed into housewife with keys dangling from her waist, and adorned, according to the *Lay of Rig:*

> With a band on her head   clasps on her shoulders,
> Around her neck a kerchief,   on her breast a yoke.

Jarl's mother was more elaborately clad:

> Ornate was her bonnet,   around her neck gold;
> Long was her train   dark blue her kirtle.

We are familiar with all the articles from our grave findings: the household keys that dangled to the knee, the oval brooches worn on the shoulder, gold and pearls on the breast, kirtle (robe), train, kerchief, headdress and bonnet.

From these descriptions and information the Viking woman emerges invested with a natural authority such as we find nowhere else in Europe. After the wedding she remained a member of her patriarchal clan; in this her social value was centered, a fact she never lost sight of. It was she, through her marriage, who helped not only her husband but also her father to greater recognition, new relatives, a broader circle of friends. To take the husband's name was something Nordic women didn't do until the eighteenth century; to be subject to their husbands was absolutely foreign to them. Through the Bible, the low Oriental evaluation of women may have reached Europe, but in the North there was evidently no reason for giving up a healthy state of affairs with the advent of a new religion. In this respect, the Viking heritage was preserved in Scandinavia, which is why the Nordic women had an impressive headstart when it came to the general emancipation of women in the twentieth century.

The Vikings lived wholly in accordance with their natural feelings. In this lay their strength. This holds good also for the life of the sexes together. The woman was by nature exempt from armed warfare; the men fought for her.

This, however, did not prevent her from taking up arms herself, usually in self-defense, though sometimes in a spirit of revenge, and also in times of war. The *Edda* is full of such warring maidens and Amazons: Sigrun, Svavo, Brynhil, Hervor, and all the other Valkyries. Among the Viking chieftains there was a "Red Maiden," who laid waste to Ulster and northeastern Ireland, and was the leader of a whole host of men. Since she seems to have been a man-woman, the numerous military expeditions of her day must have offered manifold possibilities to live according to her dual nature. We find quite a few such "red maidens" nowadays.

However, bloody feuds, wars, and *thing* assemblies were on the whole considered the concern of the male; it was up to him to resolve all unwomanly conflicts and protect his home; the female had a right to be free of such obligations. Yet living, for male or female, demanded a strong, independent personality and women often found themselves saddled with fates that demanded responsibility.

After settling on a new island, the women as well as the men could claim land for themselves; for this there was a special law. And women, of course, also had rune stones raised. A woman in Denmark called Ragnhild was apparently married twice, and had stones raised for both husbands: one "For Alle, the Pale-one, chieftain in Herd"; the other "for Gunulv, her husband, the good orator Närve's son." She was evidently married each time to an important and respected man. Or let us pick out of many examples a runic inscription from Ramsta, in Södermanland: "Auda and Inga and Erindis, the third, are eager to raise this memorial for Sven, their father, and for Gudfast, their brother. He was Auda's son."

It took forcefulness to run a farm in those restless days, whether as widow or when one's husband was on a voyage. Those women who knew how to settle the tribal hatreds their men had inflamed are praised in sagas. It could even happen that a wife hastily convened all the women on the farm. Two men might have started a bitter fight, and the women would cast their hastily gathered clothing between the drawn swords, turning the fight into something so ridiculous, it couldn't be fought.

When the Norse women voluntarily throw the full weight of their personality into the affairs of the men, they seem most sympathetic. Over and over again they cleverly manage to dissipate the hostility around them, and are given the short expression of gratitude that says so much more than a long speech. Thorborg saves Grette, the Restless-one's life, and Thorborg's husband, Vermund, says afterwards, "In many respects you are a clever woman. Thank you for what you have done."

There were women, of course, who were full of hatred and arrogance. The aforementioned Hallgärd was aflame with such wild feelings of vengeance against Bergthora, who was just as malicious as she, that the Njals Saga is full of the most dreadful events concerning them. It opens with the simple formula: "If you kill my slave, I'll kill yours." One day Hallgärd's third husband, Gunnar, boxes her ears. Later, when he is surrounded by enemies and needs a new sinew for his bow, he says to Hallgärd, "Give me two locks of your hair and braid them together for a sinew for my bow."

"Is it important?" she asks.

"My life depends on it," says he, "for they cannot subdue me as long as I can use a bow."

"Then I shall remind you of the box on the ears you gave me, and I don't care whether you can defend yourself for a short or a long time."

Gunnar defended himself for a long time, but in the end, he was killed.

Such intriguing, vengeful women are excellently suited for keeping the plot of a saga moving. Lady Macbeth would have been green with jealousy of them, although they are cut from the same cloth, for only Celtic and Nordic poetry is concerned at length with such titanic types, poisoned to the core of their souls.

Immensely talented, every inch a born ruler, is Aud the Deep-minded, whom we already know as the wife of the Norwegian King Olaf the White of Dublin. As a widowed old woman, we no longer find her in Ireland but on the north coast of Scotland, where she is having a trading vessel built:

"When the ship was finished, she got ready to sail, and had a large quantity of money with her. All her kin, all those who were still alive, went with her, and the people scarce knew of another example in which a woman escaped such warlike confusion with so much wealth and so large a suite. By this it may be already seen that she towered high above all other women. . . . She had many men of great ability and noble birth with her . . . and she sailed to the Orkney Islands. There she remained for some time, and married off her grand-daughter, Gro, from whom the entire stock of Orkney earls originates. . . . Then Aud sailed with her ship to the Faroe Islands, and remained there too for some time. Here she married off her second granddaughter, from whom the noblest clans on these islands originate, the so-called Gata men. . . .

"Again Aud readied herself for departure, and made known to her ship's companions that she intended to sail to Iceland. The voyage was good, and she took possession of land from Hvamms Fjord, as far as she desired. Finally she sailed up the innermost part, of the fjord. There her high-seat pillars had been washed ashore, which seemed to be an omen that she should make this place her residence and build her house here."

The seat of honor of a chieftain or freeholder in Viking days was carpentered as part of the house itself. The vertical front legs were continued up to the ceiling—"pillars" therefore—and were richly carved. They were a symbol of the house, and were supposed to have godlike powers. When a new home was to be founded, they were taken along to function as an oracle: at a clairvoyant moment, when land was sighted, they were thrown overboard. Whereever they were washed ashore, the emigrant landed and founded his new homestead.

"Then Aud gave many of the men a share of the land she had acquired. . . . Old age was already burdening her, so that she did not arise before noon and went early to bed. In the evening when she retired and until the time when she was dressed again, she permitted no one to discuss with her anything pertaining to the household. Angrily she replied when anyone asked her how she felt.

"On the wedding day of her youngest grandchild, she slept long, but was up when her guests arrived. She went to meet them and received her relatives with joy and dignity. In the wedding hall she said, 'I give this house with all its furnishings, as you see it before you today, to my grandson Olaf, to own and dispose of as he sees fit.'

"Thereupon Aud rose and said that she would retire to her room in which she was wont to sleep. She begged the guests to amuse themselves, each according to his own liking, and they should enjoy the house brew. They say that Aud was tall and of robust build. She walked quickly through the hall toward the door, and the men spoke among themselves how commanding the woman still was.

"Next morning, Olaf Feilan entered the bedchamber of his grandmother, Aud, and as he entered the room, Aud was sitting up in bed, propped against pillows. She was dead. The men spoke aloud their admiration of how Aud had preserved her dignity to the last. Thus both events were celebrated together: Olaf's wedding and the funeral feast for Aud. On the last day of the feast, Aud was carried to the mound which was to be hers. She was buried in a ship in the mound, and many of her possessions were placed in it with her. Then the hill was closed over her."

Whenever it was a writer's intention to malign the Vikings, he usually made a point of the fact that they practiced polygamy. At the turn of the century, scholars seemed to take malicious pleasure in depicting other "savage" traits such as concubinage and bigamy, without realizing that they were using our Christian morals as a measure for the virtues and vices of the pagan Vikings. In such a way we can never hope to understand alien peoples and past cultures. The Vikings acted in complete accord with their natural human temperament. Their moral norms were the result of experience and practice. A young girl was well sheltered in the house of her parents until she married. A young man was free to do as he pleased, and after marriage was even freer. This may have had practical reasons. A man had to see to an increase of his estate, and this included his slaves. They were a part of his legitimate economic interests. Concubines were customary, but they were always of the lowest social class. A wife could tolerate them because they never endangered her marriage; they went with the mixture of monogamy and polygamy which made up her husband's character. Instead of raising ideals to the heights to which Christianity elevated them—making them, for some men, unattainable—a moral code evolved that was more easily obeyed. We can't really say that the pagans were better or worse than the Christians, but they certainly lived with fewer conflicts of conscience than we do, without neuroses and bitter marital upheavals. At the bottom of this lies, of course, a more natural relationship to life. We hear that Queen Bodil herself adorned the inamorata of her husband, King Eric Ejegod, so that the girl might please him. This demanded the personal fortitude and generosity of mind that went with the independence of Viking women. Adam of Bremen says: "Every man has three or more wives, according to his means. But the rich and the chieftains have numberless wives."

This may have been true, and was probably the result of Arab contacts, Viking experiences in the slave trade, and the friendliness of the women in the occupied territories (fraternization a thousand years ago). In Shannon Bay, near Limerick, the Irish ravaged, in the year 977, "every site where the Normans kept women, children and harems." King Harald Fairhair had an unusually large number of wives. They are listed in the *Heimskringla,* and when he married Ragnhild of Jutland, he divorced nine wives. But these are purely Oriental customs found only in the higher social circles. On the peasant farms, the wife remained sole manager and at best may have tolerated a concubine or two.

In contrast to the *Edda* and the heroic lays, which tend to overdramatize the Valkyries and Brynhilds, we find many sayings that betray healthy, tender and altogether admirable emotions. Let us pay our respects to them. The terse runic inscriptions, with their lifelike freshness, permit us to span the thousand years that lie between us and the people who composed them, and to come almost timelessly close. A clear verdict is spoken by a peasant west of Stockholm (Parish Fläckebo):

"The good peasant Holmgöt had this stone raised for Odindisa, his good wife. She was Gud . . .'s sister.

> Ne'er shall come   to Hasemyra
> Better wife   than Odindisa.
> She was Sigmund's daughter   he who owned the village.
> Röd-Baler carved this rune."

The brief inscription on a rune stone near Ravnkilde in Denmark tells us: "Asser, the overseer, Kugge's son, raised this stone for Asbod, his mistress." (Mistress as the feminine of master.)

An isolated stone in Opedal, Norway, speaks as early as the sixth century of a sad experience. This time the rune stone is raised by a brother: "Birging, rest in peace, my sister, loved by me, Vag."

Among the by no means large number of rune stones that add any personal remarks, we can name two: "Gunvor, Eric's daughter, made this bridge for [in memory of] her daughter, Astrid. She was the most skilful maiden in Hadeland." And the words of a son from Rimsö in Rauder: "Tore, Enraade's brother, raised this stone for his mother and sister, the good women. Their death is the greatest misfortune for their son."

And finally, let us listen to Rämna, after her husband, Kjartan Olavsson had fallen in battle. The saga tells us: "She was seized by a dreadful grief, yet she bore it with great dignity and spoke amiably with everyone. After Kjartan, she did not take another man. And she lived for only a very short time after returning to her home again. Everyone believed that her heart broke with grief."

During their lives, the Vikings accumulated much human wisdom. They took particular interest in conflict wherever it occurred. How each man mastered the harshness of his fate—that was what they liked to see. The poetry concerning their gods frequently surprises us from a psychological viewpoint. They often viewed their gods humorously, even sarcastically, as for instance in the story of the giantess, Skadi, in the *Prose Edda*.

The Norse gods, the Aesirs, had killed her father. "Now Skadi, daughter of the giant Thjazi, put on helmet and byrnie [coat of mail] and other warlike weapons, and came to Asgard, citadel of the gods, to avenge her father. The Aesirs offered her compensation and atonement. First of all she was to choose a husband from among them, and choose him by his feet only, without seeing any more."

It must have been a rare beauty contest. When Skadi caught sight of an exceptionally beautiful pair of men's feet, she said, "I choose this one. In Balder, little can be loathsome." The feet she had chosen, however, did not belong to Balder, the god of light and peace, but to Njord, one of the fertility gods. Skadi got him for a husband, and with him a difficult marriage, in spite of his handsome feet! The legend goes back to an early fertility rite: where a god put his feet, the harvest would be good. In much older eras of antiquity, the soles of feet were depicted in various forms, and Njord is a very old fertility god.

Here a wedding custom that is still practiced today—with the roles reversed —has its roots. The women lie down on the floor barefoot, and are covered with only their legs showing. The young groom has to find his wife among this confusion of legs. If he succeeds, he may repair to the wedding chamber with her; if he doesn't, he has to wait for the following night.

Secondly—the gods had to make Skadi laugh. Loki had the idea of tying one end of a rope around the beard of a goat and the other end to his genitals. Robust humor. "And now the two tugged back and forth, screaming lustily. And Loki let himself fall into Skadi's lap. And then she laughed."

This is the great liberating laughter of spring, thunderous, shameless, or fresh and gay; the laughter that defies death and summons fertility, "with all its might."

And how did the marriage between Skadi and Njord turn out? Alas, she took him with her to the mountains, and he, who had lived on the coast, lamented bitterly:

> Loathsome to me   were the mountains.
> Not long was I there   only nine nights.
> To me the howling   of the wolves seemed ill,
> After the song of the gulls. . . .

So he took Skadi with him to the seashore, where she lamented just as bitterly:

> I could not sleep   at the surf's edge
> For the screeching of birds.   Each morn
> When she came from the sea,   the gull woke me.

Here we have the timeless picture of a married couple who can't agree on anything, whether to live on mountain or at seashore, whether to do a thing thus or so. Behind this episode we can also discern the old fertility ritual of the ever-changing seat of the fertility goddess, whether she is called Skadi, Persephone, Astarte, or Isis. Here, with sure instinct, the poet created, out of old fertility rites and tales, a "human interest" story that is humorous, slightly obscene, psychologically sound and comprehensible. A masterpiece of finely spun Viking storytelling.

10

≈≈≈

The Festivals
of the Vikings

THAT THE TWO solstice festivals are celebrated more intensively in Scandinavia than in southern lands is understandable. In December, when cold and snow finally make their entry and enfold the land, Stockholm and Oslo grow noticeably dark around three in the afternoon, and night lies heavily on the spirit until nine in the morning. Then the Norsemen of all times and ages have longed for light, for a return of the sun and longer days. For a period of twelve days the naked eye can perceive no evidence that the sun has reached its nadir and is rising again. For twelve days it seems to be standing still, as if hesitating to start once more on its yearly course. The Norsemen, who lived in harmony with nature, did the same thing. For twelve days they rested, ceased doing their daily chores, and avoided especially all "rotating" actions. In the peasant household, the eternally revolving flail had to have its work done shortly before midwinter; the grain had to be threshed by then. Cart wheels could stop rolling because the snow lay on the ground, and a sleigh was the more expedient vehicle for travel.

Other revolving activities were the women's—first and foremost, the grinding flour. During the Iron Age, kernels were crushed between a large, immobile stone and a revolving runner. Not until the Middle Ages did relief come in the shape of the water wheel, which did the work in two shifts—spring and autumn. In the interim—that is, in the days of the Vikings—a millstone with the runner turning in a circle was preferred. Such a stone had to turn day and night to create enough flour for a household. In *The Lay of Grotti,* the *Edda* tells us of a gigantic mill at which two maidens toiled constantly:

Now are come　　to the king's hall . . .
Fenja and Menja,　　in bondage to Frothi [the king]. . . .
These sisters robust　　as thralls are held.

He bade them not　　in their labors to lag. . . .
He wanted to hear　　the sound of their toiling . . .

They made an uproar,　　the noisy creatures. . . .
He gave them no rest;　　to grind on he bade them.

They sang as they swung　　the whirling stone;
Till all other maidens　　did fall asleep. . . .

We grind power　　for Frothi;
We grind good fortune;　　we grind his wealth
On the mill　　of good luck.

Distaff and spinning wheel were turning just as busily to make clothing and coverlets. This type of evening work had to be interrupted too. Thus, in every peasant household, all the duties of home, all "turning action" ceased for twelve days. This we can verify historically.

If we want to find out about the festivals of the Vikings, we do best to begin with the present and feel our way cautiously backward. This is difficult, because the opulent Nordic Yule is like a human creature, constantly susceptible to change. New customs creep in without making us want to abandon the old. The Yule nights grow younger with us, yet at the same time remain tradition bound. The Nordic city people happily uphold the customs of the former peasant. They buy their meat in shops now, but the form of a festivity common when pigs were still being stuck in rural households, is preserved. Now as then, a smoked pig's head is handsomely decorated, and an apple is stuck in the mouth. You will find cold ham, for everyone to cut a piece from when he likes. There is blood sausage, head cheese, the best baked goods of the year, prepared according to hundred-year-old recipes. And for twelve days all this stands ever ready in an around-the-clock buffet, a luxurious feast of pure relaxation.

Among customs such as these it is easy to recognize which ones originated in the Nordic peasant household. But how are we to know what belongs to antiquity; how the Vikings celebrated their Yuletide? The written sources are brief, but one word guides us. The Nordic winter solstice feast is called *Jul,* and in scaldic verse we are told that "Jul is celebrated in honor of Freyr." We also have the word *Jul* from the Norsemen in Byzantium, although we have no idea what its original meaning was.

We may be sure though that the Vikings were familiar with a Jul festival. It was dedicated to rest after the work of autumn was done, like so many pagan celebrations, a fertility festival at which everyone drank *"til aar og fred . . . to a good harvest and peace."* We hear of a King Heidrek who had his biggest boar led into his halls at Yuletide. The source is a late one, but we have no reason to doubt that he was honoring the fertility goddess, Freyr, whose boar, Gullinborsti, had such gold-gleaming bristles that the night all around the animal was made bright as day! With his hand resting on his boar, King Heidrek made his vows for the coming year.

In today's festival, there is always a billy goat among the Yule animals. There he stands, made of straw, or lies as a cookie among spice cakes. In former centuries he often brought gifts. Sometimes he was played by two boys under a goatskin with horns, one of Scandinavia's favorite pranks throughout the centuries. In Malmö, 1695, serious efforts were made to forbid "the so-called Yule goat games, and the running around in such disguise, since such a hideous masquerade and the shameless behavior that goes with it, can lead to nothing but nonsense and vexation." Our numerous sources for the custom don't go back further than 1543, but we may be sure that it is much older than that. How could it possibly have originated in the Christian Middle Ages? It dominates the scene so overwhelmingly that it must originally have been a Thor-goat that was allowed to live on in peasant Yule customs, just as did Thor's hammer in the bridal bed. Stripped of their heathen titles, the Christian church could sanction both of them. In such respects the priests were tolerant and practical.

One more animal stands out rather strangely in the Christian Yule—the horse. The second day of Yuletide was acted out entirely under its egis. The stableboys, up early, would saddle the horses, and off everybody went on a wild chase through the woods and across the fields, the horses' bodies streaming, their nostrils flared, through the icy nocturnal hours to a northward flowing spring into which a coin had to be thrown as sacrifice, so that the horses might drink "over silver." Then, in the same wild tempo, back to the farms, and if anyone overslept and missed the ride—God help him! The boys from the other farms shoveled the manure back into his stable and saddled his horse backwards. But the horses that had drunk from the fresh spring water, especially the horse that had drunk first, would thrive in the coming year.

The custom is attributed to St. Stephen:

Staffan, Staffan, stableboy
Waters his horses five.

Otherwise, Stephen, the martyred saint, has very little to do with horses. In Scandinavia, however, he had to jump into the breach and consecrate an otherwise heathen rite, so that it might be carried over into Christianity. In the Middle Ages we find him in church paintings in his special function of "stable-boy."

The *Jul* festival quite obviously celebrated fertility and *light*. Now there is a great difference between celebrating the solstice on the darkest *day* of the year or in the darkest *night*. For if there is a full moon on December 25, then the greatest darkness falls two weeks earlier or later. People who did not yet have any exact measurement for the length of a year counted off the winter months by the full moons and set the solstice or "sun" festival—by the moon! In Norway's shady mountain valleys, and in Iceland, so close to the Arctic Circle, the first rays of a reappearing sun must have been a decisive sign; that is why a winter—and light—festival in the middle of January have been handed down to us. The first Christians in the Mediterranean didn't know at what time of the year the Savior was actually born; they fixed their calendar according to the spring equinox, and placed the birth nine months after the annunciation, which brought Christmas so close to the pagan Yuletide of the North that it could be incorporated in the latter celebrations.

But for the Vikings it was above all a huge *family* festival, family alive and dead. Today only a small remnant of this traditional inclusion of the dead remains in a toast to "absent friends," All Souls and All Saints Day having taken over this aspect of the festival. But in the days of antiquity, a magnificent Yule table was set up for deceased relatives. A steam bath was readied for them, beds were freshly made, and the peasants slept on straw pallets on the floor so that those "from outside" could use the best rooms, take delight in all the luxuries, warm and satiate themselves. For they came out of the mounds, naturally, covered with earth or, if they had died at sea, wet and dripping. They sat with the living evening after evening, for as long as the feast lasted. We hear most often of exceptional cases, when the departed sat quietly presaging misfortune, dried their clothes by the fire and went back to their graves without having said a word. The Christian church turned sharply against this pagan form of communal life, but did not succeed in exterminating it entirely. All they could do was banish it into the realm of superstition and a reprehensible belief in ghosts. For centuries a long line of spirits and elves, trolls and ancestors, filed past during the Yule and Christmas feasts. The little farm goblin with beard and red cap grew, not quite a hundred years ago, into today's present-giving Father Christmas or Santa Claus. Thus Christian, Roman, peasant and pagan customs are interwoven to give us our twentieth-century modern, much too opulent Christmas season. But the heathen *Jul,* as we have shown, was devoted to fertility, the winter solstice and the clan. And we can differentiate quite clearly among these three functions.

The light and magical night of the other—the summer—solstice, resulted in a festival of purely Nordic character. Folklore tells us that at this time of year a bouquet made of nine different, gently scented field flowers, laid under the pillow of a young girl, would cause her to dream of her future husband. The dew that fell that night was heavenly yeast for the finest bread. Only now did the fern have huge red blossoms. To find it and not tell a soul meant a big wish fulfilled. On this night too, the grave mounds rose and stood supported on gold pillars. Their inhabitants moved freely among elves, pixies, and human beings. The magic stuff for legends about this wonderful night is endless, and it is almost impossible to separate old and new. But the essential nature of this folk romanticism is pagan, primitive and deeply in unison with nature.

How can we possibly know how far back the Maypole decorated with fresh green would take us? In Germany and America it is put up on May 1, but the Scandinavians can't very well be expected to inaugurate a "May Day" in their villages when bush and tree are still bare. In the North, the Maypole is a midsummer pole, decorated with fat garlands and wreaths, sometimes as *Maj,* in the shape of a woman; on the west coast it is rigged like a mast. In the seventeenth century the pole was often forbidden because the young people used it as an excuse for wild and highly unsuitable sport; in the nineteenth century it was also often repudiated in puritanical sternness. Today it is again beloved; you will find it wherever you go. The green branch, the green pole, the growing thing brought home, is older than all our written sources, and in some form or other was surely worshiped by the Vikings.

The summer nights in southern Europe, never as light as those in the North, did not lend themselves so well to festivity, which is why Christianity on the Mediterranean celebrates the summer solstice casually. The influence of the Church on the North remained negligible; written sources concerning Viking days are scanty. Only through later customs can we feel our way back into the past and establish that the midsummer solstice festival was also anchored firmly in the Nordic peasant household. At the end of June, all spring planting was concluded; the quiet weeks between sowing and harvest began. It was a time for healthy vacations, for hours of relaxation, for sunshine and recuperation for the farmer and his hired help. Like the winter solstice, it was dictated not by the regulation of civil law but by a natural rhythm.

And what about Easter, which, in pre-Christian Viking days must have been a great resurrection feast of fertility? We have already told of Njord and Skadi, their changes of residence, the soles of Njord's feet as a symbol of fertility, and Skadi's laughter, the laughter of spring which dispels death. Njord and Skadi, Freyr and Freya, Freyr and Gard, Balder and Nanna, Ull and Nerthus were the names of the Nordic god couples who were symbolic of love and fruitfulness in springtime. The *Edda* tells of them. We sense the age-old rituals, but we feel that the Vikings didn't practice them, since they heard about them mainly as amusing frolics.

One of our later written sources reports another prank very realistically. It was a Swedish custom to wheel a wooden statue of Freyr around in a cart. Gunnar Helming, a jolly and gregarious refugee from Norway, got into the cart one day as it was passing through a lonely spot, wrestled with the wooden god, conquered him, and took his place, even putting on the god's jewelry. He was only too happy to do this because the high priestess was young and beautiful. It made a great impression on the people of Old Uppsala to see the god Freyr eating and drinking so merrily. To be sure, this time he didn't want the usual slaughtered sacrifice, but asked for gold, silver, fine cloth and other luxury items. The enthusiasm of the people knew no bounds when they saw that the high priestess was expecting a godly son. In the end, though, Gunnar found it advisable to make a swift getaway by night, taking with him the best of the sacrificial offerings and the pretty priestess. When the Swedes saw that they had been duped, they went after Gunnar, but were unable to find him.

A festive processional that may be established with a degree of certainty is the lustration around the fruitful fields some time between the spring equinox and midsummer, later fixed on the anniversary of St. Eric's death. On the eighteenth of May, the casket containing his bones was borne in a long procession between Old Uppsala and Uppsala; reliquaries and banners were waved over field and churches, "to consecrate the harvest of the earth." Similar rogations took place in Denmark, in Norway with St. Olaf as patron saint, and in Finland with St. Martin. In Oravais, in the Finlandian Österbotten which borders on Sweden, we find written before 1852: "They took his statue from the church and carried it in festive procession around the ploughed fields. Mass and litany were chanted. This was practiced every year and was a required ritual. The saints were to intercede for blessed and beneficial weather and the grace of a rich harvest."

The "Rogation Days," as held in Sweden until 1772, coincide with the south German processionals. Among the latter, the spectacular *Blutritt* of Weingarten, during which a drop of the blood of Christ is carried across the fields, is the most famous. These processions replaced the age-old Celtic-Germanic lustrations around the crops, perpetuating them in Christian form. Numerous documents attest to this, among them one from Cloister Schildesche, Westphalia, 939:

"We ordain that every year, on the second day of Whitsuntide, with the grace of the Holy Ghost, ye shall bear the patron saint of your cloister church in a long procession, through your parochial district; that ye shall clean your houses, and that—*instead of the pagan lustrations of the fields*—ye shall make atonement with tears and in all humility, and collect alms for the poor. Ye shall spend the night in the cloister courtyard and stand festive watch over the reliquaries, and sing hymns. . . . This processional will cause the seed of the fields to grow more abundantly, and the harshness of the weather to be subdued." The original, primitive pagan ritual—which we may certainly also trace to the Vikings—shines through in every detail. Here a sharply defined custom has been preserved unchanged far better than many more important festivals.

For autumn we have only a few not very clearly defined festivals that can bear any sort of comparison with the important rites of spring. Among them we may count the so-called horse festival at the end of August. Today its equivalent—at least as far as timing is concerned—is the annual autumnal horse shows. Predominant in Viking days were the stallion fights, of which we hear much in the sagas. The Viga-Glums Saga tells us:

"In the following summer, a stallion fight was organized in which all the stallions of the area were to face each other. Those of the upper district were to confront those of the lower district. . . . There were many stallions, everybody had a good time, and the contests were fairly even. Many stallion fights took place on this day. In the end it came about that an equal number of stallions had bitten well on both sides, and an equal number had run away. It was therefore decided that the contest had been even."

More often than not the horse contests resulted in hot altercations, since the men were all too ready to take part physically in the fighting.

"Eyjolf was against it and struck the horse, but his stick rebounded and smote Bjarni on the shoulder." Or, "At the same moment, Thord lashed out with his horse-stick and smote one of Thorstein's eyebrows, so that it hung down over his eye. Thorstein took a piece of his shirt and bound his eyebrow up again."

Horse fighting was still popular as late as the beginning of the last century, when the recording of old folk ritual began. Localities such as Hästskede and Skedevi have made a name for themselves throughout Scandinavia as areas where such contests used to take place.

The Vikings felt just as much affinity for their horses as for their ships. The horse was not only a fast, reliable animal and personal friend—it was more than that—it embodied the power of the gods. Wodan's eight-footed warhorse could tear like the wind across the earth and through the air and is always mentioned when any noteworthy ride is to be undertaken. The fertility god Freyr also owned sacred horses, called Freyfaxes, on which no human might ride. Coarse, primitive phallic rites of growth and prosperity revolved around their members. Horse meat was eaten only at the most important sacrificial feasts. On this point, Christianity and paganism conflicted even more bitterly than usual. Here the new teaching knew no compromise, no clever adjustment could be made. The pagan sacrament of horse sacrifice stood in direct apposition to the Christian sacrament of the Holy Eucharist. King and peasant alike had to decide between the old and the new religion. The *Heimskringla* often touches on this central theme, and we read about it most vividly in the story of Haakon, the Good:

"In autumn, at the beginning of winter [middle of October] a sacrificial feast was held on Hlader, and the King came there. It was ever his custom, when sacrifices were being made, to eat with a few men in a small house, but the peasants complained that he was not sitting in his high seat when such joy reigned among the people. Thereupon the Jarl begged him to do so, and thus it came about that the King sat in his high seat. As they filled the first goblet, the Jarl spoke and dedicated it to Wodan, and drank to the King from his horn. The King took the horn and *made the sign of the cross*. Whereupon Kaar from Gryting said, 'Why does the King do this? Is he still unwilling to sacrifice?'

"Sigurd Jarl answered, 'The King has done what everyone else is doing who has faith in his own powers and is drinking to Thor: He made *the sign of the hammer* before he drank.'

"On that evening it remained quiet. On the next day, as they sat down at table, the peasants pressed forward and surrounded the King and demanded that he eat horse meat. The King refused to do so. Then they urged him to drink the broth, but he would not. Then they begged him to eat the fat, but that also he would not do, and the peasants were nigh unto using force against him. Whereupon Sigurd Jarl wanted to reconcile them. He begged them to stop their clamor, and asked the King to open his mouth over the handle of the caldron. Steam from the boiling horse meat was on it, so that it was a little smeared. The King went up to it, wrapped a cloth around the handle, leaned over it, and went back to his high seat. But with this no one was satisfied."

By Yuletide, the mood had become considerably more unpleasant. The heathens killed three Christian priests, and set fire to three churches. They forced the king to eat two pieces of horse liver and to drain the usual goblets to Wodan, Freyr, Brage and the clan. "The King was so angry that no one dared speak to him." A reconciliation took place much later, and only the over-all victory of Christianity put an end to bitter controversies like this.

After their conversion, the Christians declared the taste of horse meat to be horrible and considered its enjoyment unhealthy, which may be why most people shudder at the thought of it today. Horse butchers were suspected of being heathen, were despised not so very long ago, and were almost expelled from Christian communities. Convicts and so-called lost souls made a miserable livelihood in this profession, and were accursed and feared. Anything they touched had to be scrubbed or burned. One Swedish priest even used special

Mass vessels of tin for them, something, however, that his bishop soon put a stop to. Just the same, such a man's body was not carried through the cemetery gates for burial but hoisted across the wall. These successors of the heathen priests were barely allowed to lie in hallowed ground.

In the story just told, the sign of the cross could evidently pass for the heathen hammer sign honoring Thor, a fact that is highly revealing for this religious transitional period. For when the Christians raised the cross, the pagan had to find a protective symbol to oppose it. It turned out to be the Thor hammer which we find in so many Viking graves. In far-off places such as Gnezdovo-Smolensk, it testifies to the presence of a Scandinavian pagan who believed in the Norse gods or Aesirs. And just as opposites so often attract each other, we find the heathen putting two eyes in the Thor hammer, meaning that the god was present in the amulet. The visual result, though, was to make the hammer look extraordinarily like a crucifix.

We have not yet mentioned the most important Viking feast of all—the spring sacrifice of the Svea in Old Uppsala, which was so sacred that it could be held only every ninth year. Near the old royal residence with its three king barrows of the first mighty Svea kings, the Aesirs had probably been worshiped since antiquity, in a sacred grove, beside a sacred spring, under the sky. All Romans, including Tacitus, stress the fact that in the days of antiquity the Teutons had no temples but honored their gods in the open air. Just the same, there was a pagan temple in Old Uppsala. (There were pagan temples in other parts of Scandinavia as well.) It may have been built in protest against the Christian church: Everything you can do, we can do too! The Christians had a Holy Trinity; the heathen had to come up with the same thing. Wodan, Thor and Freyr were therefore assembled under one roof in the Uppsala temple, although, according to mythology, they didn't belong together at all! Churches had to stand, if possible, on the site of a former pagan temple; that was the tactic of the missionary, corroborated when excavations under the Uppsala church brought to light several stout postholes.

Adam of Bremen has described the site vividly: "The Swedes have a very famous temple called Uppsala. It lies not far from the city of Sigtuna. It is built all of gold." After a description of the three idols, he goes on to say: "The temple is encircled by a gold chain which is suspended from the gable of the building and glitters as a person approaches it, because the sacred place itself lies in a valley and is surrounded on all sides by hills, like a theater."

Could the hills be the three king barrows? And the chain a gable ornamentation like the ones found on the house shrines of those days? We don't know the answers, but we can rely on a description of the festival, because it comes from an eyewitness:

"Every nine years it is their custom to celebrate a feast for all Sweden. As far as taking part in it is concerned, no exceptions are made. The kings and their subjects send offerings to Uppsala, but . . . those who have been converted to Christianity buy themselves free from the ceremony. The sacramental rites are as follows: Nine male creatures of various species are offered, whose blood is to appease the gods. The bodies are strung up in the grove that is closest to the temple. This grove is so sacred to the heathen that every tree in it is considered consecrated by the death or decay of those sacrificed. There dogs and horses hang beside human beings, and *a Christian told me* that he had seen seventy-two such bodies hanging, all mixed up together. The songs that are sung during such a sacrifice are varied and shameful, therefore the less said about them, the better. . . . The sacrifice takes place at the spring equinox." Thietmar of Merseburg reports a similar rite in Lejre, Denmark. Thus we find out quite a bit about the religious ecstasy of the Vikings. The

113. Sacrificial tree with hanged men, on a woven cloth from Öseberg.

medieval historian, Saxo Grammaticus, supplements these accounts with reports of "female gyrations, side-shows and bell-ringing."

For the Christian it was a sad thing to have to support such a feast by payments in money; for the heathen it was incomprehensible that anyone should want to put himself outside this earthly community and god-ordained order. But the "offerings" brought by the Christians buying themselves free of all this constituted a considerable tax income for the royal coffers. Most sinister though must have been the blood, the stench, the screams of human and animal sacrifices. The wind still sighs through the groves of Old Uppsala, but no tree is old enough to have borne these hanging unfortunates in its branches. The sight has been handed down to us in one illustration of Viking days, a woven cloth found in one of the Öseberg graves, highly stylized to be sure, yet unmistakable because of the limply hanging heads and dangling feet. (*See ill. 113.*) We see only humans, and are reminded of Ragnar Lodbrok who had 111 Frank soldiers hanged on his island in the Seine, and of similar extraordinary sacrificial rites of war, of which tales were told at court.

The most glorious festivals, though, were not of this world and were reserved for only the bravest warriors. The best way to get to Valhalla was to sail there, but one could also drive or ride there if one chose. The Elysian fields were never very precisely localized. From a few picture stones, we know of wagon rides into the hereafter. (*See ill. 114.*) We find a saddled horse in graves as well as in pictures; and if it is the eight-legged horse Sleipnir, then the god Wodan is not riding her personally, but his godlike powers have

114. *Picture stone showing carts being driven to Valhalla. State Historical Museum, Stockholm. Photo: ATA.*

115. *Valkyries and riders. The figures are one to two inches high. State Historical Museum, Stockholm. Photo: E. Oxenstierna.*

moved into the horse of the dead man. He is pledged to the god of war, is, so to say, being fetched by him. In Valhalla, a Valkyrie receives him with a welcoming draught in a horn, in one case with a caldron! And a dog hastens ahead of his master. On the Ardre stone the rider, on his eight-legged horse, moves toward an imposing Valhalla-edifice. (*See ill. 12.*) Its three gates and domed roof betray the form of architecture typical of those days. But where is the dog? Evidently the artist couldn't find room for him because of the many battle scenes at the top, but he is right there on the journey into the hereafter, although until lately none of the experts were able to find him. At the very bottom, however, extreme right, you'll see him dashing off on his own!

The welcoming Valkyrie (handmaiden) is a popular motif of the stone

carvers of Gotland, but also of the master smiths. In the illustration we see
four such handmaidens assembled from various finds, all with train, cloak,
pearl jewelry, their hair in a knot, as the mode of the day prescribed. First
comes a little brisk one with a conic drinking glass; then a more regal one,
followed by one in silver, and an amusing little green one brings up the rear.
That the intention is to portray welcoming Valkyries, libation bearers, maidens
functioning as servitors of welcoming beverages, is evident not only in picture stones but also in figures like these, found in Birka graves. A counterpart
from the sister city of Haithabu are the bronze rider and Valkyrie. (*See ill.
115.*) The motif is of course excellently suited for a burial accessory.

According to Snorri, just as promising as the welcome in Valhalla was the
no less pleasant eternal stay there. Of course something had to be accomplished
during the day—laziness wasn't becoming, not even in the hereafter—so valiant
battles were fought in the environs of Valhalla. Fighting, though, produces
hunger and thirst; drinking bouts, with jovially raised drinking horns are
therefore to be found on a few picture stones and may be listed among the
established joys of Valhalla. And, again according to Snorri, the pig Sarimner
was slaughtered daily, roasted and eaten, only to rise up grunting again next
morning. (*See ills. 116, 117, 118, 119.*)

Couldn't this also be found on a picture stone? I think so. You often find
two men standing in a house—the animal heads at the top corners betray
clearly that it is meant to be a house. The men are holding a rather formless
object between them. It can quite satisfactorily be interpreted not as a live pig,
but as one that has been roasted on a spit and which they are about to carve
with long carving knives. On the Ardre stone, this Valhalla scene is clearly
discernible to the right of the sail, although the men are kneeling. (*See ill. 12.*)

116. *A Valkyrie welcomes a rider to Valhalla, while his dog hurries ahead.
From a picture stone.*

117. *Rider and Valkyrie, from a bronze casting in Haithabu.*

118. *Drinking bout on a Gotlandic picture stone.*

On the right, outside the contours of the house, the Valkyrie is moving in to do the honors. Here we have the peasant-soldier's feast of the joys of the hereafter. His pickled meat was ever ready in pantry and boat chest, but his eternal yearning was to satiate himself daily with fresh roast pork.

Only once a year could he enjoy a foretaste of these heavenly delights—at the Yule feast, which followed soon after the autumnal pig-sticking and offered fresh meat in every form, an opulent introduction to the long winter months with their salty food and unquenchable thirst. The everyday life of the Vikings at home must often have been most unattractive; the festivals, therefore, with their bounty and merriment, must have been looked forward to with a longing almost equal to the desire for adventure.

119. *Household scene, probably depicting the daily roasting of the pig in Valhalla. From a picture stone.*

11

Written History Begins

Norway: Harald Fairhair and Unification

IN OUR WRITTEN sources, Norway puts in an appearance quite early and in a clear light. Snorri's *Heimskringla,* and other documents, are rich in their descriptions of Norway's historic personalities. And at the end of the ninth century a profound event takes place—unification. We are familiar with the prologue.

Queen Asa's son, Halfdan the Black, a successful ruler, subjugated all the small lands around the Oslo Fjord and is supposed to have left four "Halfdan mounds." Snorri tells us that his people loved him so much they raised barrows for him in Ringerike, Raumarike, Vestfold and Hedemarken. We don't have to be too impressed by the caliber of this "love" of people in a recently occupied country; much more important is the fact that Snorri claims that the harvests were good, and this can be construed as an important indication of faith in the ruling powers.

Seen with political realism, the Halfdan mounds were simply symbols of might, royal courts and *thing*-forums of a sort, which the king could visit after his death whenever he so desired, and live in for a while, just as he had traveled and wielded his power in various places during his lifetime. From the archeologist's point of view, he must lie buried in one of them, probably in Borre itself, so the Halfdan mound in Ringerike, which is well preserved, may be empty, in other words—a cenotaph or "empty tomb." Halfdan's grandson, Björn Farman died on a sea voyage, yet—because his spirit had to have a place at home to which to return, had to belong somewhere, had to keep in touch with the community life of his clan and receive the sacrifices of his progeny—he was given an impressive mound, Farmanshögen. It was opened and found to be empty.

In 1939, the largest of the king barrows was opened, Raknehaugen, nearly 22 miles northeast of Oslo. (*See ill. 120.*) It is approximately 312 feet in diameter and an impressive 49 feet high. Nothing was found but three stout wooden layers, consisting of uprights, as in a charcoal kiln, which in this case never burned but, in the course of centuries, rotted. To the historian of antiquity, the wooden structure looks like a funeral pyre and might well be a royal cenotaph of Viking days, older even than the ship graves of the Vestfold kings. Of course the scholar's heart is left a bit hollow, too, with such meager findings after so much hard work: 78,480 cubic yards of earth were moved, three times as much as was necessary to uncover the entire wall of the Hammaburg, for a man who wasn't even buried in his mound!

The son of Halfdan the Black was none other than King Harald Fairhair, the unifier of Norway. He assembled his soldiers from around the Oslo Fjord,

120. *Excavation at Raknehaugen, the largest king barrow in Scandinavia. Photo: E. Oxenstierna.*

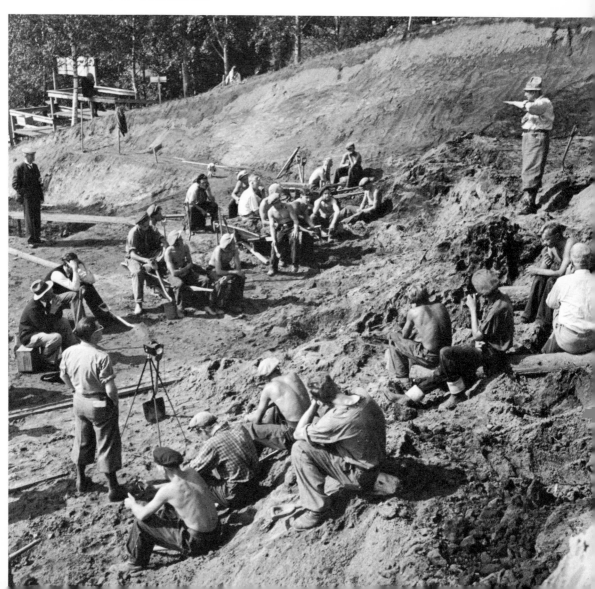

pressed forward along Norway's west coast, and was victorious over all the petty kings on that littoral in the battle of Hafsfjorden, shortly before the year 900. His timing showed great perspicacity. The best fighters were away on Viking voyages in far distant lands. One could say, therefore, that Harald Fairhair chose a propitious moment to make a Viking raid on his own people.

> From the east came ships   all eager for battle,
> With grim gaping heads   carved in gold.
> The battle began,   the berserkers howling,
> "Wolf-coats!" and wildly   casting their spears.

Although quite a few Norwegians hastened home from the British Isles, the defense proved insufficient. The defenders were even jeered at:

> Down 'neath the deck   then slid the men,
> Buttocks upended,   nose in the keel.

Concerned about his newly acquired power, and envied by many, Harald Fairhair was anxious to consolidate his claim to an all-Norwegian kingdom by being able to refer to the ancient Swedish kingdom as a part of his heritage. It therefore suited him very well when his cousin, the petty ruler Ragnvald, in southern Vestfold, he that was called the Mountain-High, chose to adorn himself with the best family tree in the north. Harald Fairhair took over the residential seats of the banished petty kings and established his own courts, in which he spent some time regularly, just as his father, Halfdan the Black, had done on the Oslo Fjord. It is interesting to note that he ordained that he be buried in his newly conquered territory, in Avaldsnes, near the Karmsund. Snorri claims to have seen the burial ground, but it seems no longer to exist.

In the Far North, meanwhile, the taxes levied on the Finns had to be collected, a levy of decisive importance for the financial policy of Norwegian unification. At the beginning of this book, we mentioned Egil Skallagrimsson's uncle, Thorolf, who carried out the rewarding function of tax collector for King Harald:

"In the winter, Thorolf journeyed to the mountains, and ninety men went with him. Once it had been customary for only thirty men, or less, to accompany the king's plenipotentiary to *Finnmarken*. He took much merchandise with him. For the most part, things went smoothly and in a friendly fashion; sometimes though force had to be used."

The account is superficial; we would like more precise details. Pelts of sable, beaver and wolverene are often mentioned. Harald Fairhair's foster mother is supposed to have lived on the White Sea—a rather legendary element of the story—and a grandson was named Harald Graycloak [the gray of squirrel fur]. "Harald Graycloak set out one summer with his army for Perm in the north. He waged war there and fought a big battle against the Permians on the Dvina strand . . . and gained for himself great quantities of booty. Glum Geirisson sings of it:

> In the north, in a burning village,   I saw the Bjarmians flee.
> The word-strong king colored   his sword red in the east.
> The leader of the warriors   won fame for this voyage.
> The young king fought   on the banks of the Dvina.

All this the Norwegians managed somehow to put up with, but when the king began levying taxes on the freeholding peasantry—that was something unheard of! That was vassalage, the curtailment of a freedom they had always taken as a matter of course, and they had no intention of putting up with it. What followed was a mass emigration from Norway across the sea. The old familiar British Isles were colonized all over again, and a second large island— Iceland—lay there, all ready to be settled for the first time. As a result of Harald Fairhair's activities, Iceland, in fifty years, received as many proud and free peasants from Norway as the earth on that island could nourish. For the most part, they were allowed to visit Norway again. And they had saved their independence, which was all that mattered to them.

Harald Fairhair was on good terms with England. The days of the big Viking raids were over; all efforts were bent now to peaceful co-existence. In England, Alfred's grandson, Aethelstan, was continuing the noble policies of his grand-father, and received the sons of princes for tutelage from France, as well as from pagan Norway. Aethelstan had to wage one big battle against the Norse-men, but it was directed westward against the Norman ruler of Ireland, Olaf Cuaran, descendant of Olaf the White and Aud, whom we have already men-tioned. Cuaran wanted to bring both islands under his rule, but his efforts failed. In the battle of Brunanburh, in the year 937, Aethelstan forced back the western Normans. Olaf Cuaran let it go at that, and continued to rule Ireland for a long time. The middle of the tenth century is undoubtedly the most peaceful period of the Viking era.

Denmark: Harald Bluetooth and Germany

For a long time, Germany formed the eastern section of the Frankish king-dom, and did not emerge as an independent state until the tenth century. The Germanic people were to be the first to demand something unheard of until

then—tribute from the Vikings. For 130 years, the Vikings had been the ones
to collect all tribute in this area, but gradually the Germans began to demand
rights in the Baltic Sea trade, which the Vikings had dominated, uncurbed, for
so long.

Haithabu's trade on the Schlei—between the Baltic and North seas—was
prospering. Possession of this port, the levying of taxes on its artisans, the
control of the Viking ships passing through it, was of immense value. At the
beginning of the tenth century, a Swede succeeded in conquering the city.
Adam of Bremen called him King Olaf, as did Snorri in his *Heimskringla;*
but the written sources of the Swedish Viking era on the subject are fragmentary. Olaf may have been a petty monarch, or a member of the Old Uppsala
royal house, with his seat in the conquered city of Haithabu.

His sons, Knuba and Gyrd, ruled after him, and they were followed by his
grandson Sigtrygg, successions which were not exactly undisturbed, for the
hour of the first Saxon kings of Germany had come. Henry I, called "the
Fowler," had turned his kingdom into a vast stronghold, erected fortresses in
the Elbe and Saale territories, and conquered the Magyars in the Southeast,
whereupon he set out on his first military expedition against the Vikings. In
the year 934, he took Haithabu—according to Widukind of Corvey—not from
the Danes, but from the Swedes. Knuba let himself be baptized and paid tribute
to Henry, the first repayment by the North!

We know Knuba quite well through his wife, who had two rune stones
raised (now in Castle Gottorp in Schleswig). The big stone stood originally
on a ford south of Haithabu, clearly visible for everyone to see, inscribed in
Swedish runes: "Asfrid raised this stone in memory of Sigtrygg, her and
Knuba's son." The smaller stone tells us a little more, this time in Danish
runes: "Asfrid, Odinkar's daughter, raised these memorial stones for King
Sigtrygg, her and Knuba's son. Gorm carved the runes." The stones are important witnesses for the correctness of Widukind's personalia.

Henry I revived the old idea of conversion, begun by Louis the Pious. For
a hundred years, nobody had given much thought to missionary work. Henry
sent Archbishop Unni of Bremen to Denmark, and from there to Birka, where
he died in 936. His body was buried there, his head lies in the Bremen Cathedral. Among the Birka graves therefore, we should someday come across a
skeleton with no heathen accessories and no head. Unfortunately we haven't
found it yet.

The rapprochement with Germany had further results. The rulers of Haithabu
began to mint their own coins. The silver hoards of the southern Baltic *after*
the year 936 often include a large number of so-called Haithabu half-
bracteates. They are "mute" or "silent" coins, because they are undeterminable;
they give no name of place or mint year, but they are so numerous around

Haithabu that there can be little doubt as to their origin. Some hoards in the Schleswig-Holstein area consist entirely of such half-bracteates. Findings in the artisans' settlement of Haithabu also corroborate the local mintage. Soapstone molds for silver bars were found in the black earth, dating from 950, but in the upper refuse strata, which was formed after 950, we find no trace of them. They had quite evidently ceased to be used as a medium of exchange. Haithabu had gone over to a purely coin currency; no other kind of silver was permitted.

The reason is simple. On arrival, traders had to exchange their hack-silber and foreign coins for the local currency, which gave the issuer a chance, in the course of the melting down and casting, to keep an appropriate amount of the "scrap" metal for himself. This was "tribute" that he had coming to him as his own personal tax levy. The local rulers in Germany and France were doing the same thing. What we witness here is a giant step toward a monetary standard. And the scattering of Haithabu half-bracteates shows a definite increase up the Oder River, where the trading interests of the city were directed.

The Vikings in turn laid waste to the German seacoast, but we know very little about this because they left no documentary evidence. There are, however, innumerable Viking finds along the entire Baltic coast in this area. Especially magnificent is the great gold hoard of Hiddensee, near the island of Rügen. (*See ill. 75.*) It is of pure Nordic origin, whereas the silver hoards south of the Baltic are often of varied (Slavonic) composition.

The Danes took the loss of Haithabu badly. Even a thousand years ago, the border across the isthmus of Schleswig-Holstein was a controversial issue. Since the old Kograben of Haithabu ran across the Treene River, and was first in Swedish, later in German hands, the Danes had to build a new fortification wall for themselves, the so-called Main Wall, the frontal course of which shows plainly that it was built at a time when the Danes were *not* in possession of Haithabu. In those uneasy days, the city people may have built the wall themselves; we hope future excavations will give us more exact information on this point.

We have spoken off and on of a Danish king, but in those days Denmark probably was still ruled by petty kings, one of whom was definitely the most powerful: Gorm the Elder, in Jutland. The name is the only thing he has in common with the rune carver, Gorm. For his queen, Tyra, he had a very interesting rune stone incised, with the imposing inscription, "Gorm, the King, raised these memorials for Tyra, his wife—Denmark's benefactor."

Here, for the first time, Denmark is mentioned by name. The runic word is TANMARKAR. And what a beautiful tribute he pays his wife, which may be translated as benefactor, salvation, blessing, or ornament. According to folklore, Tyra was the energetic woman who managed to raise the forces necessary to build the new wall outside Haithabu. Gorm is described as old, weak and frail. What is true in these tales—all recorded at a much later date than the events themselves—we unfortunately do not know. There has even been discussion as to whether King Gorm meant that "Denmark's benefactor" was himself!

It is a fact, however, that beside this rune stone, there are two king mounds which—at last also in Denmark—are of a size as impressive as those in Sweden and Norway. (*See ill. 121.*) The largest is almost 273 feet in diameter, and about 36 feet high. They lie on either side—north and south—of the church in Jellinge, not far from Fredericia and Vejle, where the royal residence used to be. A wooden chamber was found in the north mound, approximately 22 by 8½ feet, with a height of only about 4¾ feet, a meticulously constructed stave room which was examined in 1861, unfortunately not very expertly. Various objects were brought to light, among them a fine silver goblet or chalice, some wood carved objects, but no skeleton parts. And with this find began the riddles of Jellinge that were surprisingly resolved not so long ago.

By simple conjecture, Gorm and Tyra had to lie in these mounds, but antiq-

121. *The mounds at Jellinge, with reconstruction of the standing stones.*

uity doesn't always conform to simple conjecture. No bones of any description were found in the northern mound, although even the wood was excellently preserved. After various trial digs in the previous century, it could be expected that the south mound would be empty. This, of course, wasn't a very encouraging prospect for archeologists digging for results, but the Danes left no stone unturned—literally—in the year 1941, in their efforts to find out more about their first kings.

What could one hope to find in an empty burial mound of such dimensions? Broken wagon parts, a few spades and hand barrows were hardly worth the effort. From the apex, a thin post was rammed deep into the ground, apparently a marker for the center of the mound while it was being raised. The mound itself consisted of peat and grass sod, piled up with the growing side down. The results were as expected—the south mound was empty. No trace of a burial chamber this time, or of any central installation, nothing but a few very large stones, about 6½ feet apart.

They had undoubtedly been placed there for a purpose. Strange . . . but they formed two lines that ran together southward. If followed in a northerly direction, they coincided with the irregular outline of the Jellinge cemetery. A few stones of the same size had formed a part of the cemetery wall for centuries. All in all, seventy of the original two hundred large bauta or monolithic stones were found. Both diverging lines were aimed at the periphery of the north mound. They formed an enclosure nearly 179 feet long, and more than 26 feet wide at the north base. The angle at the pointed end was about 25 degrees.

No doubt about it—this was a holy *Vi,* the site of a pagan consecration or ritual ground, directly connected with the north mound. And with this, we had come upon something absolutely new, something of the most vital cultural importance.

With fresh vision, the excavator, Ejnar Dyggve, began to investigate to see if anything similar could be found anywhere else, dismantled perhaps, or damaged, and therefore overlooked. And how strange a finder's luck can be! For forty years he had owned a summerhouse in just such a *Vi.*

The church of Tibirke, in the north of Själland, lies on a natural elevation. South of it, two low earthwork walls run together to form a point, the whole area with the same dimensions as the *Vi* in Jellinge. It had always puzzled Ejnar Dyggve, and in the year 1917 he had made a few tentative digs and found nothing but stone fill. Now he made an astonishing discovery. A map of the year 1793 showed the cemetery still running along the old triangular lines. The farms of the village were situated scrupulously outside the triangle, and at the point of the *Vi* there was a sacred spring. A third ritual site of this type was found in Tingsted, on the island of Falster. Here, too, the church

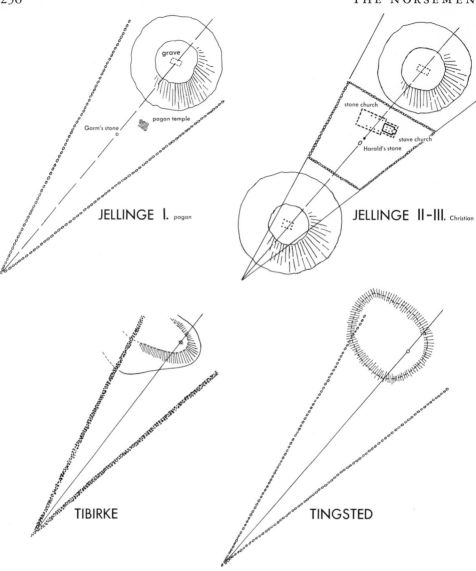

JELLINGE I. pagan

JELLINGE II-III. Christian

TIBIRKE

TINGSTED

122. *Diagrams of the ritual sites of Jellinge, Tingsted and Tibrike.*

stands on a natural height and the triangle is clearly visible on the village map of 1784. The angle is the same, the layout itself a little larger. Until 1720, *thing*-assemblies were held here. (*See ill. 122.*)

And where did the temple of the gods stand in these three places of worship? In all probability where the churches were built later. And that is how far the reflections at our desks took us. That is why Ejnar Dyggve began to dig in 1947, and again in 1951, at first under the church in Jellinge. This could be done only a little at a time or the whole stone edifice would have collapsed; and there were numerous interruptions. But in the end, under the pressed clay floor of the church, he found another clay floor with a stout posthole sunk in it. This certainly wasn't much evidence, yet we dared to conclude that here we had the foundations of a pagan temple.

This clarified the picture considerably. Gorm, the Elder, began to prepare his burial mound around 930, and added a sacred pagan grove to it at the same time. After all, in stone-poor Denmark, 200 imposing bauta stones are a remarkable achievement. He had the temple built fairly close to the middle axis, probably because the most sacred spot had to be reserved for the rites of sacrifice in the open air. His Queen Tyra died first, and was buried provisionally; he followed her into their double grave in 940. This time the burial order was reversed. But this does not solve the mystery of the southern mound. The story of their son does that.

123. *The king stone of Harald Bluetooth at Jellinge, Jutland.*

124. *Harald's conversion proclamation on the Jellinge stone.*

He bore the curious name of Harald Bluetooth, and appears in all drawings, comic and serious, with a blue tooth, although "blue" has the old second meaning of "large." It is quite likely that he had noticeably large teeth, rather than a blue one. Bluebeard, too, should be seen with a luxurious beard rather than a blue one, even if a few people feel let down at the suggestion of a change in the customary appearance of two standard historic personalities.

Harald Gormsson, or Bluetooth, immortalized his father's achievements on a rune stone which stands on the middle axis of the Jellinge triangle and gives proud evidence of having once been very beautiful. "Harald the King had this memorial stone raised for Gorm, his father, and Tyra, his mother; the Harald who unified Denmark wholly, and Norway, and who converted the Danes to Christianity."

The stone is a triangular, natural boulder. On one side is the main text. On a second side we read: "wholly, and Norway," and above this inscription we see a monumental quadruped. "The big animal" of runic ornamentation is what the scholars of antiquity call it. It is as impressive as any ruler symbol should be, with elegant animal-band interlace. The third side, with its message of the conversion to Christianity, shows an equally stylized Christ, with halo and arms outstretched; not the suffering man on the cross but the heroic conqueror in a religious struggle, the only Christ who could possibly have impressed the Vikings. Both in style and attitude, the carving is something to marvel at, unique in its conception of runic style, majesty and conversion zeal. (*See ills. 123, 124.*)

The pagans had been interested in Christianity for a long time. The colonists on the islands and in Normandy had been converted, and Christian travelers enjoyed privileges in all trading centers on the Baltic Sea. At the Synod of Ingelheim, King Otto I installed three German bishops in Schleswig, Ribe and Aarhus. Their names were Hored, Liafdag and Reginbrand. The royal residence of Jellinge was therefore almost encircled by Christianity. Around 960 came the decisive event—the baptism of Harald Gormsson by the monk Poppo and in 965, Otto declared the three bishoprics "in the Danish marshes" exempt from duty and tax free. Denmark might have become a part of Otto's empire at the time, but managed, at the hour of its birth, to summon the strength to go its own independent way. (*See ill. 125.*)

Harald Bluetooth, now a Christian king, couldn't possibly preserve the heathen grove of his father. The central area had to be rearranged, with which we arrive at the puzzling south mound. Harald had it raised over the point of the *Vi* as a grave mound for himself, and had the temple torn down, a spectacular action, since he was still surrounded by pagan administrators. The area between the mounds, he fashioned into a cemetery, and on the demolition site, he built the first stave church, which we can now reconstruct according to Ejnar Dyggve's specifications. Three postholes, and one corner, with the wooden remains of an upright board of oak were found in the clay floor covering the foundations of the temple. (*See ill. 126.*) All traces and measurements coincide with those of the earliest stave churches that we know so well: two posts for the arch of triumph, one heavy post for the four main supports and the corner between church and choir. A curious altar stone was found, a geological rarity. It is of granite, interspersed with red, rosette-shaped garnet accumulations. It could be older than the church. With the pagan's preference for extraordinary manifestations of nature, it might be a pagan sacrificial stone that was consecrated and incorporated into the church by its first bishop.

125. *Baptism of Harald Bluetooth, from a relief in Tandrups Church, Denmark. Photo: National Museum, Copenhagen.*

Harald Bluetooth did one more impressive thing for the new teachings of Christ. He ordained that he be buried in the first cathedral church in Roskilde, demonstratively on the very island where, as unifier of the kingdom, he had expanded his realm. Harald Fairhair had done much the same thing when he had himself buried in his newly conquered territory on Norway's west coast. So why did Harald Bluetooth have a grave mound raised for himself in Jellinge? The knowledge we have acquired of early Norwegian history helps to explain the enigma. Harald Bluetooth had been converted to Christianity, no doubt about that, enthusiastically, but he had been raised in pagan beliefs and remained rooted in them. He needed a mound on his home territory, which he could visit from Roskilde, and reside in, if he desired. He had no intention of cutting himself off completely from his clan after death. In this he conformed with a *social* law. Religion could not be permitted to interfere with it.

His body would live on, after death in a strange place, just like the bodies of those who died at sea or in foreign lands. With these men he had one thing in common—he had to see to it that there was a resting place for him in his clan's community. For all such men, grave mounds were raised which, upon excavation, turned out to be empty, thereby betraying all the more a devout belief in a hereafter. But why were the burial chambers of the north mound emptied, and the bones of Gorm and Tyra removed, just as in the case of the Norwegian boat graves? That is our most important concern, for which we have no satisfactory explanation as yet. The carefully planned research of the next years may offer further surprises.

Harald Bluetooth's life was stormy, as befitted a famous Viking king. When Norwegian King Harald Graycloak fell in the year 970, Haakon Ladejarl from Haalogaland in the North and Harald Bluetooth from Denmark in the South, hastened to divide Norway between them. Three years later Roman Emperor Otto I, later the Great, died, and Otto II took it upon himself to reconquer the city of Haithabu, which Germany had meanwhile lost. On the borders of Schleswig there always had been hard fighting, and in 983, Harald Bluetooth had the chance to take the good trading city of Haithabu for himself and Denmark; that was why he could proudly carve his three main achievements into the triangular boulder: "the Harald who unified Denmark, wholly, and Norway, and converted the Danes to Christianity."

His son, Sven Forkbeard, didn't honor his noble father. In conjunction with the younger generation, he started a rebellion. Harald Bluetooth fled, wounded,

126. *Reconstruction of the oldest stave church in Jellinge, on the site of the pagan temple, with foundation plan.*

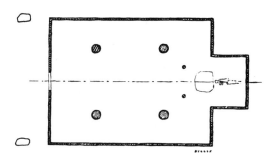

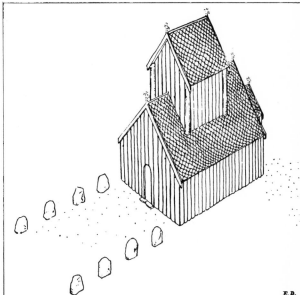

to his aerie Jomsburg, or Jumme, where he died a few days later, on November 1, presumably in the year 986, surrounded by his most loyal, bravest and toughest Vikings.

... and still no historic data on Sweden

We Swedes have to envy our Scandinavian neighbors. Our written history doesn't begin until the year 1000, or later. For the actual Viking era we don't even have a complete list of the Old Uppsala kings. It is possible that these rulers were less important than the state founders of the seventh century; they may have felt oppressed by the petty kings of other provinces. At any rate, they didn't know how to establish a reputation and insure future fame for themselves, as did Ragnvald the Mountain-High and Harald Fairhair in Norway. And how fascinatingly the new finds have succeeded in broadening the historic picture of Denmark! Gorm the archpagan and freshly converted Harald Bluetooth are suddenly turned into life-size sympathetic human figures as their religious and social consciences are revealed. But we can read nothing about their Swedish contemporaries, not even a word about such a great event as the destruction of the trading city of Birka. Only the most recent grave finds, rich in accessories, and one silver treasure, permit us to fix an approximate date for the catastrophe—the year 980, or thereabouts. The silver hoard was spread out on an iron platter in the black earth, and the most recent coin was from the year 967. Rapine and fire must have done their share in the destruction of Birka; perhaps also the slow but steady rising of the land, which may have made it impossible to get into the harbor. Even before the year 1000, the Swedish King Olaf Skötkonung found a new trading center, the city of Sigtuna. Here the black earth is very rewarding. The publicized results of the digs there may soon throw light on the destruction of Birka during a time for which we have no written documentation, just as clearly as the creation of the town was revealed to us by archeological findings.

All in all, we should not underestimate what the earth gives back to us. The Norwegian material is gigantic, and the differences in the various settlement areas are startling. In Norway, archeologists can demonstrate how the early settlers pressed forward, up the valleys, and settled in high regions that had once lain fallow. The Danes do not have such a profusion of finds in their thickly settled land, yet every now and then they come upon surprising data.

For Swedish Viking days we have to depend entirely on archeological findings. The written sources remain silent, but grave, hoard and settlement finds become more and more numerous. From 1938, they have been systematically recorded. Field archeologists rummage through one parish after the other, take notes, make surveys whenever they can, on special maps. By 1970, the work is supposed to be done. At the present the following figures for finds are available:

For the heart of the Svea region, on Lake Mälar:

Uppland	128,000
Södermanland	92,600
Västmanland	not yet recorded
The east Swedish province of Östergötland	35,100
The Baltic Sea island of Gotland	30,000 (approx.)
The Baltic Sea island of Öland	10,000 (approx.)
The south Swedish highlands, province Småland	42,000
Other recorded monuments	16,300
TOTAL TO DATE	354,000
Total for All Sweden	500,000 (approx.)

Many graves lie obscured in level ground between those that are visible, which is why the number of prehistoric monuments in Sweden may actually be twice as high. Many, of course, belong to the Stone, Bronze, or older Iron ages, but we may count on one quarter to one half million earth finds of Viking days in Sweden!

Actually they form the largest scientific archive of the nation. It can never be exhausted, but will suffice to enlarge the archeological institutes of the future enormously, pose still totally unforeseen problems for museum managements, compensate for the lack of written sources and offer us much better knowledge of that epoch. And they are only "what is left," because the historians of the nineteenth century complained bitterly of the almost incomprehensible destruction of monuments. This, however, has been effectively stopped. But in the last century, heathen graves enjoyed very little protection, and what the peasants found in them sometimes fell only by chance into the hands of collectors or historians, and from there found its way into museums. And everybody was interested only in the object itself. No one had any idea that the position of the find, to say nothing of the area surrounding it, was far more important than the artistic worth of an object.

Most of the earliest scattered finds have not yet been examined. They have been neglected because archeological resarch has been all too eagerly absorbed with the magnificent art objects found in far-off regions. Thus a research gap has formed where native material is concerned. In the case of Viking culture, the findings of not a single Swedish district have as yet been published. Is it any excuse that the enormous amount of metal objects already raised on the island of Gotland alone makes the collected material almost impossible to survey, and that in the narrow confines of thickly settled areas there are few possibilities for the precise study of settlement history? Should we condemn west Sweden as a thankless research area because the findings there are just as puzzlingly meager as those of the Danes? The scattered finds from the heart of the Svea district should be examined at once in a limited operation, to gain a better perspective for this greatest collection of Viking finds ever assembled. Only then would there be any sense in organized digging of entire village burial fields or a whole parish—which is, of course, the costly dream of research.

And what about the south Swedish highlands, that barren moraine district with its many small settlement areas? Its old finds, come upon by chance, lie arranged in an orderly fashion in cases in the Stockholm Museum, and have been catalogued. They could—and should—be studied, also in a limited operation. And this should take place soon, while the people who raised the material half a century ago are still living on their farms so that the find information, if incomplete, can be further investigated at the source.

A few of the old finds are very rewarding. In the 1890's, Pastors Palmgren and Wiblung, among others, dug with great care and wrote their report with exemplary precision. In their clear handwriting, it still lies in the museum, untouched and unexamined. With the help of such material, we should be able to gain a clearer grasp of typical settlements in inner Scandinavia.

The burial fields of Sweden frequently lie close to farms with the syllable "by" in their names, thus betraying their origin from Viking days. The 40 to 50 mounds usually found increase sometimes to more than 100 when several farmsteads lie close together, or they may have been reduced to scarcely noticeable remains by tillage. The burial fields lie on slight elevations, sometimes fortuitously in a refreshing birch grove, and are often used as pasturage. Early medieval law, as we have seen, demanded that the peasant be able to trace his ancestry back *til Haugs ok til Heidni,* and many a Scandinavian could still do so in the eighteenth century. And the mounds mutely unite the peasant of our highly technical age with the Vikings of a thousand years ago. These barrows are not only research material, also form an integral part of the historical development of a still existing community. They demonstrate that the Scandinavian cultural landscape is more than a thousand years old, and—something that could turn out to be almost unique in world history—that the peasants of today are rooted spiritually, socially and economically, in the Viking era.

12

The Discovery of America

New Lands . . .

WHAT THE CONTINENT of Europe had to offer fitted aptly into the world viewpoint of the Vikings' pagan faith: *Nifelheim* and *Muspelheim*—ice in the North, heat in the South. Between the two, in *Midgard,* the homestead in the center, it was pleasantest to live. Now why couldn't there be other lands, far away, beyond the ocean, beyond the continents they knew? All sorts of stories were circulated: eyewitness accounts, misinterpreted conjectures and purely boastful yarns. Not that the Vikings had any specific urge to explore the four corners of the earth; sometimes a discovery would be made by chance. One of the dragon ships might be buffeted by a violent storm. To keep the open boat from becoming waterlogged, to repair damage, just to stay on top of the waves, took all the strength the crew had. Water would grow scarce; there was nothing to hope for but to sight land. . . .

This was the fate of a typical cosmopolitan of his day—Gardar Svarvarsson. He was born a Swede, but he owned a farm on the Danish island of Seeland, and was married to a Norwegian. One day he set out to claim an inheritance on the Hebrides, but he was caught in a storm off the Orkney Islands and driven off course. At last he sighted land, and by sailing around it, ascertained that it was a large island. He named it after himself—Gardarholm.

At about the same time, in the 860's, a Norwegian named Nadd-Odd was cast up on the same island. From a high mountain, he saw that it was uninhabited, sailed southward, reached his homeland and told of the island. He called it Snowland.

The thought of the island tempted a man from west Norway, Floke Vilgerdsson, who took cattle on board his ship and sailed in search of Snowland. He found an abundance of fish and bird's eggs on the island, but he had

127. *The Vikings in North America*

forgotten to take along hay for his cattle, so that winter the animals died. He also lost one dinghy. The spring was cold, and from the mountains he could see many glaciers in the north. Disgruntled, he called the island Iceland. But a young peasant called Thorolf, who was there with Floke Vilgerdsson, saw the newly discovered territory with different eyes, and declared when he got home that "in the land they had discovered, butter dripped from every blade of grass," which is why he was called Thorolf Smör (butter).

Norsemen may not have been the first discoverers of Iceland. The Irish geographer Dicuil, who wrote about the Faroe Islands, also gives us the following account:

"Thirty years ago (*circa* 795) I spoke with some pious men who had visited the island of Thule (by which Dicuil means Iceland) from February to August. They said that the summer nights there were strangely light. The sun went down, but it was as if it had only hidden behind a hill. It didn't get dark; you could go right on working, even pick lice off your shirt. Higher up in the mountains, the sun perhaps also shone in the night. According to these pious men, the open sea lay all around Thule, but north of the island, a day's journey away, they came upon icebergs."

This coincides with the report of an Icelandic historian, Are Frode: "In those days there were Christian men here whom the Norsemen called *papar*. These men later moved away because they did not want to live with the heathen. They left behind Irish books, bells and croziers, from which we may deduce that they came from Ireland." We also have the names of places such as Papefjord, Papö, Paperbo and Irerbakke on Iceland, to give support to the story. Irish hermits may well have preceded the Vikings in Iceland.

The year 874 saw the beginning of the Norwegian landfalls. First Ingolf and Leif of Firdafylke set out on a voyage of discovery. Ingolf had his high-seat pillars on board and threw them into the water when he sighted land. He didn't find them again until his third winter on Iceland; then, like a true Viking explorer, he let himself be guided by them, and moved to the shore where they had been washed up. He named the spot Reykjavik, or Warm Springs, because close to the bay there were springs from which steam was rising.

Iceland is an island of contrasts—geysers and glaciers, rich sheep-pasture land and desolate mountains, summer light and winter darkness close to the Arctic Circle, a land for the proud peasants who did not want to submit to the sovereignty of Harald Fairhair. To them, the mere interference in their personal independence was a far more heinous thing than any tax they would have had to pay. The latter was a negligible factor in their impetus to get away. This is why the great emigrations of 874–930 took place simultaneously

128. *Picture stone from Gotland, depicting an exchange of land. State Historical Museum, Stockholm. Photo: ATA.*

with the unification of Norway. By far the greater part of this migratory wave flooded Iceland, creating there a community of independent peasants.

The first who came could still take as much land as they wanted, especially on the desirable south and west coasts, which were washed by the Gulf Stream. Those who came later could either buy some of this land from the pioneers, or be satisfied with the north and east shores, which were influenced by the Polar Stream. How the actual parceling out of the land was legally settled has been handed down to us. Harald Fairhair's edict reads as follows:

"No one is to take more land than he and his crew can circumnavigate with fire in one day. He is *to light a fire when the sun is in the east.* Then other smoke fires are to be lit, so that one fire can be seen from the other. But the fires that were lit when the sun was in the east are to burn until nightfall. *Then he is to walk until the sun is in the west,* and again light a fire."

Such a distribution of land was immortalized on Gotland picture stones. (*See ill. 128.*) We see the low sun and the jagged edges of a fire; also three men with spear, spade and sickle, their backs turned on sun and fire. The picture could represent the transference of land to an heir. If so, the latter is depicted at the top of the stone, taking a spear from the hands of an old man (his father?), a gesture symbolizing an exchange of property. The tribal *fylgja,* or Nordic guardian spirit, in the form of a bird, sticks its head through the wall at this solemn moment, while the mother expresses her grief with her hands in front of her mouth.

With a grasping of the spear and a procession—according to medieval law, "with ratification and procession"—a transference of land was legalized. It required two witnesses who cut into the earth with spade and sickle. Out of this custom, which was general on all farmsteads and estates at home, a similar tradition developed and was applied to land acquired on new islands. Important information is here passed on to us on these Gotland picture stones. The inheritance may very well have been disputed and the heir might have wanted its legality confirmed with a stone picture.

We have already mentioned two Iceland immigrants—at the beginning of this book, Skallagrimsson; in a previous chapter, Aud the Deepminded. The names of a thousand men are inscribed in the land register. Around 930, the population must have been from 16,000 to 20,000; toward the end of the tenth century, more than 20,000.

In approximately the year 900, a voyager seeking land was driven off course, westward, and made landfall on several islands which he named after himself —Gunnbjörn Islands. But it wasn't until the year 982 that anyone paid serious attention to this vast, unexplored North Atlantic area, although it was frequently mentioned. Then there came Eric the Red, a man easily aroused, who lived in a constant state of hostility with his neighbors in northwest Iceland, and had few advocates at the *thing*. After he had slain two sons of one of his enemies, he was outlawed for three years.

He made brilliant use of his banishment by exploring an unknown land that lay westward [Greenland]. No nineteenth-century explorer could have done better. He must have sailed southward along the east coast of the island, and noted how huge its dimensions were, and that it was highly uninviting. It could only get pleasanter and warmer the farther south he sailed, and shortly after he had rounded the southernmost point of Cape Farewell, he came upon the friendly fjord area of Julianahaab, which he named Osterbygden, or Eastern Settlement, although it lies on the west coast. It is situated, however, more to the east than another landfall he made in that area, near Godthaab, which he named Vesterbygden.

Eric lived by fishing, hunting, birding; he sailed up every fjord, but was careful not to spend any winters inland because he might have found himself locked in by pack ice. He took his time about all this, until the three years were over, then he returned to Iceland, and reported on the two new settlement areas. Lumber was missing there, but the little timber the Norwegian emigrants had found in Iceland had been cut long ago, anyway. There was fruitful pasture land in the new regions, and good hunting for those Icelanders who had been apportioned land too meagerly. He called the new territory Grönland, or Greenland, "for he felt that many would go there if it had a good name."

In this we have evidence of his psychological astuteness. Erik the Red and Quarrelsome, developed into a splendid leader and organizer, who knew how to apply his excess energy where it was most useful. Enthusiasm for the new land was great. In 986, in the spring, 25 ships sailed westward in an organized emigration, carrying 500 to 700 men, women and children. The remaining shipping space must have been needed for cattle, horses, farm equipment, wood and cooking utensils. It was a fabulous achievement, this penetration of the ocean, especially in the light of the perils of such a journey. And they did not fail to materialize. The migrants encountered a violent storm; only 14 ships reached their destination. The others were driven back or foundered.

Eric the Red was, of course, the leader, and he took the best land for himself. On the Eriks Fjord in Osterbygden he built his homestead, Brattalid, and divided the land. He created a *thing*-assembly and founded a free peasant republic according to the Icelandic pattern. Gradually up to 200 farms were settled in Osterbygden, 100 in Vesterbygden. At times the population may have reached 3,000.

But life so close to glaciers, at the foot of towering mountains, on a narrow green strip of coastal fjords, was undeniably arctic. From October to May, the population was cut off from the outside world and lacked many things that, even in those days, were considered necessities of life, above all grain, wood

129. *Remains of Viking settlement in Osterbygden, Greenland. Photo: National Museum, Copenhagen.*

130. *Small settlements in the Arctic Circle and Arctic hills of Greenland, today as they were in Viking days. Nordisk Press Photo, Copenhagen.*

and iron. Iron could be obtained from Iceland, and washed-up wood played an important role; but the cattle-pasture lands were the vital element, with the fodder they provided for the barns in winter. In the excavations of old settlements, we can read in the remains of bones how important hunting was. The land was rich in fish, whale, seals, birds, hares, bears and reindeer; wolves, of course, were less welcome. Life was hard, but bearable, and made more so by barter and regular voyages to Iceland and Norway.

And what became of this newly discovered oceanic island? During the Christian Middle Ages, Greenland experienced an era of prosperity; there can be no doubt about that. We count 16 churches, 2 cloisters, and 1 bishopric near Gardar in Osterbygden. Among the export articles, walrus tusks were the most valuable item. In 1327, the papal legate received 250 tusks from the Greenlanders as tithe and "Peter's Penny." The Greenland *knorr* was the trading vessel used for such traffic until it was shipwrecked in 1367. The last Icelandic historians report that Eskimos were often seen in Greenland. In the fourteenth century came the great Eskimo migration across Smith Sound, southward along Greenland's west coast. The Greenlanders had to relinquish the walrus hunting grounds which were so important to their trade and traffic with Europe. They had to evacuate Vesterbygden. Everywhere they were routed by fleets of kayaks. Innumerable sagas corroborate this influx, in which the successors of the Vikings had to give way and see themselves overrun by a strange people.

Grain they had lacked anyway. When even the pasture lands were threatened, no one could hope to hold out on a European economy basis.

From the middle of the fifteenth century, there is an ominous silence in all written sources. The Greenlanders might as well have been living on a desert island; no one paid any more attention to them. Trading with them apparently no longer paid. Something fundamental and dreadful had evidently happened to them. In 1540, an Icelander was still able to sight people in the fjord interior, but a man was lying dead on the stony ground with a knife in his hand, and no one had bothered to bury him. A few years later, a caravel from Hamburg, under skipper Gert Mestermaker, reached the settlement, saw no sign of life, and turned back.

Early in the eighteenth century, Greenland was rediscovered. For a long time there had been hope of bringing aid to the survivors on the far-off isle. A guilty conscience—because they had been forgotten—may have played a part. But the explorers looked in vain for Osterbygden on the east coast. In the end, digs proved the unhappy ending of this Viking settlement: houses, kitchens, graves could be studied. Interred in ground frost, in graves that had been dug during the few weeks in summer when the ground thawed out, the dead on Herjulfsnes lay in costumes that were still intact, as we see them in illustrations of the Middle Ages. In their unmistakable way, the skeletons tell a story of human beings, sick and in need—deformed spines, rickets, tuberculosis, mental retardation, tooth decay, dwarflike build and a very low average lifespan—all the results of hopeless malnutrition. A woman not yet thirty years old was delicately built and only 4 feet 6 inches tall. Her back was crooked, her buttocks were flat. Another woman, 5 feet 2 inches, was the tallest, but she was hunchbacked and sterile, due to the extreme narrowness of her pelvis.

In astonishing apposition to all this misery were the elegant styles of 1400: woolen robes down to the ankles, with full shirts for male and female alike, and the typical cap with the point dangling. It would go beyond the framework of this book to describe them in greater detail, but it is quite evident that the forlorn inhabitants of Greenland picked up the latest continental modes from the last seamen to reach their island, and copied them in their own sheep's wool, even a Burgundy bonnet, and other stylish features of approximately the end of the fifteenth century; a convulsive escape into elegance by starving cripples to whom in the end no voyager gave a thought.

. . . and a New Continent

Eric the Red's fleet had just left Iceland in the year 986, when there arrived on the island a young man who wanted to see his father again. The young man's name was Bjarne Herjulfsson. He was told that his father had migrated to Greenland with many other people, but Bjarne stuck to his resolve. His crew stood by him, thus the twenty-sixth ship sailed off in the wake of the big migration fleet. All alone across a completely uncharted ocean!

Westward—that much Bjarne knew, and he had probably gathered detailed information orally: that the mountains on both islands were so high and the air of the north of such unparalleled clarity that he would sight Greenland's coast very soon after Iceland's coast had been lost to view.

But things didn't turn out as predicted. After three days, Bjarne sailed into fog and his ship was driven aimlessly hither and yon, apparently with the southward-flowing Polar Stream. Suddenly, one day, he sighted land, wooded land, with no mountains, only low-lying hills. Though Bjarne knew it couldn't be Greenland, this didn't seem to worry him; nor did the fact that other islands now began to appear on the ocean. They didn't even interest him. After all, he was looking for his father in Greenland!

But we are interested, because he had come upon a very large island. Bjarne had discovered America! America, at a point southwest of Greenland. For five days he sailed northward, sighted land twice more, and at last saw the mountains and glaciers he had been promised. But he didn't wish to land; the country looked "pretty useless" to him. He confirmed the fact, however, that it was an island. We may assume that he had arrived at Resolution Island at the southernmost point of Baffin Island.

With a southwest wind, Bjarne sailed on for four days, and for the fourth time sighted land.

"And now the crew asked Bjarne if he thought this could be Greenland. Bjarne replied that this looked most like what he had been told about Greenland, and here it was his intention to disembark. They did so toward evening, on a spit of land, and on it they found a boat. And on this spit of land lived Herjulf, Bjarne's father. And from this the spit of land got its name, and has been called Herjulfsnes ever since. So then Bjarne went to his father and stayed with him for as long as he lived, and continued to reside there after the death of his father."

It is almost incomprehensible that Bjarne should have taken it into his head to seek his father somewhere along the oceanic coast and found him! Evidently all the North American littoral meant to him was that he had been driven off course. So on he sailed, away from it, until he hit his target—bull's eye! In the course of the voyage land had been sighted on another continent. And who should be more suited to explore this new continent than the son of Eric the Red, Leif Ericsson? And what ship could be better suited for the voyage than Bjarne's, which had already made the trip? With thirty-five men on board, Leif sailed from Greenland according to Bjarne's precise instructions. He was able to make good use of the currents, first along the island coast northward, then southward down the coast of the new lands. This got him off to a fine start. First he came to the glaciers and smoothly cut rocks, made landfall, and called the land Helluland (Baffin Island), or Land of Flat Stones, *hell* meaning "rocky plateau." The English later named it Table Land, which oddly enough means practically the same thing. It was good for nothing.

Leif also found the second land, which was wooded and had white sandy shores, and named it Markland, meaning Woodland. Now he was on the Labrador littoral. Still farther south he came to a third land, and this he named Vinland. And now the terse accounts vie frantically with each other over how pleasant this last region was. The rivers were overflowing with salmon. The grass didn't wither in the frostless winter, and they had never tasted anything so sweet as the dew. There were grapes out of which wine could be made, (hence the name?). The men felled the "grape trees" and dragged the trunks on board to take back to treeless Greenland. They also took the wine they had made.

A lot of this is nonsense. Such Utopian descriptions discredit the entire report. We are reminded of Thorolf Smör who saw butter dripping from every blade of grass. So why not honey? Or take the first letters nineteenth-century immigrants wrote home describing the United States: they told of pigs that gorged themselves on the raisins and almonds that grew wild everywhere, and said one could drink wine from fountains! The grass grew so high, all you could see were the horns of the cattle, which let themselves be milked by anyone. Sugar rained down from sugar trees, and the rivers were full of syrup. In the sixteenth century, similar fantasies streamed out of China, Japan and India. Pessimists like Floke Vilgerdsson saw only ice, toil and failure everywhere, but the staunch explorers were optimists who praised the bounty of the land they discovered. Let us, however, examine these early reports for any possible truth to be wrested from them. For there is no denying the fact any longer that the Vikings discovered America, settled on the American continent, and undertook several expeditions from their homelands to the newly discovered territory.

Leif's brother Thorvald was the next one to set out on a voyage of discovery, again on Bjarne's ship, in the year 1004. They reached the *Leifsbodarna* (Leif Settlement) as planned, and spent two winters there.

"They found the land beautiful and wooded. The distance between wood and sea was short, and there was white sand, many islands, and shallow water."

But now came an embarrassing surprise, something totally unexpected after the undisturbed settlement of Iceland and Greenland. The Norsemen were met by a native population. They killed eight of them; a ninth man escaped. And the results of this slip were immediate. Masses of canoes made of hide appeared; there was a battle during which Thorvald was killed by an arrow. He was buried where he fell.

Time passed. In Iceland and Greenland people spoke of the new land, and decided on an organized expedition to it in grand style. In the year 1020, this took place under the leadership of Thorfinn Karlsefni. The same vigorous activity was displayed as in previous expeditions to other oceanic islands. Three ships were outfitted, with crews numbering 160 men in all, with cattle and all the necessary gear. One advantage was that no wood had to be taken along. They followed the tried and true way over Helluland and Markland, and settled down along an inlet which they called Straumfjord, on an island which they named Straumsöy, since the current there was very strong. "There were so many birds, that a man's foot could scarcely find room between the eggs." There is also mention of grapes and wild wheat. More wishful thinking of a far off land of milk and honey?

Adam of Bremen has the same story to tell in his Hammaburg History, since he counted all the oceanic islands as a part of his diocese. Couldn't a small kernel of truth perhaps be hidden behind the "wheat that grew by itself"? Couldn't this be the "corn" of the Indians, the wild maize that astonished the pioneers of a later era because it grew so easily and apparently without cultivation? How otherwise could the Norsemen, in whose country grain, especially wheat, could be grown only with the greatest difficulty, assert something that came so close to the truth?

Soon, of course, the inevitable happened: nine boats made of hide approached. They were manned by "ugly little men; their hair was stringy. They had big eyes and wide cheekbones." In a few words, a not very flattering but recognizable portrait of an Indian. The Norsemen called them *skrälingar,* or skraelings.

These "ugly little men" were willing to negotiate, and the Vikings arranged a peaceful trade agreement according to the familiar pattern. The savages offered pelts and gray squirrel skins and accepted, for a black fur, nine inches of red material which they tied around their heads. But Karlsevne forbade the sale of swords or spears.

The Norsemen's stock in trade was not large. Soon they had to cut the cloth in finger-wide strips, but still it went the way of all rare merchandise—the skraelings were willing to pay the same amounts as before, even more, for these narrower strips. Then misfortune overtook the newcomers. One of their oxen broke loose and stampeded, bellowing, into the woods. The skraelings fled, frightened, but soon came back again, this time with hostile intentions. They dragged along with them a peculiar catapult-like weapon, and the sound was frightful when heavy clods from it flew through the air. One of the Viking women tore off her shirt, baring her breasts, and began to belabor the skraelings with a sword. This terrified them.

On the battlefield the natives found an iron ax. "They picked it up and struck on wood with it, one after the other, and found it to be a valuable thing with a sharp blade. Then they struck on stone with the ax and it broke. So they decided that the ax was a useless thing since it could not withstand stone, and they threw it away."

All our written sources come from Iceland. The Greenland Saga is the most important one. The scene just described is true, every word of it, no doubt about that. We can read, in many documents written throughout the Middle Ages, what the European thought the peoples in far-off islands were like. Adam of Bremen tells of a land where the young men had the heads of dogs and barked instead of spoke, but the maidens were very beautiful. In another place there were bloodthirsty, insatiable men, born with gray hair; or pale green men who lived for a very long time. In the skraeling stories, however, we have nothing wildly implausible, but a highly convincing, surely eyewitness report of the encounter of Europeans with a primitive native population. The sale of the red material is recounted with accuracy. We have meanwhile learned more about the catapult. The Algonquin Indians used it in later times. They sewed the stones that were to be used as missiles into wet leather, which dried tightly around the stones. They painted the leather. It took more than one man to use the catapult.

During this meeting of a Stone Age tribe with peoples of the Iron Age, the former could have taken the giant step from one evolutionary period to the other, but the Indians lacked the rudimentary knowledge for evaluating an iron ax. When a simple stone proved stronger than the curious instrument the stranger had brought with him, they elected to remain in the Stone Age.

I think the point has already been made, that we archeologists take pride in the fact that the results of excavation so frequently complement and augment written sources. In this case we have evidence from the sagas that an actual Viking settlement was established on American soil. The Norsemen called it the *Leifsbodarna.* For years 160 people lived on the Straumfjord. Children were born on the new continent. Thorvald Ericsson died in America and was interred there. The iron ax was wrested from the hand of a fallen Viking who was surely buried after the battle. But all early efforts to find evidence of the Vikings in America failed. In 1930, a sword, an ax, and the remains of a shield boss or kettledrum were allegedly found in a typical Viking grave near Beardmore, not far from Lake Nipigon in Canada. The three iron instruments were undeniably authentic, but could very possibly have been brought over from Norway at a much later date. Various other scattered finds and discoveries served no better purpose. A round tower in Newport, Rhode Island, for a while was thought to be a round church of the early Middle Ages, but strong arguments, and the remains of modern settlements, discovered in 1949, speak against it. The most startling find was the Kensington Stone, supposedly discovered between the roots of a tree in Minnesota in 1898. That it is a forgery may be proved by various factors.

The inscription ends with the date 1362, a time when runes were still being carved, but no rune stones of that era can be found anywhere in Scandinavia. The finder of the Kensington Stone sent a copy of the inscription to O. J. Breda, Professor of Scandinavian Languages at the University of Minnesota, which gives every evidence of having served as a rough draft of the actual inscription. Modern influences are blatantly evident in it, conscious archaizations and Anglicanizations. Anyone interested in more detailed and technical proof that the stone is a forgery will find a sound explanation in an article by Professor Sven B. F. Jansson, our finest expert on Swedish rune stones, in the *Nordisk Tidskrift,* Stockholm, 1949. The conclusions of scientific examinations and discussions in 1949 and 1950 rule the stone out as an authentic object of research.

Historians searching for clues gave a good deal of thought to the fact that the southern limit of salmon is 41° latitude, the northern limit of grapes, 42°. As a likely meeting ground we arrive at the coast between Boston and New York City. Icelandic documents inform us that on Vinland the days were much more alike than they were in Greenland. The daylight lasted many hours longer, even at the winter solstice, and there was little frost. Without doubt, therefore, Leif penetrated farther south in America than did his predecessors. But how could one possibly identify scarcely noticeable irregularities along such an endless coastline? No wonder all early attempts to verify the presence of Vikings on the American continent were inconclusive.

The Norwegian Arctic explorer, Dr. Helge Ingstad, familiarized himself with the northeast American coast as no one had done before. He studied its nature to determine what possibilities it might have offered to the ancient mariners, in what way it could have fulfilled their specific practical needs. With an expert on languages, he made a study of the word *"vin."* Did it have to mean wine? Wasn't it far more likely that in the Norse language it could have been used to designate "grass," or "pasturage"? In which case the oldest name for America could be interpreted as Grassland, or Grazing Land. He felt he had to seek the landfall where the coast offered good feeding grounds for the cattle the settlers took with them.

He was also on the lookout for ancient foundations of houses, probably scarcely visible in today's earth. He looked on Rhode Island, along the Massachusetts coast, elsewhere—all in vain. He decided not to follow any more leads that restricted him to latitudes or longitudes. For the sailor of those days, the vast coastline must have been incalculable. Any such knowledge had to be of a later date. He began to think his way into the world of Leif Ericsson. "He could sit in his hall in Brattalid in Greenland, and in the concise way of speech that is reflected in the sagas, tell one of the sea captains what landmarks, and on what schedule he would reach Vinland." First, aided by the warm currents, northward along Greenland's coast as far as Godthaab; then across Davis Strait to the rocky coast of Helluland (Baffin Island) ; then down the wooded shores of Markland (Labrador). The saga of Thorfinn Karlsefni tells us: "They sailed along the land for a long while until they came to a cape. The land lay to starboard; there were long beaches and sands there. They rowed ashore and found there on the cape the keel of a ship, so they called the place Kjalarnes (Ship's Keel Cape). The beaches they called Furdustrandir (Wonder Strands) because it took such a long time to sail past them."

Cape Porcupine, where the waters of Labrador's inland lakes flow into Goose Bay, forms a triangular silhouette, like the keel of a Viking ship. Such things could impress the superstitious mariner of olden days. Ingstad felt sure that Cape Porcupine was Kjalarnes. The point was followed, absolutely correctly, by sandy beaches 30 miles long, with woodland directly behind them. "Grassland" would have to be the next visible feature. And there it was. "You can't miss it. . . ."

Of course the procedure wasn't quite so simple, especially during the reconnoitering that went on in the 1950's. Dr. Ingstad had to weigh all imaginable possibilities, carefully interpret every word of information, each concept and natural phenomenon he came across in the course of his search. He had to examine them critically and draw comparisons before he was gradually able to arrive at a clarification which drew him to the Island of Newfoundland. Here he asked questions and sought doggedly in the vicinity of St. Anthony. One day a fisherman told him that he had heard another fisherman speak of ruins in L'Anse au Meadow, a little village on the 10-mile-wide northern tip of the island. No highways lead to it. Here live 11 families who speak an antiquated English dialect. George Decker was the name of the fisherman who led Dr. Ingstad to the traces of former houses, now scarcely visible on the earth's surface, and assured him, "No stranger has seen them, and here at Lancey Meadow nobody tramps around without me knowing it."

This was in 1960 and seemed so promising that Dr. Ingstad started excavating in the summer of 1961. With him was an "expeditionary force" of nineteen participants from the United States, Canada, Iceland, Norway and Sweden.

Close to the ocean, protected by a small peninsula, not far from a fresh water brook, outlines which the layman wouldn't recognize, gradually emerged. For the expert who is familiar with the way houses were built on Greenland and in Scandinavia a thousand years ago, these outlines were priceless evidence. Dr. Ingstad could see the low remains of turf walls, he found postholes, he could visualize the former peaked roof made of long, vertical tree trunks. The largest house in L'Anse au Meadow measures 70 by 55 feet. It has the great hall that was so popular with the Vikings, and four rather unsymmetrical smaller rooms adjacent to it. It is just like Brattalid on Greenland where Leif Ericsson dwelt. The hall has a floor of hard-packed sand and clay, several hearths, and a slate-lined ember pit, less than a foot across, which kept coals glowing through the night for next day's fire. Around this foundation the traces of six more houses were uncovered.

On a nearby natural terrace there was a hollow which looked very much as if it had been formed by human hands. Dr. Ingstad's wife, Anna Stine Ingstad, dug here with a colleague and soon raised treasures more priceless than gold: hundreds of pieces of slag weighing approximately 30 pounds, as well as scraps of iron and some natural bog-iron ore. No doubt about it—she had found the Viking smithy. Close by, in another pit, she came across a thick layer of charred wood. Charcoal was requisite for the primitive processing of iron as practiced in Scandinavia in Viking days.

The charcoal find was of exceptional importance because, by the Carbon-14 method, we are able to date such finds precisely. One carbon reading resulted in the year A.D. 860, plus or minus 90 years; another in A.D. 1060, plus or minus 70 years, the time of the Viking expeditions to North America. It is impossible therefore for this smithy to have originated after Christopher Columbus' day; impossible, too, that it might have been an Indian camp, since the Indians, we know, didn't have iron. In the houses, ember and cooking pits corroborated the same dates.

An iron nail was found, the kind that turns up in all Viking settlements, but on the whole, finds were rare and we cannot expect too many because the soil is very acid and has destroyed even bones, except those that were burned and therefore calcined. A sensational addition, found some time later, is a soapstone spindle whorl. It is typically Scandinavian and was certainly used by Norse women. It was found rather indicatively just where a woman might be expected to sit and work in the sunshine, beside the hall of her house. A long piece of copper also deserves mention. Chemical analysis proved it to be metal that had been smelted in a primitive fashion.

Every one of the L'Anse au Meadow finds speaks for the acceptance of Dr. Ingstad's theory that here we have a Viking settlement on American soil, perhaps the *Leifsbodarna* itself, and that Leif Ericsson may have dwelt in the big hall. Not a single find points to a settlement of Indians, Eskimos, whaling men or fisher folk of a later period. Dr. Henry Collins, expert on primitive cultures of Arctic America, visited L'Anse au Meadow and declared: "The sites are definitely not Eskimo or Indian."

The government of Newfoundland has erected walls and roof over these excavated remains of houses to protect them, since exposure to the elements has made them vulnerable. President Johnson has decreed that America will celebrate Leif Ericsson Day as well as Columbus Day.

Leif Ericsson's arrival in the New World as described in a saga called the *Flatey Book,* suddenly rings true:

"They returned to the ship forthwith, and sailed away upon the main with northeast winds, and were out two days before they sighted land. They sailed toward this land, and *came to an island* which lay to the northward of the land. There they went ashore and looked about them, the water being fine, and they observed that there was dew upon the grass, and it so happened that they touched the dew with their hands, and touched their hands to their mouths, and it seemed . . . that they had never before tasted anything so sweet as this."

How would it be if we were suddenly to take these Norsemen literally, with a feeling for the gentleness and beauty of nature, something modern technical man is scarcely capable of?

The saga proceeds more precisely: "They went aboard their ship again and sailed into *a certain sound, which lay between the island and the cape,* which jutted out from the land on the north, and they stood in, westering past the cape. At ebb tide there were broad reaches of shallow water there, and it was a long distance from the ship to the Ocean; yet they were so anxious to go ashore that they could not wait until the tide should rise under their ship, but hastened to the land, where *a certain river flows out from a lake.*"

That is how these alert observers of nature reported on what they found. They took delight in the sandy beach, the protection offered by shallow beaches, the fresh water close by, the grass, and the trees, which they felled, just as whaling and fishermen lumbered off the wood along the coast in later days.

And what about the legendary wine?

A man called Tyrk took part in Leif's expedition. One day he was missed. Twelve men set out to look for him and found him totally drunk, lolling gaily, glassy-eyed. He was a small fellow, nothing to look at, but a good artisan.

"At first and for quite a long time, he rolled his eyes, made faces, and spoke German. So they didn't understand what he was saying. A little later he spoke in a Norse dialect: 'I did not go much farther than you,' he said. 'I have something new to tell. I found grape vines and grapes.'

" 'Can this be true, O my foster-father?' asked Leif.

" 'Of course it is true,' said he. 'For I was born where grape vine and grapes are not lacking.' "

According to the Greenland Saga, Tyrk had lived for a long time with Eric the Red, which is why Leif addressed him as "foster-father." As a German, coming from a wine region, he knew just what to do with the berries he had found; exactly what immigrants of the seventeenth century did—squeezed the grapes with their hands and let the juice stand for five or six days. The beverage did a good job on Tyrk who, in a gay mood, lapsed into his mother tongue, a very usual effect of alcohol.

The story sounds convincing and free of any fantastic elements. But grapes never grew in Newfoundland.

This problem, too, Dr. Ingstad managed to solve. The region is still rich in various types of berries. Tyrk took some of these berries, let them ferment, and in due course they intoxicated him. In later versions of the story they became grapes. But the decisive word in the thoughts and vocabulary of the men around Tyrk was "*vin,*" not the wine but the juicy dew-fresh grass that would feed their cattle. And George Decker knew of one fisherman who used to keep cows outside much of the winter. That is why the Vikings could report: "The nature of the land was so choice, it seemed to them that none of the cattle would require fodder for the winter." And when the Indian's arrow felled Thorvald Ericsson, he is supposed to have said, "There is fat around my belly! We have won a fine and fruitful country, but will hardly be allowed to enjoy it."

Thorvald was right. The aggressive action of the skraelings prevented the Vikings from completing their conquest. How could a handful of Europeans have hoped to hold out against a hostile native population? They would have had to bring over more and more iron and people from their homeland. When we think how much blood had to flow on the American continent before the European was able to settle on it, even with the help of firearms, we have to realize that even if the Vikings had mustered all their strength, they would never have succeeded in subjugating and colonizing the new continent.

A few flint instruments found in L'Anse au Meadow were made by Indians. They corroborate rather than contradict our conclusions, for we know that the Vikings traded with the redmen. A flint spearhead of typical Indian formation was found in Leif's homestead, Brattalid in Greenland. Anthracite coal was lying in Thorfinn Karslefni's house in Godthaab and may very well have come

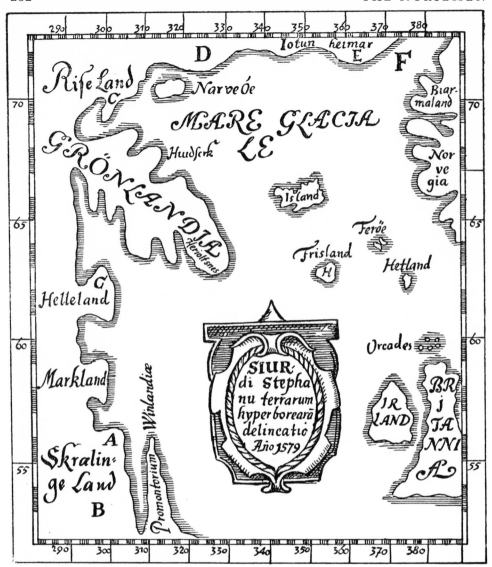

131. *Map of the Icelander Sigurd Stefansson, 1570. In those days the lands discovered by the Vikings were thought to be one connected continent surrounding the Atlantic Ocean.*

from Newport, Rhode Island, brought back to Greenland from a Viking expedition that penetrated that far south on the North American coast. Thorfinn and Gudrid's son Snorri was the first European to be born in America. He became the founding father of a prominent Icelandic clan.

Voyages across Davis Strait must have been frequent. In the year 1121, Bishop Eric traveled from Greenland to Vinland. It was important to bring lumber to treeless Greenland, and American larch has been found—indisputably

—in the churches and coffins of Herjulfsnes in Greenland. The last written account of a ship from Markland arriving in Greenland is dated 1347, but in the year 1637, the Icelandic Bishop Gisle Oddsson wrote that the Norse inhabitants of Greenland had "turned to the people of America."

According to Dr. Ingstad's outstanding achievement, the map of Icelandic Sigurd Stefansson (1570) may be considered more reliable than was formerly realized. Markland, Skralinge Land—which we may take to mean the Labrador coast running into the St. Lawrence River delta—and the Winlandiae promontory (presumably the northernmost peninsula of the Island of Newfoundland) are here depicted awkwardly, but with their relationship to one another just what it should be; and that was what the Vikings depended on. No doubt about it, the men of the North were well acquainted with the American continent. They read, discussed and interpreted all the information available to them: classical sagas, maps, to say nothing of the lore that was handed down to them orally.

In the fifteenth century, the great powers were searching for a northwest passage to India. Fortunate archive findings make it possible for us to prove that, in 1476, a Norwegian pilot named Jon Skolp pointed out to a Portuguese expedition a sea lane that led across the Atlantic Ocean, past Greenland, to the Labrador coast. So Norsemen were using this route to America sixteen years before Columbus!

In 1477, Christopher Columbus was in Iceland. The purpose of his journey was to find out more about the "islands" beyond the ocean. So why didn't he undertake his long voyage on the *Santa Maria* westward via Greenland to Labrador, which would have been shorter, less dangerous, and far more conclusive? Because in those days one did not proceed so systematically. Not for a moment did Columbus doubt the existence of all sorts of islands where others thought there was nothing save "night and horror," but the ice-cold waters of the north, with their perhaps numerous and certainly obstructive islands, did not interest him. His purpose was not to discover new islands, much less a whole continent. All he wanted was to find an easy sea route to India. That was the only undertaking for which he could raise either interest or money.

Christopher Columbus, Leif Ericsson and Thorfinn Karlsefni all were striving for the same Utopia, where wheat grew all by itself, rivers flowed with wine, dew was sweeter than honey, and mountains were pure gold. Reality, however, was different. The land was a new world. Only by hard labor could the conquest which the Vikings had planned be consummated.

13

~~~

From Vinland
to Baghdad

THE VIKINGS were the first people to visit four continents of this globe, a staggering fact, made all the more astounding when we take into consideration how far off the beaten track their Scandinavian homeland was. They fought and traded with American Indians and Saracens; with Eskimos and Florentines; with Finns, Turks, Slavs; with Irishmen, Franks, Spaniards, English and Germans, and frequently among themselves. The Emperor of the West knew them just as well as the Emperor of the East. They had trading privileges in Byzantium, and permission to roam in the noisy bazaars of the Caliphate city. The range of their expeditions reached incredible dimensions—from Vinland in the west to Särkland in the east, and finally to Baghdad.

In order to reach the latter, they had to pass through the city of Itil (today Astrakhan) where the Volga flows into the Caspian Sea. The king of the Khazars gave them permission to do so, but demanded as reward half of any booty they might take.

"Then the peoples round about the [Caspian] Sea cried out loudly, for in the days of old they had never known an enemy to find his way to the Caspian, which was plied only by trading vessels and fishing boats. The Rus therefore sought battle with al-Gail, ad-Dailam, and with Ibn-abu-Saga's governor, and they reached the sources of naphtha, in the empire of Sirwan, which is known as Baku."

A thousand years ago, therefore, before Alfred Nobel's exploitation of the Baku oil fields, the Swedes already had taken possession of this famous crude-oil area. According to a recently discovered written source, they laid waste to the town of Berda'a in the Caucasian Mountains in the winter of 943, and in the course of other military expeditions landed in Abasgun, Sari and Jorjan, on

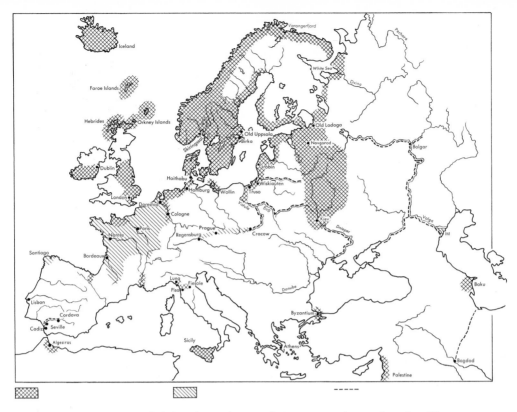

132. *States founded by the Vikings, their routes of travel and military expeditions.*

the southern shores of the Caspian Sea. Ibn Khordadbeh reports: "Sometimes they transported their merchandise on camels from the city of Jorjan to Baghdad. Here Slavonic eunuchs served them as interpreters."

Strange to think that the Vikings exchanged their dragon ships for ships of the desert to cross the Persian highlands (today Azerbaijan) and turned up on the Tigris. Could this be the farthermost point reached by them in Asia? In 1955, some archeologists carefully examined the earth of the Swedish trading center Helgö, on Lake Mälar. A bronze object was found and laid bare. Everyone was breathless at the unexpected sight of the sculptured figure—it was a Buddha! The statue was extremely well preserved, an art object of the finest caliber, a little over 3 inches high, the caste mark of gold, the legs crossed, the soles of the feet turned up, the whole figure seated on a lotus flower. Experts are still examining the fine stylistic details with a view to establishing the period to which it belongs. (*See ill. 133.*) How could this Buddha have reached Sweden from India or Afghanistan?

In a north Swedish grave, a well-preserved purse of fine lizard skin was found. (*See ill. 134.*) The raw material had been contributed by the lizard *varanus salvator,* which is found in India, Indonesia and China, or, possibly, by

133. *Buddha found on the island of Helgö, Sweden. State Historical Museum, Stockholm. Photo: ATA.*

the *varanus bengalensis*, found in India and Baluchistan. It may therefore be considered a sensational guest in Sweden. And we have the Chinese silk found in Birka graves. From the Silk Road it must have been traded farther by Arabian middlemen. Among all the Viking finds, these are the objects from farthest away.

In the north, the Vikings were at home as far as the White Sea. Here, too, they apparently felt their way along the Asiatic coast. Saxo Grammaticus, "the Lettered," notable Danish historian of the Middle Ages, tells of a voyage in 1180, a hundred years after the end of the Viking era, when many trade routes already existed in this area:

"Nether Bjarmaland is filled with constant frost and covered by high masses of snow so that it cannot even enjoy the power of the summer's warmth. The area is rich in virgin forests but scarce in fruit, and there are many animals that are hardly known anywhere else. There are supposed to be numerous rivers which pose hazards for the ships with their reefs and hissing, foaming whirlpools."

I think we can safely say that the Vikings got as far as the Pechora River, perhaps even to Novaya Zemlya, although the names of places in the report of the voyage are unclear. One thing though we may be sure of—the Bjarmaland voyages customarily undertaken by the Vikings were highly profitable. We know, for instance, that Thore Hund sailed with a few comrades to Bjarmaland in 1026, where they held a market, with great success. This was followed by the usual brawling with the native population and finally several instances of manslaughter among the participants. What interests us is the fact that Thore Hund returned to Norway from the White Sea, and four years later made his way far south:

"Thore Hund left home shortly after the death of the king. He went to Jerusalem, and there are many who say that he never came back."

I leave the reader to figure out the distance between Archangel and Jerusalem, in all probability not by way of Gibraltar, but across Lake Ladoga to Byzantium; how long it would take to make the trip by ship; how great the climatic changes must have been en route. What could men capable of such exploits really have been like?

134. *Fragment of a purse made of Indian lizard, found in Sweden. State Historical Museum, Stockholm.*

A few runes were carved into a whetstone that was found in Gotland's earth a few years ago. The row of words could serve as title and criterion for the entire Viking era. The original reads: *Ormiga :ulfuair :krikiaR :iaursaliR :islat :serklat.* The translation gives the philologist no trouble: "Ormika, Ulfair, Greece, Jerusalem, Iceland, Särkland."

First two Gotlanders are mentioned by name, after which are listed the lands they visited, a register of localities that men spoke of and which merited being inscribed. Once these men must have taken the route across the Russian rivers to the Black Sea, or across the eastern Mediterranean; another time they may have crossed the North Sea and Atlantic Ocean to Iceland, and from both trips they returned home safely.

Just as expressive in its way is a rune stone which commemorates the fate of an entire family whose members seem to have been driven far afield, as happens in periods when there is much warfare. The stone stands near Mjölby, in Östergötland:

> Thorgärd raised this stone for Assur, her uncle. He died in the East, in Greece.
>> Gulle, a good peasant, had five sons.
>> Asmund, the brave fighter, fell near Fyris [near Uppsala]
>> Assur died in the east, in Greece.
>> Halfdan was killed on Bornholm.
>> Kare died by Dundee [in Scotland?]
>> Dead also is Boe.

135. *Siegfried etching on the Ramsunberget stone, Sweden. Photo: ATA.*

The Vikings also introduced their poetry, their legends, and the world of their gods, into the far-flung corners of the earth. We have already met the smith, Volund, vengeful Hild and Gunnar in the snake pit. Most popular of all, probably, was Siegfried the dragon killer, especially well depicted on the famous rune stone southwest of Stockholm. Here again a woman ordered the stone raised. The inscription tells us: "Siegrid made this bridge. [She was] Alrik's mother [and] Orm's daughter. For the soul of her husband Holmger. . . ."

So the soul is mentioned; Christians have already made their influence felt. The legend is not in anyway dependent on pagan religion, and the woman is announcing before anything else that she has had a bridge built, by which she doesn't mean a bridge across a river but a stone-paved way across a damp depression. Traces of it have been established. This stone stands at a bridgehead, easy for every wayfarer to see. Originally the figures on it were painted in clear colors. Traces of color have been found on some rune stones that were protected by earth. And the similarity of the names Siegrid and Siegfried was probably what motivated Holmger's wife to invoke just this legend.

The inscription band serves ingeniously as the serpent's body. The hero rams his sword into the dragon, Fafner, from beneath. This is the essential point made by the descriptive pattern. The dragon killer is crouching in a pit. His husky biceps end in a spiral, in accordance with the style of the design. The helmet is conic, the sword easily bears comparison with those found in weapon graves. (*See ill. 135.*)

Siegfried roasts the dragon's heart over an open fire; burns his thumb in the process, sticks it in his mouth, thus gets dragon fat on his tongue and can suddenly understand the language of the birds. The birds are perched on the tree to which Siegfried's horse, Grane, is tethered. The birds twitter and say that the smith Regin is up to no good. He wants to kill Siegfried and get possession of the dragon's hoard. Whereupon Siegfried makes short shrift of the treacherous smith and chops off his head. That the headless man is really supposed to be the smith, we can tell by the instruments: hammer, tongs, anvil and bellows. On top of it all—an animal. This is the otter (son of the giant, Rodmar), in its mouth the ring Andvarenautr, symbol of the treasure that is under such a terrible curse.

Less well known is a clumsy copy of this fine carving, almost ridiculous in its awkwardness. (*See ill. 136.*) The stone carver seems to have had special difficulty with his human figures. The dragon killer is a failure; the headless man is nothing more than a clumsy body with hands, and Siegfried as cook is a lascivious sybarite, incomprehensibly holding a hammer in his hand. The horse fares no better; it looks like a camel. But we can have a good laugh at the expense of this bungler, who is an isolated case.

136. *Copy of the Ramsunberget Siegfried etching, Gökstenen, Sweden. Photo: ATA.*

Of much greater importance is the profusion of fine Siegfried illustrations. The Ockelbo stone shows numerous figures arranged in a pattern that was used on a whole group of north Swedish stones. (*See ill. 137.*) Although slightly damaged at the top, we can still recognize the sword stabbing upward into the dragon band. Below it, on the right, the hero is probably being stabbed in the back; to the left, Brynhilde, riding to the funeral pile in a four-wheeled horse cart, meets a bent-over giantess. This interpretation of the legend should be examined scrupulously. Below, two men are enjoying a game on a board and drinking out of horns. In all probability, Siegfried and Gunnar's friendship is here being symbolized. What interests us most is the impressive central tree, with Grane and a bird, as we already know them. To right and left a man and woman who turn up again on four rune stones: the female with a drinking horn, the man holding a ring behind him. The woman must be Krimhilde, offering the draught of forgetfulness to Siegfried; the man, Andvari, with the ring, Andvarenautr. An alternative would be Gudrun, welcoming her brother at Atli's (Attila's) court, and the messenger Vinge, with a warning

137. *The Siegfried Saga crudely depicted on the north Swedish rune stone of Ockelbo.*

138. *Carvings of the Siegfried legend, showing the hero with his sword and Andvari the ring bearer in various combinations.*

139. *Scenes from the Siegfried legend on the stone cross of Kirk Andreas, Isle of Man.*

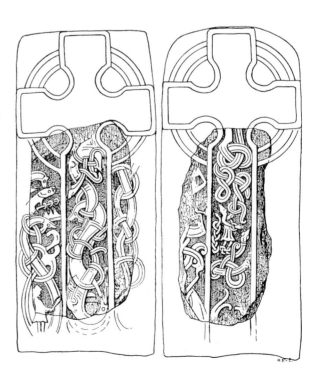

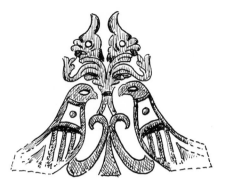 

140. *Scenes from the Siegfried legend on an ornate ax found in Vladimir-Suzdal, Russia.*

wolf's hair in the ring. Be that as it may, we can see how popular the Norse legends were, and how familiar the Norsemen were with them. (*See ill. 138.*)

We find similar motifs on stone crosses on the Isle of Man. Let us take a look at the damaged stone cross of Kirk Andreas, where we catch a glimpse of Siegfried in the lower left corner, sticking his sword diagonally upward into the dragon ornamentation; above it, the fire with the dragon's heart sliced on a spit. In the center of the opposite side, Gunnar lies in the snake pit, his arms and legs bound. A monster is biting him in the breast. (*See ill. 139.*)

We find illustrations of the Siegfried legend in Russia, on a magnificent ax from the Vladimir-Suzdal region. (*See ill. 140.*) It is richly inlaid with gold, silver and niello. On one side a dragon is writhing, a sword stuck upward in

141. *Andvari with the ring, cast as a piece of jewelry found in the Latvian fortress of Daugmale Pilskalns.*

his body, unmistakably Fafner. On the other side, two birds are sitting, symmetrically, demurely, on either side of a tree, a motif we come across quite often. This is an age-old Oriental, late Roman-Christian design, but, when it is combined with a dragon slaying, it is clear that the two birds in a tree of the Siegfried legend are being depicted.

Today we can add one more figure to this type of illustration. (*See ill. 141.*) The author of this book participated as a pupil in his first dig—the excavation on the Lett fortress-mountain, Daugmale Pilskalns. The drawing is after a casting of the original, which was given him as a present, but was not available at the time. It shows a Viking in a typical shirt down to his thighs. The sword hilt is Nordic. The only thing no one could find an explanation for was the big wreath the man was holding behind his back. But if we hold the figure up against the Ockelbo Stone, we recognize immediately that the wreath is the ring Andvarenautr; the Viking is the dwarf Andvari. This gloriously situated mountain with fortress had a commanding position over the broad sailing route of the Southern Dvina, inland to Russia. The Letts could demand tribute, or the Viking hordes could fight their way through by force. Somehow this illustration of a Nordic heroic legend found its way into the earth of the mountain, and today helps us to demonstrate the popularity of the motif. It moved through Europe with the Vikings.

We have numerous illustrations of the beliefs and legends of the Vikings, many of them older than our Icelandic, German and other written sources, and the way in which they are scattered geographically is highly revealing. That is why it is so regrettable that all this evidence has not yet been properly organized. If it had been, we would no longer have to put up with such random and often fantastic "interpretations," as we unfortunately still do, every year. Historians should classify the material, date and evaluate it according to style, just as we archeologists do when we catalogue and publicize our finds. Only then could the experts of the various branches of knowledge approach the many illustrations with confidence. Their interpretation is not always as simple as was the case with the Viking from the Dvina, or the stone of Sanda. The heroic lays, legends, laws and Valhalla themes of the Vikings merit objective, up-to-date interpretation.

Toward the end of the tenth century, a new generation of Vikings was ready to set out, eastward and westward. In the Nestor Chronicle, we can read that Rurik's two great grandsons quarreled, and that Vladimir (Waldemar) fled across the sea, *i.e.*, to Sweden, where he raised an army. With it, he returned to Novgorod in 980, and from that city succeeded in reconquering Kiev. His brother fled and was killed. The soldiers he brought with him from his original homeland called themselves *Varingar* (Varangians). The word is pure

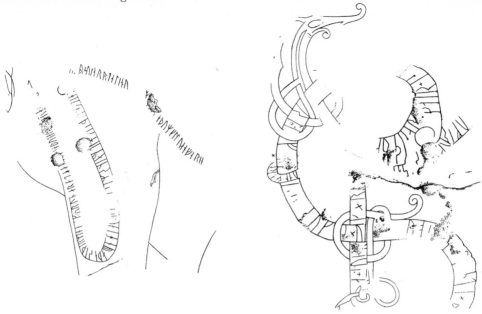

142. *Runic loops on the marble lion of Piraeus, now in Venice.*

Nordic. The syllable "-ing" is typical, and *"Var"* means loyalty. They were therefore confederates, co-members of a merchant guild, but first and foremost sworn brothers in arms. Ad.Stender-Petersen, scholar of Danish legend, believes that the Varangians didn't move into Russia until 980. He draws a clear dividing line between them and the Rus. According to him, they represent two quite independent thrusts from Sweden. If the name of these confederates turns up in the Nestor Chronicle quite often before the year 980, it is because the Varangians had a feeling of solidarity with the earlier settler, the Rus. They identified themselves with the Rus to justify their presence in the East. They adapted the legend of the three brothers to their own requirements. The beautiful invitation, "Come and rule over us," was their main moral and diplomatic excuse for their presence in Russia. The turn of the second millennium was stamped by what they did or left undone in that country. After their victory in Kiev, "the Varangians said to Vladimir, 'This is our city. We have conquered it. We therefore want a ransom. . . .'

"He gave them nothing. Whereupon the Varangians said, 'You deceived us. Show us the way to Greece.' He said, 'Begone!' and he chose from their midst, good and reasonable and brave men, and divided cities among them. But the others moved on to Greece and Byzantium."

There they entered the service of the Byzantine Emperor. Soon they formed his bodyguard and became responsible for his personal safety. They were always on the alert and were used in whatever capacity the daily situation in the

143. *Rune stone near Stockholm, in commemoration of a man who was chief of the Emperor's Guard in Byzantium.*

restless eastern Mediterranean area demanded. In the harbor city of Athens, there was a garrison. Today the place is called Pireaus; before that it was named Lion-gate, after the marble lion in the harbor entry. Here the Emperor sent only reliable soldiers, who had proved themselves in battle. The Varangians carved an elegant dragon loop and runes into marble for a fallen comrade.

(*See ill. 142.*) The stone has become so weathered that we can't read every word, but it is undoubtedly the most distant of all the Southeastern runic memorials. Today the stone can be seen in front of the arsenal in Venice. It is complemented by no less than twenty-six Swedish rune stones for men who fought in Greece. The aforementioned Assur was one of them. In a wood south of Sigtuna lies a moss-covered erratic boulder, looking primordially Swedish in its shadowy evergreen forest. (*See ill. 143.*) On it we can read, to our surprise: "These runes were carved by Ragnvald; he who was chieftain of the Varangians in Greece." A man, therefore, who had held the highest position in the Emperor's guard in Byzantium, but had returned to his home north of Stockholm on his retirement.

On another stone, not far from Stockholm, we can read: "Astrid had this stone raised for Östen, her husband. He went to Jerusalem and died in Greece."

Twenty-five rune stones name a military leader called Ingvar, of whom we know that he led an impressive Viking expedition to the east in the year 1041. Perhaps Ingvar the Far-traveled was a member of a Swedish royal family. They spoke at home of the troops he levied, of whom many never came back.

In Byzantium you could find men from every part of Scandinavia. The Icelandic sagas often mention emigrating Icelanders or those returning home. In Ravnkel Freysgode's Saga, a man called Torkel writes: "I am a free man. Last summer I came here to Iceland. I was away for seven years, out there in Miklagard (Byzantium). I have sworn fealty to the King of Gardarike [Russia]." And in the Njal's Saga: "Now we can tell of Kolskegg, that he sailed from Iceland to Norway and Denmark. . . . There he was baptized. But he did not do well, and wandered off eastward to Russia, and spent one winter there. Then he moved on to Byzantium, where he entered military service. The last news from him was that he had taken a wife there, and was the leader of a northlandic army."

The most famous chieftain of the Emperor's bodyguard in Byzantium was the Norwegian king Harald Haardraade, or Hardruler, whom we met at the beginning of this book. He was the pert little boy who tugged the king's beard. He spent his childhood (1034–1044) in Russia and the eastern Mediterranean. Snorri created a whole novel of adventure out of Harald's heroic deeds. It forms a part of the *Heimskringla*. Harald came to Miklagard with a large entourage:

> Forward the black prow,   driv'n by cold primeval breezes,
> Sails billowing smartly,   armed men sailed strand lengthwise.
> Greece's Emperor could see their ships   radiant light playing round
>   them,
> As the bright shimmering ships   floated to his fort's battlements.

"At the time, Empress Zoe the Powerful was ruling Greece, in conjunction with her lover, Michael Katalaktes. When Harald came to Miklagard, he entered her service, and in the autumn his ships, manned with soldiers, took off for the 'Greek (Aegean?) Sea.' Harald had not been in the army long before the Varangians flocked to him, and wherever there was fighting, they stuck together. . . . He moved his army to Särkland, and took 80 fortresses. Some surrendered, others had to be stormed. Then he moved on to Sicily, where he took a great amount of booty in the form of landed estates, gold and all sorts of valuable treasure. Everything that he didn't need to defray his expenses, he sent to the North, with his loyal followers, to Holmgard (Novgorod), into the safekeeping of King Jarosalv (Vladimir's son). Soon a tremendous amount of weath had accumulated there, as was to be expected, since he was ravaging a corner of the earth that was rich in gold and luxury; and was always undertaking such vast enterprises. . . . He also went to Jerusalem, and wherever he went, castles and forts capitulated before his might."

The man who was to be Norway's king headed all these military excursions. Snorri tells us that Harald and the Varangians put out the Emperor's eyes after a battle, but this horrible fate overtook Michael Kalafates (son and successor to Michael Katalaktes) in the year 1042.

Blind was the master of Greece . . . smitten with horrible wounds.
The quick warlord won gold and rich booty.

Did Snorri play around quite a bit with historic data? No, not Snorri—he was much too conscientious. He recounted only what he was told. The Varangians were the ones who embellished the meager historic facts. Eighty forts in Särkland alone? Here we are probably dealing with Syria, citadels in Palestine, and an absolutely legendary amount of booty, the value of which was left to whatever fantasy chose to see. These are the stories that originate around a camp fire. The Saga of Harald the Ruthless is a gold mine for the historians of legend, and in the narrative that is concerned with his expedition to Sicily, the most ingenious ruses of warfare are strung together like pearls on a chain. Before taking a particularly strong fortress, he is supposed to have caught birds, tied wood shavings, wax and sulphur to their tail feathers, and with their fluttering—as they flew back to their nests in the fort—they started a fire! The many small flames led to a big conflagration, and the occupants of the fort had to capitulate. "Harald spared all those who begged for mercy," is the last naïve line of the story.

Before the days of societies for the protection of animals, a few scientists experimented with the idea, and succeeded in thoroughly debunking the incident, but it turns up again in the Nestor Chronicle, in the Dünaburg (Dvinsk) and in the Irish city of Cirencester. Together with all the other fantastic tricks of warfare, it is and remains a tall tale.

Actually King Harald the Ruthless didn't do so well in southern Italy because he met up with compatriots, tribal brothers. Normans from Normandy had moved down there in ever-increasing numbers, settled in various areas, and begun to threaten even Byzantine properties. Western and eastern Vikings met in the year 1042 in a Mediterranean sea battle. Harald was defeated by the Normans, who didn't have to be persuaded to accept the cedar apples, almonds and gilded nuts of Sicily. They arrived without invitation, in good old Scandinavian style. Tankred of Fort Hauteville in Normandy had twelve grown sons, eight of whom emigrated to Sicily. Robert Guiscard (the Sly) and Roger were the founders of a Norman dynasty on the island.

Their colorful fates were determined by a polyglot world consisting of Romans, Greeks, Arabs and French-speaking Norsemen. The most famous offspring of this dynasty is Roger's great grandson, Holy Roman Emperor *Deutscher Nation,* Frederick II of the Hohenstaufen dynasty, and dominant ruler of Europe in the thirteenth century. The Normans brought a Nordic strain to Sicily which added color to the life there. It is not the purpose of this book to follow the administration, laws and customs of this area further, but here undoubtedly is one of the most fascinating projects for future research.

The Varangian troops in Byzantium gradually underwent a change of formation. After the Battle of Hastings in England, 1066, many Englishmen who no longer felt at home in their native land fled to Byzantium and were accepted as soldiers in the Emperor's bodyguard. Soon you could hear, with Greek as the official language, the same mixed Norman tongue as in the Viking-occupied territories of England. Gradually, however, the stream from Scandinavia died down. In the end we hear only of English members of the bodyguard which became, one might say, a Swedish Guard with no Swedes! Until the end of the Byzantine Empire in 1453, the English were the sole guardians of peace and safety at the palace.

The chiefs of the Rurik dynasty had moved meanwhile from Kiev to Novgorod. The royal house was bound with as close ties to the Nordic ruling houses as were the Scandinavian rulers among themselves. This can be studied most easily on a family tree:

Rurik (ninth century)	Emigrated from Sweden.
Igor (tenth century)	Married Helga-Olga, born of Nordic parents in Pleskov.
Svyatoslav (died 972)	Married Malmfrid-Malusa, keybearer to Queen Olga.

Vladimir (Saint 972–1015)	Married Ragnheid-Rogned, daughter of the chieftain Ragnvald in Polotsk, who emigrated from across the sea.
Yaroslav (died 1054)	Married 1019 to Ingegärd, daughter of Swedish King Olaf Skötkonung.
Ellisif-Elisabeth	Married King Harald the Ruthless of Norway.
Holti-Vsevolod (ruled 1078–93)	Married a Byzantine princess of the Monomachos dynasty.
Valdemar-Monomach (ruled 1113–25)	Married Gyda, daughter of Harald Godvinsson in England.
Harald-Mstislav (ruled 1125–32)	Married Kristin, daughter of Swedish King Inge Stenkilsson.
Ingeborg (twelfth century)	Married King Canute Lavard V of Denmark.
Malmfrid (twelfth century)	Married King Sigurd Jorsalafar of Norway, the Jerusalem voyager; later married her brother-in-law, King Eric Emune of Denmark.

We see that the princes of Novgorod usually had two names, a Nordic and a Slavonic one, according to the bilinguality of their dynasty and milieu. Every generation married a Nordlander. Ingegärd's wedding in 1019 seems to have been particularly impressive. Her picture was found not so long ago under the chalk plaster of the Sophia Church in Kiev which her husband, Yaroslav, had built. Ingegärd is walking ahead of her three daughters, all of them queens-to-be—Queen Elisabeth of Norway (see family tree), Queen Anne of France, Queen Anastasia of Hungary. It is the earliest contemporary portrait of a historic person from the Viking era.

With all these events, Sweden might well have been converted to the Greek-Orthodox faith. We find traces of "Resurrection Festivals" in Sigtuna, also in the last graves that contain furnishings very similar to those popular in Russia. "A bishop with no head" is said to have been at the Swedish king's court around 1055. "He is supposed to have ruined the newly converted barbarians by an incorrect teaching of our faith." This points to a schismatic trend toward the orthodox faith. We find the chief saints of Russian ikon painting—Maria and Nicholas Chudatvoritch—on small reliquaries in a late silver hoard on

144. *Russian-Orthodox reliquaries from a late silver hoard in North Sweden. State Historical Museum, Stockholm. Photo: ATA.*

the north Swedish coast, an *enkolpion*—i.e., a crucifix used as a reliquary—in Byzantine style, just outside the city limits of Stockholm, as well as other proofs of conversion to the Eastern faith. (*See ill. 144, 145.*)

In the course of two hundred years, the Viking character underwent great changes. The peasant raiders who, at the beginning of the Viking era, sailed across the sea to Lindisfarne, were followed by the "seasonal" Vikings, who

145. *Russian "resurrection eggs" of baked clay, found in Gotland. Similar eggs are found often in the vicinity of Kiev. State Historical Museum, Stockholm. Photo: Iwar Anderson.*

sailed forth in the summer and made life difficult for the Frisian merchants. They in turn were replaced by hordes of emigrating Vikings, forcing their way through to foreign lands to win living space for new settlements. Their children grew up to found states and cut themselves loose from the mother country to face independent fates of their own in their newly adopted lands. Then came the peaceful Vikings of the middle of the tenth century.

Their strength lay in the freedom of the community life of soldier and peasant. It took only a few men and a quick bold decision to master the most difficult situation. They may have tolerated now and then a king—allegedly descended from a god—but they granted him no godlike powers. As subjects they felt any interference in their independence as individuals to be intolerable. In a last wild resurgence of militarism, we find a Viking soldier who subordinates himself to an organized command and with that renounces his true nature, his independence. Warlike excursions had become so numerous, and assumed such dimensions, that a more complex administration and greater discipline had to be achieved, in coastal defense as well as in planned attack, in defense as in offense. And this turned out to be a major psychological problem, because it conflicted with the specific Viking mentality.

When the Varangians set out for the East with fierce intentions, the smoldering Viking peril flared up once more in the West, a parallelism we have been able to demonstrate all along. At the same time as in the East—in 980—the storm broke over England again. Southampton was plundered. On every coast,

146. *A reconstruction of the Viking Encampment of Trelleborg, Seeland. Photo: National Museum, Copenhagen.*

also in the Irish Sea, the dragon ships appeared again, this time brilliantly organized and in unbelievable numbers. Olaf Trygvasson, scarcely returned from Russia, won his first great victory near Maldon, in 991. Harald Bluetooth's son and successor, Sven Forkbeard, rushed to help him. They laid siege to London, ravaged the south of England, and made a minor foray into the Elbe district, to "Saxland." This was the powerful prelude.

Only rarely can military expeditions be proved by archeological excavation, but for these excursions the finds of the last decades have been highly satisfactory. First we found the circular wall of Trelleborg, on West Seeland, in the following casual fashion. Some buyers turned up who wanted to purchase a certain piece of land for a motorcycle race track. It included a ringed slope which they intended to use as a grandstand. Nobody had given the site a thought; suddenly it seemed worth investigating. (*See ill. 146.*) And this turned out to be far more rewarding than most excavations, for it established facts about Viking administration of which no one had ever dreamed. The postholes alone—those thankless but, in this case, revealing remains of buildings—within the ringed earthwork, showed that 16 elliptical houses had once stood there, four together in four squares, and fifteen houses in an arc outside the wall. And the exactitude of geometric measurement was astounding. The Roman foot—11.54 inches—had formed the unit of measure.

Inner radius from center to wall	234 ft.
Radius from center to gable end of row of houses	twice 234 ft.
Distance from inner to outer wall-ditch	234 ft.
12 house corners meet at an outer right angle, the side of which measures	272 ft.
4 house corners meet at an inner right angle the side of which measures	72 ft.
The houses have a length of	100 ft. each

This is no number magic. Whoever has done any measuring outdoors knows how difficult it is to proceed with any sort of exactitude. Deviations in precision proved to be less than 1/2 per cent. And this is a bureaucratic pedantry we hadn't expected of the Vikings. Architects and surveyors must have been at work here with lines of sight, must have staked out measurements, focused, trued, until all lines were accurately adjusted.

The houses themselves were astounding because of their flat, elliptic form, yet we already knew them from the shape of the small whalebone caskets from Cammin and Bamberg. (*See ill. 147.*) For these wonderfully ornamented caskets are shaped like houses and give us a general impression of what the buildings must have looked like. There is still a lot of controversy about their technical construction, because the postholes tell us little about the walls and

147. *A reliquary casket found in Cammin, Pomerania. The casket is in the shape of a house, elliptical, like the foundations uncovered in Trelleborg. The original was destroyed in World War II. Photo: ATA.*

nothing at all about the roof. The ringed wall gave the entire enclosure the shape of a pool. After every rainfall there must have been a terrible morass under the planks, which is probably why boardwalks ran between the houses.

We know of no fortification like this in any other lands. After the Danes had finished excavating Trelleborg, they began to look around for more circular walls, and soon came upon Aggersborg, on the Lim Fjord. Whoever may not have been astonished by Trelleborg could be now at sight of the 12 squares found in Aggersborg, with 48 houses, each 110 ft. long. (*See ill. 148.*) Finally Fyrkat, near Hobro, and Nonneborg on Fünen were also discovered. But we have no publications concerning them as yet.

These fortifications are pure military encampments of the early years of Sven Forkbeard's reign. The barracks were probably laid out with the same precision with which the Viking soldiers were being drilled. Due to the fact that Viking expeditions at last moved with mutually agreed upon goals, they gained a great deal in striking power, yet—as already mentioned—the individual Viking gave up something invaluable—his independence, thereby disavowing himself. And the ensuing abrupt end that had to follow such disavowal did not fail to materialize. The Vikings experienced military victory at the moment of their downfall as clear-cut individual personalities.

In historical accounts, the victories at first follow hard one upon the other. The vacillating English King Aethelred trembled, and in the years 991 and 994, bought his freedom for 10,000 and 16,000 pounds of silver respectively. Danegeld it was called. But the Vikings came back, fought and conquered, and in 1002 departed with 24,000 pounds of silver. In his confusion, Aethelred murdered every Dane residing in England, calling down Viking wrath on his head all over again. Tribute payment rose to 36,000 pounds of silver. One Viking chieftain, called Torkel, was able to raise the price to 48,000 pounds.

Sven Forkbeard landed in Five Boroughs with a new fleet. He found the population passive and neutral. After all, they were of Danish origin. He conquered almost all of England—but not London. Helpless, Aethelred again paid up—this time 21,000 pounds—and fled the country. What the Great Army had been unable to do, because they had been opposed by Alfred the Great, the Vikings now accomplished with ease. More than that—London was being defended by one of their own kind, the aforementioned Torkel, who had gone over to the English king and become his vassal. Naturally he remained loyal only as long as there was a king in England. So London, too, opened its gates, and the Vikings entered. The island's fate lay in the hands of the Danish king, Sven Forkbeard, who, on February 3, 1014, fell from his horse—and died.

For four years, Sven's and Aethelred's sons fought for the mastery of England, until young Canute won near Assandun and became the undisputed North Sea ruler over all Denmark and England. He paid his Vikings off with 82,500 pounds of silver.

148. *Plan of the fortifications of Aggersborg, on the Lim Fjord.*

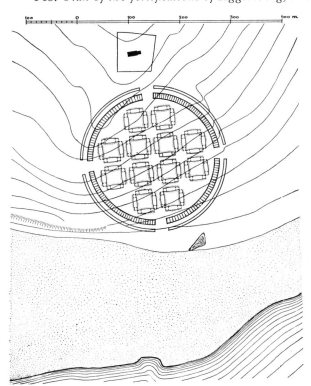

149. *Rune stone in North Sweden. The inscription reads: "Dan, Huskarl and Sven and Holmfrid, mother and sons, had this stone raised for Ulfrik, their grandfather. He received tribute twice in England. God and God's mother save the souls of this father (Ulfrik) and his son (Halfdan.)" Photo: Gösta Lundqvist.*

150. *English silver coins, tribute paid by King Aethelred, found in Sweden.*

The black earth of Trelleborg betrays, by an oval brooch and a Haithabu half-bracteate, that the fort was built *circa* 990. The ring wall had gates in all four directions, each of them 10 feet wide.

With so much talk of so much silver, one would expect to find traces of it preserved for posterity, and we do. Even the east Swedish rune stones tell of it: "Karse and Ambjörn had this stone raised in memory of their father Ulf. God and God's mother have mercy on his soul. But Ulf received tribute (*kial,* money, fire tax) three times in England. The first time Toste paid him, after that Torkel, and finally Knut (Canute)." (*See ill. 149.*)

This soldier from east Sweden therefore fought from 1009 to 1018 under Torkel and Canute, about whom we have already read. We know less about Toste. Snorri mentions a man by that name, "the mightiest and most respected in Sweden of all those who did not bear a princely title. He was a great Viking, and was away a long time on military expeditions." At first Swedish Vikings in England may have been under his command. The formulation is interesting —according to it, the Nordic leaders are mentioned as the paymasters of the Danegeld. Three other rune stones give us similar information:

"Ale received Canute tax in England."

"Ulfrik twice received tax in England."

"Gudvir was in the west; in England he received his share of the taxes; in Saxland he cleverly stormed fortresses."

Another comrade didn't do so well. "He died in Jutland, just as he was setting sail for England."

We could hardly expect to find Frankish silver payments of the ninth century in Scandinavian earth, but something is left of these enormous tribute payments. We are dealing here with, all in all, 240,000 pounds of silver, or, if we are going to count only Aethelred's payments—158,000 pounds. Since scarcely any trading was taking place during his unfortunate rule, we can look upon practically all the coins minted by him and found in Scandinavia as Danegeld. (*See ill. 150.*) The largest hoard, found near the church of Igelösa,

151. *Viking ship on the Bayeux tapestry, depicting the invasion of England by William of Normandy.*

contained 828 coins. In their way, they are just as telling witnesses of the participation of Viking soldiers as the rune stones. The coin finds are still being examined, which is why we do not have a total for the Aethelred coins. And for the present we also have to take into consideration that many coins must have been melted down to make rings and other silver objects.

In Ireland, Olaf Cuaran's son once more assembled all resident soldiers and roving seafarers into one gigantic army and pitted them against the assembled might of the Celtic kings. On Good Friday, 1014, Sigtyrgg Silkbeard decided to attack near Clontarf, not far from Dublin. If he had been victorious, if Sven Forkbeard hadn't fallen off his horse ten weeks before, the history of the oceanic islands might have been . . . Speculations such as these are frequent when we study the numerous decisive Viking battles. And so we arrive at the last bloody defeat of the Normans in Ireland. Their strength was broken. In the confusion of the many minor skirmishes that followed between petty kings, we see no great guiding line, only the beginning of a more felicitous fusion between Normans and Celts.

In 1018, Canute the Great sent his Vikings home. In his short life he created, to the best of his ability, a prosperous England and a peaceful Denmark. And from the Vikings—no protest. They obeyed. They had become soldiers. Subordination to a royal command had dispelled their *élan*. They were not conquered by Christianity, as Louis the Pious had hoped two hundred years before, but by administrative order, by Roman discipline, by southern bureaucracy.

In exchange they received—a fatherland. The wide world became stranger to them, and they to it. They belonged *at home*, that is to say—in Denmark, in Sweden, in Norway, in Iceland. From now on they were to fight and die at home; there—not across the seas—lay the future.

And yet . . . England was flooded again by Norman armies. They no longer came from Scandinavia, however, but from Normandy. In 1066, William the Conqueror, a successor of Gange-Rolf, landed in the south of England with his invasion fleet, defeated the British in the Battle of Hastings, had himself declared the new ruler of England and, according to the age-old pattern, began to divide the land among his soldiers. This final event is immortalized in fascinating detail and with marvelous pictorial liveliness on an approximately 230-foot-long tapestry in Bayeux. (*See ill. 151.*) Thus two ultimate state foundations emanated from the Scandinavian-founded state of Normandy: Sicily and England.

14

The Viking Heritage

WHAT IF THE economic foundation of the far-flung Viking expeditions east and west, north and south, were to shift? Then the very basis of Scandinavian world power would be shaken. In the tenth century, Viking trade was still organized according to conditions that had prevailed 150 years before. Purses were still filled with Arabic silver, fur and natural produce from the Arctic were being traded, luxury items were being bought and sold in Europe and the Far East, and the Norseman enjoyed complete supremacy of the oceans and rivers. Suddenly the Saxon kings—with the intention of strengthening the young German Reich—began to work the Harz Mountain silver mines. Hammer blows could be heard in the pits of the Saxon mountains. At last the Occident's dependency on Arabic silver could be overcome.

Goslar, the natural center for this new, fast-growing traffic with silver, began to thrive. The metal was transported westward on the Hellweg, via Soest and Cologne. Saxon coins found their way northward as currency for the Scandinavian fur trade, and the Vikings could do nothing but welcome their prosperous trading partners from Germany. Soon the new Harz silver mines make their presence felt in archeological findings which are such a delicate instrument for this sort of data. Up to the year 950, the Scandinavian silver hoards consist exclusively of Arabic coins and hacksilber. Suddenly the first German coins turn up—until 980 only in isolated cases, then they begin to increase. The evidence of German coins in Scandinavia is infallible, and important for a study of the history of the Saxon kings. We can demonstrate the increase of Saxon coins exactly with the Danish finds that have been examined:

	Year	Arabic Coins	German Coins
Coin hoards buried in	950–980	2,336	22
(The year given in the case	980–1000	738	457
of large hoards is the one	1000–1020	129	1,184
of the most recent coin.)	1020–1050	20	2,994
	1050–1070	4	3,030

The tabulation shows that Arabic silver grows scarce as Saxon silver increases. And the change is rapid. Only a few Arabic coins minted after the year 1000 reached Scandinavia, and the most recent one for all Scandinavia was struck in 1010. The Arabic coins disappear just as fast as the German coins take over.

Decisive events took place in the southeast, which still have to be studied more extensively. But we can safely say now that the silver mines in the Eastern Caliphate seem to have been exhausted just as the Harz mines became active. This is a strange coincidence. Certainly it served to prevent a dreadful inflation and a tangible lack of silver in Europe. The era of heavy trading with the Arabs was over. One of the Vikings most prosperous trading partners dropped out, and this defection shook the entire system.

In their stead, we find the fortuitous new buying power of Germany and France. Christian lands could not traffic with slaves, but they paid good Saxon silver for furs from the North. All major trade efforts therefore had to be channeled in new directions, away from the Caliphates, from Särkland, and southern Russia, so that the jingling silver might be collected in the West instead of the East. It is our special pride that this turn of events can be read nowhere so clearly as in archeological findings. At last, the hour had drawn nigh for a closer co-operation between the Western states—with an energetic new Germany across the Baltic, between a thriving Frankland and a healthy Scandinavia, already partially converted to Christianity. But the trade monopoly of the Norsemen was broken. We can see the evidence in startling new finds in Lappland and Karelia.

In the world-wide sphere of Viking interests, we have so far failed to mention their closest neighbors, the Lapps—hunters, fishermen, reindeer breeders —who had existed, isolated, in the north Scandinavian tundra since prehistoric times. Graves in the area are attributed to them, but are so poor in content that it is often difficult to make a sure statement concerning them. They took over some of the essential elements of Nordic pagan beliefs even before the Viking era. Until now we knew little of their ancient history.

At his desk, historian Gustav Hallstrom was working on some scientific deductions in a purely theoretical way. It seemed that in the seventeenth century, a few Swedish administrators and pastors had discovered that there were still heathen people within the borders of their own land—the Lapps. The discovery was followed by great conversion zeal. All sites of pagan sacrifice were to be wiped out. But these were so sacred to the Lapps that they often misled the Christians, showing them the wrong locality as a place where their gods had been worshiped. The real ones, Dr. Hallstrom decided, would probably be very old. Ancient sacrificial objects might quite possibly be found there.

After having come thus far in his reflections, historian Hallstrom chose
Rautasjaure, between Kiruna and Abisko, as a likely locality, and went there.
Due to a stone slide, the sacred site can be seen from far off, a sacrificial stone
of huge dimensions, beautifully located on an icy tarn. The stamped down,
littered surface of the ground didn't seem to offer much hope, but the first dig
brought an English coin to light, minted under Canute the Great, and from
then on success was assured.

All in all, 11 sites proved to be authentic, and the latest publication (by
Dr. Inga Serning, 1956), with its list of sacrificial objects in metal, is astonishing. The Lapps were wont to sacrifice the antlers—also the blood and flesh
—of reindeer at their altars. We can find proof of this today in the peatlike
black earth of these sites. They also sacrificed bear teeth, the bones of oxen,
a horse's tooth, wreaths wound in birch, pieces of clothing, wool threads; but
all these objects are of little value to us because they don't tell us *when* the
sacrifice was made. What we had to find were metal objects to which we could
attach a date, and this happened in all eleven of the sites just mentioned.
(*See ill. 152.*)

Again coins of various origin give us the most precise dates—all in all 165
German coins, 36 English, 400 Scandinavian, 1 Arabic (struck in Turkestan
in 967) and 4 copies. The isolated Arabic coin managed to find its way to
Lappland when the last dirhems had disappeared from the Nordic market—
in the second half of the first millennium. The most recent coins are not dated
so easily, but they must have been minted around 1250, and were buried, at
the latest, shortly after 1300.

In exactly the same time span fall the many thousand sacrificial objects, the
oldest among them originating in the final phase of the Viking era, most of
them from the Nordic Middle Ages. Swedish oval fibulae were found in fragmentary condition only; pieces in the style of rune stones turned up. We find
objects in the Gotlandic decorative style; but the Finnish oval, convoluted ring
and round fibulae are more numerous. East Baltic, Russian and Finno-Ugric
pendants are also plentiful; so are Lapp ornamental crosses and tinwork. This
does not mean that the Lapps felt any affinity for Christianity, only that they
knew that an uncanny strength was inherent in the cross, making it practical
to offer also some sacrifices to its power.

The astonishing, the unexpected thing—and this can be read only in the
results of archeological research—is to see the Lapps, shortly after the year
1000, becoming visible through their places of sacrifice, which were probably
age-old at the time. We see them for a little more than 200 years, as if through
a window frame, filing by, after which they disappear again completely from
our findings. What they did before or after this period, we do not know. All
we can report is that during this time they enter our archeological range of

vision in the same places of sacrifice at which they turn up again later, and that they seem to have been well off economically. They had just entered the European metal era when we meet them again, from 1050–1300, and had been incorporated into the world trade of those days, just as they have been in the last thirty years of our day and age. Today tasty reindeer meat is a desirable delicacy, and indestructible reindeer leather a highly durable raw material for the tanner. In exchange for it, the Lapplanders buy canned goods, steel knives, sewing machines, battery radios, and so on. The furred animals of those early days, which had not yet died out in the north Swedish inland areas, also enter our field of vision. Suddenly they were in demand. Buyers were looking for new markets along the Swedish rivers and inland. The Lapps brought down their furs, and became in turn rich in useful and decorative metal articles, of which their gods were to have their share.

The Finno-Baltic-Karelian-Russian participation in these finds is remarkable. A definite metal culture becomes evident in east Finnish Karelia at the same time. The two new fur dealers—Lapp and Finn—were closely allied, and demonstrate that the most important trade route no longer ran through the hands of the Svea, along the Bothnian seacoast, but across Viborg and the Gulf of Finland. This new economic flowering tended *eastward,* and bypassed the Svea. The old heart of the Viking lands was left lying off to one side.

152. *Lapp sacrificial objects from the end of the Viking era. State Historical Museum, Stockholm. Photo: ATA.*

Conversion to Christianity imposed harsh demands on the Scandinavian people, and was a major distraction. The Norwegian kings required all of the eleventh century for it; in Sweden the way to Christianity wasn't clear until the burning of the pagan temple in Old Uppsala in the 1080's. But whatever happened to the supremacy of the Norsemen in the Baltic? To our great surprise, we hear of Wendic Slavs sailing the high seas in boats copied from the Vikings, starting with the year 1050 and reaching a height of sorts in 1135, when Slavs plundered the city of Kungahälla on the Swedish west coast, after which 7,000 captive Nordlanders were auctioned off as slaves in Mecklenburg. The flowering isle of Gotland evidently wasn't spared either; the Danish islands of Falster and Lolland were hard hit; finally Waldemar Sejr and Bishop Absalon destroyed Arkona on the island of Rügen in 1169. In 1187 the Slavs laid waste the trading center of the Svea, the city of Sigtuna. Pribislav of Wagrien is supposed to have complained about the pressure of the Saxon princes:

"What is there left for us to do but leave the country and take to the sea and live on the wave? Is it our fault if, in flight from the land, we disturb the sea and live by robbing the seafaring merchants of the Danes?" In the hour of their downfall, the Slavs apparently saw no other avenue open to them.

This time it was not—as it had been a thousand years before—the east Germanic peoples, Burgundians, Goths, Vandals, but guilds of traveling German merchants who began to penetrate ever more actively into Mecklenburg, Pomerania and East Prussia. This took place in the crisis-ridden years from 1050–1150, which we archeologists call the "dark" century of the Baltic Sea lands because the find material in heathen graves begins to slough off and the written sources of the Middle Ages are so sparse. In the tiny corridor to the Baltic, the City of Lübeck was founded in 1143; in 1157, Henry the Lion took possession of it and gave the town a charter with tariff and mint privileges. It became the natural center of a swiftly developing German Hanseatic League, which now burst in on the north European trade.

Were the Scandinavians—exhorted to a love of peace by a new religion, ravaged by the Wends, pushed aside by the Hanseatic League—to sit back and let all this happen? After all, didn't they still have their incomparable ships whose grinning dragon heads and square sails were feared on every littoral whenever they hove in view? But their time was over. The Hanseatics—even their predecessors—sailed with new ships: koggs. The Scandinavian shipbuilders looked down their noses at these heavy tubs that lay deep in the water and moved slowly. But the Viking ships had disadvantages, which were to spell their doom. Because they lay so lightly on the water, a starboard or portside wind could drive them off course, whereas the koggs, just because of their depth, could make good use of a lateral wind. In fact, it was soon decided to enlarge the size of their sails. A foremast was used, which was found to be even more useful when fastened to a bowsprit that stuck out over the prow. A square-cut stem with rudder at the rear was also good only for a heavy, deep-lying ship. For a new era, an entirely new sailing principle evolved.

The Viking ships had been the swift greyhounds of the ocean, invented by warriors anxious to reach their destination as speedily as the wind, and ready to strike just as fast and hard. They were suited to traders carrying a small cargo of luxury items. But when traders and guild brothers began to transport practical and bulky merchandise as peaceful, orderly freight from harbor to harbor, the Viking ships became obsolete.

It was in the tradition of the Hanseatic merchant not only to trade but also to promote production in the East, and to raise the economic standard of the old German Reich. They stimulated agriculture in the land of the Wends, took empty barrels and Lüneburg salt to the herring fishers in Öresund, brought smiths and miners to the middle Swedish iron mines, organized the Balto-Finnish fur trade, and saw to the sale of this natural produce in overpopulated Flanders and the Rhineland. And for all this they needed sturdier freighters than the Vikings ever had. An old Hanseatic verse lists quite different merchandise than that with which we have been dealing in this book:

Lübeck, a warehouse	Lüneburg, a salt house
Cologne, a wine house	Stettin, a fish house
Braunschweig, a honey house	Halberstadt, a women's house
Danzig, a grain house	Reval (Tallin), a flax house
Magdeburg, a bakery house	Cracow, a copper house
Rostock, a malt house	Wisby, a pitch and tar house

New ships, new merchandise, new seller and buyer, newly organized guilds —these were the four essential changes through which north Europe's trade slipped out of the hands of the Scandinavians and fell to the German Hanseatic League. What the Vikings had built up, the Hanseatic League continued, on a new basis. Just the same, they chose to use the trade routes that had been broken in by the Vikings. This development, which took place in the afore-mentioned "dark" century, has not been examined with any thoroughness, but its outlines lie clearly before us.

The Hanseatic traders moved the vulnerable crossing place between the Baltic and North seas about sixty miles southward, from Hollingstedt-Haithabu to Hamburg-Lübeck, so that it should not lie in borderline territory, but well within the safe protection of the Reich. In 1161, Henry the Lion signed an agreement between the Gotlanders and "all the merchants of the Holy Roman

Empire who visit Gotland," according to which Wisby was founded as a Hanseatic city for German merchants. Gotland continued to lie in the path of Baltic Sea traffic, with the only difference that now *German* trade was moving *northward* from Lübeck. The "remaining Germans" on the island—that is how they signed themselves—sailed eastward with their Gotlandic Guild brothers, and to their own advantage. They sailed on the old established river lanes, up the Neva and Volkhov. *Vorschkerle* helped them across the rapids; in the most important trading centers, a Guild Hall was at their disposal. Or they took the familiar Southern Dvina route to Smolensk, and signed trade agreements with the princes there.

The majority of the Hanseatic merchants came from the Rhineland and Westphalia. This remarkable fact can be more precisely established by a thorough study of genealogy. We find in one and the same register the following typical family names which clearly display their origin: Westfelinc, Gruiten, Kölner, Kamen, Essen, Lennep, Koesfeld, Münster, Duisburg, Lippe, Warendorf, Hameln, Wipperfurth and Neuss. Guilds and families moved eastward, slowly, always leaving a member of the family in the old Reich, in Lübeck, on Gotland, in Reval, in Riga. Artisans and technicians moved right along with the merchants. They colonized the southern Baltic seacoast; they created lasting and competent minority groups in the Baltic area, in Gotland, in the Swedish Hanseatic cities of Kalmar, Söderköping, Stockholm, and in Norwegian Bergen. In their calm, thorough Westphalian way, they never moved faster than their ability to cope with the district in question.

How differently the Vikings had behaved in the same waters! Swedes, Norwegians and Danes had swept across the borders of what was their known world at the time, arrived at and colonized new islands, countries, continents, without even troubling to safeguard their own waters. And all the states they founded in foreign lands were dissipated. In the year 800, the borders of the land peopled by Scandinavians were the same as in the years 1060 and 1960. In spite of their gigantic conquests, the Vikings were never able to broaden the dimensions of their countries by so much as a few acres.

Today we have the tendency to want to know, at the end of a book like this, the historic importance in an enduring sense, the lasting value of an achievement. Shouldn't we perhaps regard the achievement as an end in itself? After having recognized all the causes for the Viking expeditions, now that we know what their resources were and after having told of their brutality without glossing it over, the recognition of their spectacular and fundamentally unfathomable human effort remains with us.

Insofar as they were a constant threat to Europe, we may say that they were politically active, and in this respect contributed to world history. They did so more constructively through the numerous states they founded; most of all, though, through their administrative policies, their laws, social order and the customs they introduced in these lands. They did not delay European unity for centuries, as is so often stated. That is how the history of the early Middle Ages is painted for us; in beautiful, romantic colors all blame is taken from the Christian and placed on the devilish heathen from across the sea. But things are not so simple. The Vikings were neither worse nor better than all other Europeans. They behaved like their adversaries, like all the Germanic-Celtic Western tribes. They fought among themselves; they allied themselves with a ruler, only to support his opponent a year later; they became vassals and rebelled against their patron. The bloody deeds registered in the constantly fluctuating battle formations on the continent and on the British Isles prove one thing clearly—that war and politics, then as now, were unpredictable and subject to constant change.

This is our Occidental fate, so different from the Roman. Never were we able to create for any enduring length of time a unified empire, like the Roman Empire of the German, Frank and other European nations, and to assemble all our strength collectively. It is probably our painful good fortune never to march as one, like the Romans; never to practice contemplation like the Orientals. Our creative pursuits are so dynamic, we have at our command intellectual and artistic powers of such brilliant versatility, no Roman Empire or any other major power on earth has ever experienced anything like them. Ours is a free and impetuous spirit.

It has not been the purpose of this book to judge all this in detail. We have neither glorified nor condemned the Vikings. Our efforts have been bent on dealing with them seriously, as human beings with as much right to a true evaluation as any other people. We have tried to understand them as far as our sources of information permit. We have seen descriptions in which blood flows, taken from dramas that may be counted as some of the most outstanding works of world literature. Often we are offered vistas of historic dimensions or vivid social pictures, but more often than not only as marginal notes, jotted down by chance. *For the Vikings dominated the scene, but not the times.* They lacked a uniform plan for their historic stake in Europe. They didn't know how to think historically.

We have had to seek their historic place and progression in written sources, and in the findings of archeology. We have considered their world-encircling expeditions together with the achievements going on at the same time, as evidence of a subtle European unity. Only thus could we sense and evaluate what was inherent in the continent of Europe at the hour of its birth in the way of strength, spirit and dynamic forces, the same human values that make it possible in the twentieth century to populate ever greater continents, to move into outer space, to penetrate our own psyche—in Faustian exploration and conflict. Only thus could we hope to come to a closer understanding and appreciation of the Vikings.

BIBLIOGRAPHY

Viking History

ARBMAN, HOLGER, *The Vikings, Ancient Peoples and Places.* Praeger, New York. 1961.

BRØNDSTED, JOHANNES, *The Vikings.* Penguin Books, Baltimore, 1960

KENDRICK, T. D. *A History of the Vikings.* Scribner, New York. 1930.

KLINDT-JENSEN, OLE. *Denmark, Ancient Peoples and Places.* Praeger, New York. 1957.

LEWIS, A. R. *The Northern Seas, Shipping and Commerce in Northern Europe, A.D. 300–1100.* Princeton University Press, Princeton. 1958.

SAWYER, P. H. *The Age of the Vikings.* St. Martin's Press, New York. 1962.

STENBERGER, MÅRTEN, *Sweden, Ancient Peoples and Places.* Praeger, New York. 1962.
  The Vendel and Viking Age. Det forntida Sverige. 1964, pp. 579–832.

The Vikings in Britain and Ireland

BAKKA, EGIL, *Some English Decorated Metal Objects Found in Norwegian Viking Graves.* Årbok for Universitetet i Bergen. 1963, pp. 1–66.

BRØGGER, A. W. *Ancient Emigrants.* Oxford University Press, London. 1929.

HODGKIN, R. H. *A History of the Anglo-Saxons, II.* Oxford University Press, London. 1952.

ROUSSELL, A. A. *Norse Building Customs in the Scottish Isles.* Levin and Munksgaard, Copenhagen. 1934.

SHETELIG, HAAKON, *An Introduction to the Viking History of Western Europe. Viking Antiquities in Great Britain and Ireland.* Oslo. 1940.

ARBMAN-STENBERGER, *Vikingar i Västerled.* A. Bonnier, Stockholm. 1935.

STENTON, F. M. *Anglo-Saxon England.* Oxford University Press, London. 1947.

WALSH, A. *Scandinavian Relations with Ireland during the Viking Period.* Talbot Press, Dublin. 1922.

The Vikings in Iceland, Greenland, and in America

BRØNDSTED, J. *The Norsemen in North America before Columbus.* Smithsonian Institution, Annual Report, Washington. 1953, pp. 367 and following.

GJERSET, K. *History of Iceland.* Macmillan, New York. 1925.

HERMANSSON, H. *The Problem of Wineland*. Islandica. 1936.

HOVGAARD, W. *The Voyages of the Norsemen to America*. American Scandinavian Foundation, New York. 1914.

INGSTAD, HELGE, a book on the discovery of Viking settlement in Newfoundland, not yet published.

JANSSON, SVEN B. F. *About the Kensington Stone Falsification*. Nordisk Tidskrift, 1949.

JONES, G. *The Norse Atlantic Saga*. Oxford University Press, London. 1964.

NØRLUND, P.-STENBERGER, M. *Brattahlid, Researches into Norse Culture in Greenland*. Meddelelser om Gronland, Copenhagen. 1934.

The Vikings on the Western Continent and in Spain

ROBINSON, C. H. *Anskar, The Apostle of the North*. London. 1921.

SHETELIG, H. *Vikingeminder i Vest-Europa*. 1933.

STEFANSSON, J. *The Vikings in Spain*. Saga-book of the Viking Club VI. 1909.

The Vikings in the Baltic, in Russia and the Orient

ARBMAN, H. *Svear i Österviking*. 1955.

ARNE, T. J. *La Suède et l'Orient*. 1914.

NERMAN, BIRGER, *Die Verbindungen zwischen Skandinavien und dem Ostbaltikum in der jüngeren Eisenzeit*. På Akademiens förlag, Stockholm. 1929.

PASZKIEWICZ, H. *The Origin of Russia*. Allen and Unwin, London. 1954.

RAUDONIKAS, W. J. *Die Normannen der Wikingerzeit und das Ladogagebiet*. På Akademiens förlag. Stockholm. 1930.

THOMSEN, VILHELM, *The Relations between Ancient Russia and Scandinavia and the Origin of the Russian State*. Revised edition. Burt Franklin, New York. 1964.

TIKHOMIROV, M. *The Towns of Ancient Rus*. Moscow. 1959.

Important Settlements and Early State Foundings

ARBMAN, H. *Birka I, Die Gräber*. 1943.

BLINDHEIM, CHARLOTTE, *The Market Place in Skiringsaal*. Acta Archaeologica, Copenhagen. 1960, pp. 83–100.

GEIJER, AGNES, *Birka III, Die Textilfunde*. Stockholm. 1938.
Oriental Textiles in Sweden. Rosenkilde and Bagger, Copenhagen. 1951.

HOLMQVIST, W., B. ARRHENIUS, P. LUNDSTRÖM, *Excavations at Helgö*. 1954–9, I–II. Stockholm. 1961.

JANKUHN, HERBERT. *Haithabu*. K. Wachholtz, Neumünster. 1956.

KAUPANG-EXCAVATIONS. Universitetets Oldsaksamlings Arbok, 1958–9, pp. 78–120. 1960–1, pp. 143–159.

NERMAN, B. *Grobin-Seeburg*. Almqvist and Wiksell, Stockholm. 1958.

NØRLUND, P. *Trelleborg*. Gyldendal, Copenhagen. 1948.

SCHINDLER, REINHARD, *Ausgrabungen in Alt-Hamburg*. Verlag Gesellschaft der Freunde des vaterländischen Schul- und Erziehungswesens, Hamburg. 1957.

SCHULTZ, C. G. *Aggersborg*. Vikingelejren ved Limfjorden, Fra Nationalmuseets Arbejdsmark. 1949.

Graves and Other Find Sources

BRØNDSTED, J. *Danish Inhumation Graves of the Viking Age.* Acta Archaeologica, Copenhagen. 1936.

DYGGVE, EJNAR, *The Royal Barrows at Jellinge.* Antiquity. 1948.
Gorm's Temple and Harald's Stave Church at Jellinge. Acta Archaeologica, Copenhagen. 1954.

RAMSKOU, TH. *Viking Age Cremation Graves in Denmark.* Acta Archaeologica. Copenhagen. 1950.
Lindholm, Preliminary Report. Acta Archaeologica, Copenhagen. 1953, 1955, 1957.

STENBERGER, M. *Das Gräberfeld bei Ihre auf Gotland, der wikingzeitliche Abschnitt.* Acta Archaeologica, Copenhagen. 1961, pp. 1–152.

Art of the Viking Age

ARBMAN, H. *The Skabersjö Brooch and some Danish Mounts.* Meddelanden från Lunds Universitets Historika Museum. 1956, pp. 3 and following.

BERG, GÖSTA, *Sledges and Wheeled Vehicles.* Nordiska Museets Handlingar 4. 1935.

BRØNDSTED, J. *Early English Ornament.* Hachette, Ltd. London. 1924.

GALSTER, GEORG. *The Cuerdale Find and the Danish Viking Kings of the Ninth Century.* Aarboger for nordisk oldkyndighed. 1962, pp. 1–36.

HOLMQVIST, W. *Germanic Art during the First Millennium, A.D.* 1955.

KENDRICK, T. D. *Late Saxon and Viking Art.* Humanities Press, New York. 1948.

KERMODE, P. *Manx Crosses.* Bemrose and Sons, London, 1907.

SHETELIG, H. and H. FALK. *Scandinavian Archaeology.* Oxford University Press, London. 1937.

SHETELIG, H. *The Norse Style of Ornamentation in the Viking Settlements.* Acta Archaeologica, Copenhagen. 1948.
Classical Impulses in Scandinavian Art from the Migration Period to the Viking Age. 1949.

SKAARE, KOLBJORN, *Anglo-Saxon Coins in the History of British Coinage and in Norwegian Viking Age Finds.* Viking 1963, pp. 81–122.

King Ships and Ship Graves

BRØGGER, A. W.-SHETELIG, H. *The Viking Ships.* Dreyer, Oslo, 1951.

PEDERSEN, O. KRUMLIN. *The Steering Oar from Vorza.* Kuml. 1960.

SJØVOLD, T. *The Öseberg Find and the other Viking Ship Finds.* Oslo. 1957.

Rune Stones

JANSSON, SVEN B. F. *The Runes of Sweden.* Bedminster Press, Totowa, New Jersey. 1962.

INDEX

Editor's note: The names of places and people in this early historical period often appear in varying forms. The biographical and geographical entries in this index have been identified as accurately as possible throughout.